SLOVENIA

in your hands

2013

Ljubljana

Gorenjska

Primorska & Western Slovenia

South Slovenia

Northeast Slovenia

Authors
Vladimir Dulović
Adele Gray

Editor
Ivan Kovanović

Managing Editor
Branko Andrić

Cover photo
Miha Gantar

Photos
Miha Gantar
Luka Esenko
and others

Maps
Dušan Broćić

Design & Layout
Ivan Grujić

Published by
KOMSHE d.o.o. Beograd

COPYRIGHT © 2013 KOMSHE

For information and distribution
info@komshe.com

Acknowledgements:

We reserve special thanks for the Embassy of the Republic of Slovenia in
Belgrade and the Slovenia Tourist Board without whose generous assistance this project would not have been possible.

We are grateful to Oscar Mulej for his help with researching and writing
the Practical Help section.

For help with collecting together photographs and additional information for the project we would also like to thank the following people and
organisations:

Jöerg Heeskens, Uršula Kordiš; Prof. Mladen Bogič of the Slovenian Rail-
way Museum; The Development Agency of Idrija and Cerkno (with photo-
graphs by Jani Peternelj and Samo Trebižan, see p 149); The City Museum of
Ljubljana; TIC Vipava; TIC Brda; The Idrija Municipal Museum; The Zaprikraj
Open Air Museum (with photographs by Tamino Petelinšek, see p 138); The
Idrija Military Museum; The Lipica Stud Farm; Father David of Kostanjevica
Monastery; LTO Laufar Cerkno (with photographs by Bojan Tavčar, see
p 149); TIC Izola (with photographs by Jernej Filipčič, Jaka Jeraša, Ubald
Trnkoczy and Matej Mitruševski, see p 162); Planinsko društvo Jesenice; TIC
Kobarid (Archive www.visit-soca.com with photographs by Matevž Lenarčič
and Tamino Petelinšek, see p 135, 136, 138); Gostilna "Pri Lojzetu", Zemono
Manor; The Tourist Organisation of Koper (with photographs by Ubald
Trkoczy, see p 157); The Archive of the Bogenšpek Castle Public Institute
(with photographs by Darinka Mladenovič, see p 179); Planinsko društvo
Cerkno; The Slovene Museum of Christianity; The Otočec Rock Festival;
Terme SPA Rogaška d.d.; The National Museum of Slovenia (with photo-
graphs by Matija Pavlovec, see p 61); TIC Podčetrtek; TIC Črnomelj (with
photographs from the Development and Information Centre of Bela Krajina
by Anita Jamšek and Robert Glazer, see p 209); The Tourist Board of Novo
Mesto (with photographs by Marko Pršina, Marko Habjan, Tomaž Grdin
and Tomaž Levičar, see p 185); The Museum of Dolenjska, Novo Mesto; The
Celje Regional Museum; TIC Murska Sobota; TIC Luče (with photographs by
M. Lenarčič, A. Šiljar, D. Turnšek and S. Ramšak, see p 246); The Municipal-
ity of Murska Sobota; TIC Brežice; The Regional Development Agency of
Koroška (with photographs by Tomo Jeseničnik and Aleš Fevžer, see p 249);
TIC Rogatec; The Institute for Entrepreneurship, Tourism and Youth Brežice
(with photographs by Hrvoje Oršanič, see p 248); Hotel Kračun (with photographs by Janez Kotar, see p 242); Postojna d.d. (with photographs from
the Postojnska Jama Archive); The Maribor-Pohorje Tourist Board (From the
archive www.maribor-pohorje.si and with photographs by Marko Petrej
and Gregor Mursec, see p 230); TIC Slovenske Konjice (with photographs
by Tomo Jeseničnik, Jurij Popov and Andraž Korošec, see p 230); The Walk
of Peace in the Soča Region Foundation (with photographs from the www.
potmiru.si archive by Tomo Petelinšek, see p 135).

CONTENTS

BASIC FACTS

Slovenia at a Glance

Slovenia's beautiful coastline

Slovenia is a country so varied and engaging it is as though it was created for the enjoyment of visitors. It abounds in natural beauty, picture-perfect Alpine peaks and valleys, clear mountain rivers and lakes, the wondrous caves of the Karst region, the blue Adriatic and rolling hills dotted with vineyards. And all these sights are within easy reach, just an hour or two's drive apart. There are also quaint towns and villages, merging German tidiness with Italian charm, perched on stony hills or nestled in glacial vales, countless medieval castles, relaxing spas, top notch modern architecture and – last but not least – great hotels and superb restaurants. If all this is not enough, Slovenia's tourist centres are dearly treasured and immaculately maintained by this small but proud nation.

In Slovenia everything looks modest but nothing lacks style. Megalomania of any kind will seem but a distant memory as you discover that everything here is made to suit a human scale and pace. Even the country's capital, Ljubljana, manages to combine the pleasures of a fashionable and arty Central European city with a gentle, almost rural, calm. Surely this Eden-like place must have its problems but it is hard to imagine that the people, who throughout their history have reaped some good from every evil, will not manage every crisis with style.

From its flawless highways and neat towns and villages to its varied and imaginative cuisine, Slovenia seems to have wrapped up the best of Europe within a manageable, budget-friendly experience. From culture to hiking, to taking the waters or roaming the wine roads, beaches or ski slopes – Slovenia has it all. Be sure to set aside a few extra days for your stay in Slovenia. You will need them.

The Robba Fountain in Ljubljana

The view from Slovenia's highest peak, the indomitable Triglav

THE PEOPLE

With just over two million people, Slovenia feels like a cosy place. Don't be surprised to hear locals call their country "Our Little Slovenia"- size does not matter, it's the quality of life that counts. Within such a small and easily navigable country, Slovenes have a developed friendly sense of community. This is apparent in a number of ways, not least in polite every day communication: it is totally normal to say *Dober dan* (Good Day) to complete strangers, just as in a small village (and let's not forget half of all Slovenes do live in villages!).

One of many small picturesque towns in Istria

Children playing in Ljubljana

The locals love and care for their villages and towns to an extent that often seems quaintly naïve to outsiders. Through schools and media Slovenes are taught that what nature endowed to them needs to be respected and tended in order to flourish; and they have taken this message to heart. This is indeed a close and amiable society

and Slovenes take their warm and open approach to friends and family, and indeed guests, very seriously. Seldom does a Sunday go by without a family lunch or a holiday without a large gathering of friends, family and guests.

For such a small country there are very distinct differences between Slovenes from different **regions**. While the Alpine Gorenjci are seen as relatively closed, hard working and frugal, the Štajerci from the East are thought to be more open, lovers of good wine and song. Of course, the Mediterranean lends an easy-going air to all activities and the Slovenes from the coast share a carefree attitude to life with their neighbours from Italy and Croatia. The folks from Prekmurje in the North East are perceived as the most different with their almost unintelligible dialect and unusual customs and cuisine more akin to those of Hungary.

Unfortunately, even though its economy has until recently been very robust, many have felt that their salaries were not

Traditional costumes in Trnovo near Ljubljana (see p. 68)

Slovenes from Maribor in traditional dress

following the rising costs of life. The main reason people leave Slovenia, therefore, is in search of better jobs. The slack is taken up by immigrants coming into the country and approximately as many people make Slovenia their home every year as leave. Most come from former Yugoslavia (mainly Serbia, Bosnia-Herzegovina, Croatia), for them the language is easy to master, things still seem familiar and there are plenty of relatives and compatriots around. The locals

The Kurentovanje festival in Ptuj (see p. 229)

have a love/hate relationship with this slow but steady phenomenon: referring to these newcomers as *naši ljudje* ("our people", slightly ironically intonated, of course) and seeing them as the least inconvenient form of immigration.

Young Slovenes hanging out in Prešeren Square, Ljubljana

LANGUAGE, RELIGION & CULTURE

The official **language** is Slovene, a South Slavic language, similar to Croatian and Serbian, but which has kept a lot of its unique features. It is, for instance, one of very few languages that, in addition to the singular and plural, also retains the dual form (a trace of this remains in English in the form of 'both', 'either' and 'neither'). Mastering a few phrases is not complicated but be warned, learning the grammar is far from easy. Considering that it is the mother tongue to only 2.5 million people learning it would be a labour of love, but one into which Slovenia might easily charm you. There's no cause for concern, however, if you are not a gifted linguist, Slovenes are well aware of their linguistic isolation and are very enthusiastic about learning foreign languages. Almost everyone speaks English

and German and other European languages are well represented too.

Apart from Slovene, on local level there are two other official languages – Italian in the coastal communes and Hungarian in Prekmurje. However, the third most widely understood and spoken language remains Serbo-Croatian, and speakers of any other Slavic language will find their knowledge very useful.

Traditionally, almost all Slovenes were once Roman Catholics. For a nation firmly rooted in the countryside **religion** was closely connected with everyday living and one of the basic manifestations of identity. To see the legacy of Slovene devotedness and the influence the church has had on people's lives look no further than the fact that there is barely a hilltop without a chapel or a church. However, the Church has not managed to regain the influence it enjoyed before communist times. Nowadays, the young are less and less attracted by the conservative nature of the Church and only half of all Slovenes declare themselves as Roman Catholics, a figure that drops roughly one percent every year. The second largest religious denomination is Islam with 2.4 percent of the overall population, followed closely by the Serbian Orthodox Church.

Slovenes are proud of their Central European **cultural heritage**. Suggesting that they belong to Eastern Europe, or worse the Balkans, is considered a serious *faux pas* and some people might take offense. Slovenia has always proudly kept

Pope John Paul II on a visit to Maribor

pace with the main cultural trends in Europe, even during the communist period. From its Roman and Celtic legacy to Expressionism or top notch contemporary design, Slovenes have always been ready to embrace new styles, above all because they did not see them as alien. Strange perhaps for a nation that has kept so in touch with its traditions, but there exists a constant duality of Slovene spirit: on one side is the love of this small corner of

Ljubljana looking resplendent in its Christmas lights

Sometimes controversial, always entertaining, Slovenia's most eminent philosopher, Slavoj Žižek

Provocative Slovene band Laibach have now achieved international cult status

Europe and its local customs, on the other an eagerness not to let it become isolated.

This is one of the reasons Slovenes are passionate about **science**. A lot of attention is paid to education and there are more than 115,000 students at the country's three universities, resulting in 23 percent of adults completing some form of higher education. There may not be any world famous names among Slovene scientists but the nation's innovative spirit is beyond reproach. The 18th century mathematician Jurij Vega and the Slovene-Austrian chemist and Nobel Prize laureate Fritz Pregl are but two scientists worthy of note. Perhaps the most famous Slovene today is controversial philosopher, Slavoj Žižek, a passionate social commentator and opponent of Neo-Liberalism.

In **popular culture** the biggest impression was made by rock groups from the 1980s that combined New Wave creativity with anti-regime activism. The most famous of these is Laibach, with a proto-industrial sound and provocative presence both on and off the stage. Not to get carried away: not all Slovenes listen to progressive rock and you will find a sort of tacky Euro pop with a folksy twist hugely popular, especially in the countryside.

POLITICS & ECONOMY

Slovenia is a parliamentary democracy. The head of the state is the president, elected in a popular vote for a five year term. The parliament is bicameral, consisting of a National Assembly of 90 members that elects the prime minister and his government. The other chamber is the National Council, made up of different social, economic and local interest groups who advise and monitor the National Assembly.

Until recently, Slovenia was hailed as an example of successful adaptation to a

Slovenia is a parliamentary democracy

SLOVENIA IN A NUTSHELL
Population: 2,058,130 (2012)
Area: 20,273 km²
Capital: Ljubljana (pop. 272,300)
Ethnic make up: Slovene (83%), Serb, Croat, Bosniak
Religion: Roman Catholic, Islam, Orthodox Christian
GDP per capita: $22,461
Inflation: 1.8 (2011)
Unemployment rate: 8.4% (2012)

free market economy and EU norms (*see also p. 22*). However, the global economic crisis has hit the small country hard and has paralysed its growth. In 2009 Slovenia's GDP fell by almost 8 percent and has not recovered since. Though it only threw the country back down to the EU average, the crisis has shattered public faith in the system. In part this is due to many high profile cases of corruption and nepotism. The sudden end to its economic boom has left many in Slovenia demoralised. Since the start of the crisis and the governmental attempts to curb it, the country saw large, mostly peaceful protests – something not seen in recent Slovenian history and a clear sign of the depth of the crisis.

In early 2013 the government was ousted by large-scale but largely peaceful protests

SPORTS & RECREATION

It should come as no surprise that a nation located in such a breathtaking natural setting should be a nation of lovers of the great outdoors. On a sunny weekend Ljubljana empties out as it seems almost everyone has dashed off to the mountains or the seaside.

The two most popular sporting activities are hiking, in the summer, and skiing, in wintertime. Around 4 percent of the whole population are members of the national Mountain Association (established back in 1893!) and a much greater number make use of the excellent

Skiing at the Cerkno Ski Centre (see p. 150)

Hiking is not so much a national pastime as a national passion

network of marked trails and well kept mountain huts on a less formal basis. It is said that every true Slovene patriot should climb the country's highest peak,

Slovenia vs. Croatia at Eurobasket 2009

the iconic Mt Triglav, at least once in their lifetime. What is more, all Slovene towns, including Ljubljana, are bike friendly and many people cycle both to commute and for pleasure.

With the first snow, people of all ages and walks of life pack their skis and head for the slopes scattered throughout the northern half of the country. The ski resorts offer a myriad of pistes catering for all ability levels, miles of cross country skiing tracks and, at Planica, the largest such centre in the world, ski jumping. Consequently Slovenia, despite its size, is a veritable winter sports super power. Sportsmen and women such as cross country skier Petra Majdič and ski racer Tina Maze (to name but two) making headlines of sports sections well beyond Slovenia's borders.

The largest crowds are, however, drawn to popular team sports, especially football and Slovenia's national team has taken part in two World Cups and one European Championship since independence. A close second is basketball; Slovenia came second at the European basketball championships, Eurobasket, in 2009 and is hosting Eurobasket 2013. There is also a respectable ice hockey league and national team. Last, but certainly not least, there is handball: the Slovene national team has missed only one European championship since independence and won a silver medal on home ground in 2004.

The Slovenia national football team

Top Sights in Slovenia

Triglav

Rising high above the other mountains of the Julian Alps, at 2,864m Mt Triglav is the heart of Slovenia's only national park, a medley of awe-inspiring cliffs, lakes and valleys. Triglav is a veritable pilgrimage site for this nature loving nation

Lake Bled

Slovenia's most famous destination, picture-perfect Lake Bled with its fairytale island church, medieval castle nestled atop a jagged rock and glorious mountain backdrops will keep even the most active visitors busy for days

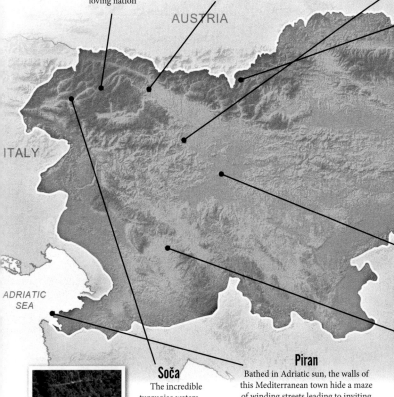

AUSTRIA

ITALY

ADRIATIC
SEA

Soča

The incredible turquoise waters of this fast flowing river are as much a sight on their own as a haven for all devotees of active sports, but its Alpine surroundings with historic sights from WWI are equally appealing

Piran

Bathed in Adriatic sun, the walls of this Mediterranean town hide a maze of winding streets leading to inviting squares and intriguing Medieval churches

Škofja Loka
Don't miss this tiny but perfectly preserved medieval town, complete with a hilltop castle, squares lined with burghers' houses and a stone bridge high above the waters of its mountain river

Logarska Valley
The breathtaking crescendo of the Savinja Rvier snaking between mountain peaks, this picturesque corner of the Alps is just the beginning of a dream-come-true for hikers and outdoors enthusiasts

HUNGARY

Jeruzalem
Hilltop villages and inviting solitary wineries, like islands lost in a sea of infinite vineyards, producing some of Slovenia's best white wines

Ptuj
Two millennia of uninterrupted peaceful existence have endowed Ptuj with an idyllic old town, numerous historic churches as well as a castle brimming with art and archaeological findings

ƆATIA

Karst Caves
The highlight of the Slovenian Karst region, the Postojna and Škocjan Caves never fail to amaze and are among the best loved and most visited European caves. Visit the Postojna Caves for amazing cave wildlife or Škocjan for Tolkienesque underground rivers.

Ljubljana
A capital city but on a human scale, Ljubljana is both a dynamic hub of culture and the arts and a place where one can unwind, be it in its verdant parks, in front of Plečnik's architectural masterpieces or in one of its relaxed riverside cafés

History of Slovenia

THE ARRIVAL OF THE SLAVS

The Slavs who settled in modern-day Slovenia and the surrounding countries in the 5th century came from an area between the Baltic Sea and Carpathians, aound present day Poland, Belarus and western Ukraine, beyond the scope of Roman geographers and historians. Taking the opportunity to settle areas abandoned by other peoples moving onto the rich lands of the crumbling Roman Empire, the Slavs slowly pushed West, South and East from their ancestral home. Around the same time the Germanic **Lombards** came from the North to settle in the Alps and the Asiatic **Avars** arrived in the plains of Pannonia to the East. As the Slavs were divided up into a number of unorganized tribes, the warlike Avars easily took the upper hand and came to treat Slavs as second class allies, numerous foot soldiers to supplement their army of horsemen.

The wild Avars must have been too dreadful as neighbours for the Lombards who moved away in **568**, crossing into modern-day Italy. The Avars and Slavs immediately filled the void left by the Lombards at the foot of the Alps, advancing up the Sava, Drava and Mura rivers, following the old Roman roads and settling one Alpine valley after another until they clashed with the Lombards (eager to defend their new lands) and Bavarians coming from the North. The Avars were less interested in these unfamiliar areas and preferred to remain close to the plains around the Danube. The Slavs, on the other hand, the forefathers of the Slovenes were here to stay. They occupied nearly all the land between the Danube and the Adriatic, from present day Vienna to Trieste.

THE FIRST STATES AND THE AGE OF SLOVENE RULERS (623-874)

Remaining habitually divided into smaller entities, the Alpine Slavs were united for the first time under the leadership of **Duke Samo** (623-658), a Frankish merchant who fled to the Slavs. He managed to organize the various tribes into one state stretching from the River Elbe to the Adriatic. Though short lived, this new state was strong enough to ward off attacks both by Samo's countrymen and the Avars.

Samo left no heir and after his death the Slavs returned to their old ways. Those living in present day Slovenia elected their own leaders known as *vojvoda* (literary "army leader") to lead them in battle as well as to resolve internal quarrels. The most prominent of these archaic mini-states was **Carantania** (future Carinthia). A Caranthian duke would be inaugurated by a chosen peasant who would ritually question his abilities and remind him to look after his people. The ceremony centred around the *Knežji Kamen* («Duke's Stone»), still preserved as a symbol of the Slovene proto-state.

Choosing the lesser of two evils, the Alpine Slavs decided to the seek help of their former enemies, the Bavarians, in order to fight the Avars; in return they accepted the supremacy of the Germanic tribe. During this joint effort the first German-speaking **Christian missionaries** ventured in amongst the Slavs. They were most successful in converting the leaders and their families; the first Slavic Christian known by name is Gorazd, the son of Vojvoda Borut. It is not known whether the pagan majority was aggravated by suppression of their gods, the growing German influence or most probably both, but they rebelled against their Christian dukes. With the help of the Bavarians the pagan uprising was crushed in **772** and Christianity gained a firm foothold in Slovene lands.

When **Charlemagne** took control of Bavaria soon afterwards, the lands of the Slavs became part of the budding Frankish Kingdom. In **791-96** Charlemagne destroyed the Avar Khanate, eradicating its people and annexing Slav-inhabited territories all the way to the Danube.

The Knežji Kamen

A decade later he also wrestled **Istria** from Byzantine control. In his far-flung provinces Charlemagne wisely left the locals to rule as they saw fit but grouped them in to two 'marches' under his control. At this time Christianity was spreading rapidly in the region, coming from the Archbishops of Salzburg in the North and from the Patriarch of Aquilea in the West. Slavic lands were now truly a part of the Central European story, converted to Latin Christianity and controlled by Germanic overlords.

This situation was not to everyone's liking. **Duke Ljudevit**, ruler of the neighbouring Pannonian Slavs, rose up against Frankish control in 819. The Dukes of Carantania and other Slavs under Frankish tutorage joined him but were eventually defeated. As a consequence the Franks replaced the disobedient dukes, who would from now on come only from German ranks. At the same time the first wave of German colonization of the eastern Alps started, significantly reducing the territory inhabited by the Slavs.

Eventually Slavs would come to be tolerated as feudal lords again as long as they did the Germans' bidding. One of those willing to play by the rules was Duke Pribina of Lower Pannonia, taking in German settlers and helping their Latin rite churches, but his son **Kocelj** decided on a different course.

He welcomed Byzantine monks, Cyril and Methodius, who came to translate the Holy Scriptures into Slavic. In 870 Kocelj founded a diocese separate from both Salzburg and Aquilea in which the liturgy was read in Slavic. Such heresy could not be tolerated for long and in **874** Kocelj disappeared from the annals of history, noted as the last Slavic ruler of the Slovenes for more than a thousand years.

MIDDLE AGES: FEUDALISM AND GERMANISATION

Around **896** a new foe appeared, the fearsome **Hungarians**, the last in the long line of Asiatic peoples that descended on the plains of Pannonia. They quickly overcame the Slavic and Frankish outposts in Pannonia and made the area a base from which they routed most of Central Europe over the following half a century. Cornered from the West and North by the German advance and now from the East by the Hungarians, the Alpine Slavs were cut off from their brethren in the North and effectively hedged into a grouping that would eventually come to be known as the South Slavs. Though there was nobody

Language reformers and Christian missionaries, Cyril and Methodius

to notice at the time, their language was developing its own particular forms and their relative isolation would slowly render them a separate ethnic group.

Hungarian incursions were halted in **955** the victory of Emperor Otto I at Lechfeld after which the Eastern Slovene lands, most gravely affected by the wars, were resettled. The land was carved up into Marches that eventually became the duchies that shaped Slovenian history – Carniola/Kranjska, Carinthia/Koroška, Styria/Štajerska and Istria. The language of the church and education at the time was Latin, the language of administration, the aristocracy, of trade and the towns was German. Slovenes were reduced to peasants, almost invisible to the eye of history.

As the power of the German Emperors waned, during the course of the next two centuries various noble families such as the Babenbergs, Andechses or Spanheims tried to carve out more control over the provinces for themselves, submitting the region to petty feudal wars and battles for the control of trade routes. In the background of these events we see a growth in the population and the rise of the cities. German demographic pressure on these peripheral Slovene lands meant that round the year 1400 the main dividing line between the two ethnic groups ran slightly North of the present Austrian-Slovene border, where it remained until the mid-19th century.

In an ambitious drive in the 1260s Ottokar II of Bohemia, one of the most successful nobles of the German Empire, managed to unite a string of lands from Bohemia and Moravia to Carniola under his control. His success was short lived, however, and in **1278** the lands that he

The coat of arms of the Counts of Celje

enormous number of people to flee their homes. Some estimates set the number of people lost in these raids as high as one third of the overall population. On the other hand, refugees from the South poured in: Horvat ("Croat") remains the most common surname in Slovenia and a few villages of Orthodox Serbs who arrived at this time survive in Bela Krajina to this day.

united now passed to the **Habsburgs**. In the next 250 years this shrewd noble house took hold of all the lands the Slovenes inhabited and continued to rule over them until 1918.

Their rule was, of course, contested by many. Amongst their early rivals the best remembered in Slovenia are the **Counts of Cilli** (that is, of Celje). From minor nobles in the course of the 14th century they managed to acquire large estates across Slovene lands, but also in the neighbouring Croatian lands of the Hungarian Kingdom. In the early 15th century they intermarried with the kings of Hungary, of Bosnia and the rulers of Serbia. The most powerful Count of Celje was Ulrich II who became the Regent of Hungary in 1452. He was, however, reckless enough to walk into a trap set by his numerous adversaries in Belgrade where he was assassinated in 1456. His kingly possessions were inherited by those crafty Habsburgs. All that remained of the glory of the Counts of Cilli was a romanticized memory of anti-Habsburg lords whose marriages and connections in the South Slavic lands later gave rise to fantasies of a South Slav state. Their most prominent legacy today are the three stars, taken from their coat-of-arms, which feature on the Slovenian national emblem.

THE 1500s AND 1600s: THE OTTOMANS, REBELLIONS AND REFORMATION

The **Ottoman Turks**, that great force that radically reshaped the history of South Eastern Europe, also had a huge impact on Slovene lands. Their first raids were recorded at the start of the 15th century and, after the fall of Bosnia in 1463, their attacks became a regular occurrence. Their tactics entailed prolonged pillaging of the countryside starving the fortified towns and castles. These raids caused an

The situation became especially grave after the Ottoman conquest of Hungary in **1526**, the event that also meant that Ferdinand I of Habsburg inherited the Hungarian crown. In order to protect the heart of his empire from the raids, Ferdinand started organizing a military frontier in Croatia. Peasants were armed, castles linked together and manned by soldiers paid by the Emperor. The system soon reduced the number of raids and brought hope of turning the tide. The **1593** battle of Sisak in Croatia in which the imperial forces routed the Ottomans marked the end of the worst of the Turkish scare.

As always, it was the peasants who bore the heaviest burden of the Empire's problems. In addition to higher taxes and the loss of lands that they previously rented from feudal lords, there came a period of insecurity and calls to arms against the Turks. The first larger peasant revolt came in 1515 but the largest and best remembered remains the one of **1575**. It erupted just over the border in Croatia but spread like wildfire to neighbouring Slovene lands. Led by the legendary **Matija Gubec**, the peasant army initially had some success but was mercilessly destroyed by a Baronial army after only ten days.

As elsewhere in the Empire, the teachings of Martin Luther found fertile ground in Slovene lands. The first followers of the **Reformation** were the intellectuals and then the nobles and townsfolk. It was,

"The Execution of Mateja Gubac", by Oton Iveković

however, the son of a simple miller from the area around Ljubljana that became the most notable figure of the Reformation in Slovenia. Just like Luther, **Primož Trubar** was a young, well educated priest. Gradually leaning towards Protestantism, he was expelled from Ljubljana and found refuge in Tübingen where in **1550** he published the **first books in the Slovene language** – *Catechismus* and *Abecedarium*. Bearing in mind the fact that the total sum of previous writings in Slovene didn't number more than a dozen documents, this was a truly revolutionary moment. In doing so Trubar disproved the then common assumption that Slovene is so crude and barbaric it cannot be either written or read. What's more, Trubar was the first to use the term *Slovenec*, "a Slovene" in his books. Protestant Slovene literati flocked to Ljubljana, which in the 1560s became a thriving centre both of Protestantism and of Slovene publishing and the Carniolan dialect became established as the literary standard for all Slovenes. In the span of just 45 years the Slovene reformers produced more than fifty books and laid the foundation for a future national culture.

Through sermons, printed books and, above all, their fervent idealism, the Protestants achieved a great deal. At the peak of the movement, in 1578, the reformed nobles pressed the Catholic Habsburgs to grant them freedom of religion. This they were granted but they did not enjoy for long: by 1590 the dark clouds of the **Counter-Reformation** were already looming over Slovene lands. Under the influence of the Jesuit Order

A woodcut of Primož Trubar

the Habsburgs took up a more aggressive stance, forcing conversions and expelling protestant preachers, first from the towns (1598) and then from the whole of the country (1599-1604), leaving Slovenes in the firm clasp of Catholicism once again. Some of the richest families, especially burghers, as well as many of their best educated sons, were forced to flee Habsburg controlled lands. The triumph of the Counter-Reformation was also the triumph of absolutism over the noble estates. Previously relatively politically independent, from now on the nobles would be no more than officials of the state.

Entrusted with the re-Catholicisation of Carniola, the Bishop of Ljubljana, Tomaž Hren (1599-1630), gathered a number of Italian (or Italian educated) artists to build and decorate new Jesuit churches, replacing those destroyed by the Turks with a new style – the **Baroque**. In the arts the victory of the Counter-Reformation represented a victory of populism, ensuring a lot of work for artists and craftsmen on the highly detailed decoration designed to impress the masses. Due to the intensity of construction in the 17th and 18th centuries, the vivacious lines of Baroque artists such as Francesco Robba, Andrea Pozzo or Giulio Quaglio left a deep impression on Slovene art.

THE 1700s: AGE OF REFORM AND ENLIGHTENED ABSOLUTISM

After their defeat at the gates of Vienna in 1683 the Turks were on the retreat and the border between the two belligerent Empires was pushed southwards. Wealth,

Bishop of Ljubljana, Tomaž Hren

Empress of the Hapsburg Empire, Maria Theresa

previously squandered largely on war, could now be directed to other needs as well. During the reign of Emperor Charles VI (1711-1740) **new roads** connecting Vienna and the Adriatic ports of Trieste and Rijeka were built across Slovene lands. **Trieste** became the darling of the Habsburgs, their big project designed to choke the aging Venetian Republic and soon enough it also became the biggest city of the Slovene-inhabited provinces.

The next two Habsburg rulers, Maria Theresa and Joseph II, strove to create a strong centralised state by means of *enlightened absolutism*. For Slovenes, still by and large peasants, this meant that their taxes were now prescribed by the state, the noble estates were put under central government supervision and the powers of the baronial courts were curtailed. The state was not, however, only interested in protecting the tax-paying peasants from the temperamental feudal lords, it also wanted to advance its bureaucratic system. From 1771 it became obligatory to send children to German-language state schools and simultaneously an agricultural revolution was under way, with new crops such as corn and potatoes and new agricultural associations. A few years later, in 1781, serfdom was abolished and the peasants became all but free. Lastly, Joseph II abolished all non-productive monasteries (meaning almost all of them) and established a network of parishes complete with educated priests.

With such brave changes and ideas, a new era beckoned; the needs and ideas of ordinary Slovenes were brought to the fore. Their main allies were the lower clergy, parish priests and monks, often the best educated Slovenes. In order to be able to teach and preach to parishioners they pushed for the introduction of the Slovene language into schools and books. Out of this effort came a new grammar (1768), dictionary (1781), collections of folk poems, the publication of the first Slovene poems and, to top it all, the first Slovene language newspaper– *Ljubljanske Novice* (1797-1800).

THE 1800s: LANGUAGE, NATION AND POLITICS

Napoleon's rise and reshuffling of the old Euroean order meant, in this corner of Europe, the disappearance of the Venetian Republic and the organization of the Carinthia, Carniola, Istria, half of Croatia and all of Dalmatia into an administrative unit called the **Illyrian Provinces**. The provinces were named based on the belief that the South Slavs were the descendants of the ancient Illyrians. Though short lived (1809-13), the provinces were a transformational: Illyrian (Serbo-Croatian) became one of the languages of administration, Slovene was used in newly opened primary and secondary schools and new roads were built. The legacy of this ephemeral administrative unit, combined with the age of Romanticism, meant that not even the chancellor of Austria, arch-conservative Prince Metternich, could extinguish all of its influences. On the other hand, new taxes were also introduced which meant that only a few far sighted intellectuals could see the overall benefits of this rule while the peasants remained indifferent or indeed hostile to the "blasphemous" French.

The contest between several types of orthography - the so-called "Battle of the Alphabets" - that raged in the 1830s resulted in the adoption of the same alphabet recently introduced by the neighbouring Croats - a victory for those counting on closer ties with Croats and Serbs. For their part, the Carniolians secured the use of their dialect as the literary language of all Slovenes. While intellectuals fought over matters of the mind, poet France Prešeren (1800-49) captured the hearts and imagination of his countrymen. His poems showed the literary potential of their neglected language to a gentry that still spoke German better than Slovene.

1848, the year of revolution across Europe, caught most Slovenes off guard but they swiftly joined the flow. Peasants rebelled and, in consequence, were finally freed from the last vestiges of serfdom. The heroes of the day were Slovene students

Bishop Anton Martin Slomšek

even in higher primary school grades and there was not one Slovene language high school, not to mention that calls for a Slovene university fell on deaf ears.

That political action resulted in so few successes was partially due to the economic weakness of Slovene lands. Most local industry was driven by foreign money or owned by the town-dwelling ethnic Germans. Even worse, industry developed at a much slower pace than in the rest of the Empire and was not able to absorb the landless peasants moving into the towns. While the rest of Austria enjoyed population growth equivalent to the European average, the Slovene population grew at a half of that rate. Wherever Slovenes lived or mixed with Germans they were losing ground and the border between the two peoples was moving Southwards with every new census.

THE GREAT WAR AND THE FIRST YUGOSLAVIA (1914-1941)

in Vienna who drew up a plan to bring all Slovenes together into one region under the Habsburg Emperor and even managed to get it to him through his brother Johann, who spent most of his time amongst Slovenes on his estate just outside Maribor. Nevertheless, the revolutionary potential of the young nation was not strong and the conservative elite decided to cling to its tried and tested strategy – obtaining smaller privileges and rights one at a time, so as not to alarm Vienna.

After the initial darkness of the post-revolutionary Bach period (1849-61), Slovenes gradually became more involved in politics. Led by the clergy, the conservatives or the "Old Slovenes", preached that, in the words of bishop Martin Slomšek, "one's duty is first of all to be a good Catholic, then a good Austrian (in terms of citizenship) and only then a good Slovene." In practice this meant staying within the system and not rocking the boat. The opposing camp, the liberals, or "Young Slovenes", wanted to speed up reforms and supported the unified Slovenia proposed in 1848. Most of the activities of both fractions were focused on the use of language and education through schooling and literature. Though there were some successes, the pressure of Germanisation annulled most of them. Starting from 1882 Slovene was permitted in primary schools, courts of law and local administration, however, until 1918 German was predominant

As war broke out in Europe in 1914 Slovenes duly joined their Imperial Army units and were sent off to fight the Russians. Lured by the promise of Austro-Hungarian territories, however, Italy joined the Triple Entente in 1915 and attacked its Eastern neighbour. Their offensive soon ground to a halt and the front stabilised in the Alps, just above the Soča River. Not only was the war now fought on Slovene land, resulting in the resettlement of thousands of civilians, it was also fought by Slovene troops. When casualties were counted at the end of the war it was established that some 30,000 Slovene soldiers had perished.

As the war dragged on support for the Habsburgs waned. In 1917 a club was formed in the Viennese parliament petitioning for a separate crown land of the South Slavs. Its actions were supported by 200,000 signatures but the Habsburgs failed to react. Workers strikes followed in **1918**

Troops on the Isonzo Front

and in May of that year some Slovene army units rebelled. As the Austro-Hungarian Empire started to crumble, South Slav members of parliament declared themselves to be a National Council and at the end of October broke all ties with Vienna. A month later they joined Serbia in a new **Kingdom of Serbs, Croats and Slovenes**.

The first problems of the new state were its borders: ethnic Germans took control of the border towns while the Italians were pushing in from the West, taking not only what they had been promised by the Allies but anything they could grab, including Ljubljana itself! Through a joint effort by liberating Serbian soldiers and local volunteers the Italians and Austrians were pushed back. Borders were drawn up in 1919 with the exception of south Carinthia. Here a referendum was organized in 1920 and though Slovenes constituted a majority of 59%, the population opted for stability and voted to stay in Austria. The largest single set back of WWI for the Slovenes was that 330,000 of them ended up in Italy, a state that immediately closed down all Slovene schools and organizations, arrested all of their leaders and prohibited any inscriptions in Slovene.

For the Slovenes living in the Kingdom of the South Slavs, things changed overnight: German disappeared from all schools, institutions and streets, its place taken by Slovene and Serbo-Croatian and in 1919 a Slovene-language university was founded in Ljubljana. Compared with the rest of the new state, Slovene lands were by far the most industrialized and prosperous and Slovene industrialists began making profits in the large new market to the South.

Not everything about the new state was to Slovenes' liking, however: their political parties voted for a decentralised country but the Kingdom of Serbs, Croats and Slovenes (from **1929** renamed to **Yugoslavia**) adopted a centralising constitution in an attempt to overcome the differences between newly acquired provinces. The official view was that the Serbs, Croats and Slovenes were merely three tribes of one nation, something that many Slovenes could not really envision. Furthermore, Slovenes were left divided across several administrative units until 1929. On the other hand, Slovenes were by and large left with the broadest cultural autonomy and their culture prospered.

OCCUPATION AND RESISTANCE (1941-1945)

In **April 1941** Nazi Germany and Fascist Italy together with Hungary and Bulgaria attacked Yugoslavia. The country was defeated in weeks and then partitioned among the victors. In Slovenia the Italians took Ljubljana and all the land South of it, the Hungarians Prekmurje, and the rest was annexed to the German Reich. The occupiers set out to reverse all that the Slovenes had achieved in two decades of relative freedom and they reversed it with a vengeance. There was no place Slavs them in the new Germany: all things Slovene were banned, intellectuals were sent to camps or deported and whole regions were emptied to make room for German colonists. The Italians were at first more permissive but as they encountered resistance they decided to implement many of the same methods.

Some Slovenes collaborated with the occupiers but it was obvious to the vast majority that the only way to survive was to fight back. The sweet taste of freedom was on the lips of the young nation and for the first time in its history it was willing to fight for it. There were several resistance groups but the single largest was the **Osvobodilna Fronta** ("Liberation Front") made up of Christian Socialists, Communists and other left-leaning groups. After Germany attacked the Soviet Union the Communists, already skilled in underground tactics, took the lead in attacking the occupiers. For them this was not only a war against occupation but also an ideal chance to take power. Reprisals forced more people into the woods and hills and soon the Communist Partisans (*Partizani*) numbered hundreds of members all over Slovenia. In **1943** delegates of the Liberation Front met in liberated Kočevje in what was hailed as the first Slovene assembly. Here they

Osvobodilna Fronta pamphlet, "He who votes 'black' is an enemy of the people"

reaffirmed their will to coordinate actions with Communists in the rest of occupied Yugoslavia, led by **Josip Broz "Tito"** (himself half Slovene on his mother's side) and set their goal - a Slovene republic, a separate unit in the new, federal Yugoslavia. Wary of the rising power of the Partisans and capitalizing on their ideological zeal, the occupiers turned to organising collaborationist units, such as the Slovene Home Guard, and spurred a bloody civil war. Yugoslav Communists were, however, by now backed not only by the Soviets but also by the Western Allies who saw them as the only effective fighting force against the Nazis.

In **May 1945**, at the very end of WWII, the People's Liberation Army of Yugoslavia liberated Slovenia. All but a few Germans fled. Yugoslav units preceded westwards taking control of all the Slovene inhabited territories of Italy, including the prize catch – Trieste. This, however, brought them into prolonged conflict with the Allies. Slovenia also got access to the seaside where the majority Italian populations of the towns were expelled. Similarly, most of the retreating collaborators, returned to them by the British, were executed next to the Austrian town of Bleiburg. Thousands of others who were seen by the Communists as potential enemies (including ideological enemies), bankers, industrialists, and members of the pre-war political parties, were dealt with in the same way.

SLOVENIA IN SOCIALIST YUGOSLAVIA (1945-1991)

At first it seemed that the communist Yugoslavia was going to follow all the excesses of Stalin's Soviet Union but in 1948, to everyone's surprise, Yugoslav president Tito decided not to bow to Soviet demands and to lead Yugoslavia on its "own path to socialism". Such a U-turn was gladly supported by the West and Tito was aided in his confrontation with Stalin with everything from tanks to American loans. Soon enough socialist Yugoslavia became a darling of the West without having to become a capitalist country – a model for potential renegades from the Stalinist camp. While the economic and political systems remained under strict communist control the cultural sphere was allowed more freedom and to open up to the West.

What started in 1945 as a formal federation of six republics under strict supervision by the Communist Party developed into a loose union of national states whose only unifying factors were the Party (now under a more benevolent name the Yugoslav League of Socialists), the Army and its lifelong leader, President Tito. Slovene grievances against Socialist Yugoslavia were above all economical. Most developed from the start as the little republic carried the greatest burden in helping out the poorer republics and regions to reach the proclaimed goal of equality. Despite that levelling, due to its good organization and agile population, the gap between Slovenia and the other republics was actually widening: it had a GDP 2 1/2 times higher than the Yugoslav average and as much as 7 times that of the poorest province. In a cryptic bureaucratic manner typical for that era Slovene politicians were making the point that Yugoslavia had become a burden.

When in **1981** Tito passed away in Ljubljana's state-of-the-art Clinical Centre, Yugoslavia lost its utmost authority, its almighty arbiter between bickering republics. There followed a decade of gradual claiming of freedoms, be it in culture or in politics, developing against the backdrop of a prolonged economic crisis. The first to voice Slovene complaints were its intellectuals, who were quickly followed by the local party leaders ready to ride the wave of long silenced discontent. The year 1990 kicked off with the first multi-party elections and ended with a referendum for independence, supported by the vast majority of Slovenes.

The federal authorities, paralyzed by the break-up of the state, did little to

The life-long president of Yugoslavia, Marshal Josip Broz "Tito"

Largely peaceful demonstrations have been an increasingly common form of voicing opposition in Slovenia

prevent any of this. It was only a day after Slovenia declared its **independence** on **June 25, 1991**, that the Yugoslav People's Army decided to act in an attempt to retain Slovenia by force. Its reaction, however, came much too late and had little chance of success. The ensuing **Ten Day War** only reaffirmed the obvious – Slovenia was independent and Yugoslavia was no more. Unfortunately this muscle flexing came at the price of 53 lives lost on both sides.

EPILOGUE: INDEPENDENT SLOVENIA (1991-PRESENT)

After a rough take off, Slovenia's independence was recognized by the world in 1992. The period up to 2004 was marked by the dominance of LDS ("Liberal Democracy of Slovenia"), a centre-left party whose achievement was the gradual introduction of a market economy whilst trying to retain elements of the welfare state and labour rights. The policy seemed to work and when in 2004 Slovenia joined the EU it was considered a success story of the Union's Eastward expansion. GDP grew steadily, inflation and unemployment were low and falling. LDS lost the 2004 elections to the conservative SDS (Slovenian Democratic Party) that thought the time ripe for the liberalisation and privatisation of the public sector, which it saw as too influenced by state intervention. Fuelled by the enthusiasm of EU accession, the new government over-borrowed from foreign banks and, in 2008, faced with a credit crisis, the voters ousted SDS from power. Instead the Social Democrats (SD) were elected but their attempt to implement reforms that would curb the crisis was met by trade union and student protests. In the end SDS came back to power in 2011 leading a centre-right coalition with the goal of approving a set of Merkel-styled economic measures. These are resolutely opposed by public sector workers as well as the country's youth.

Food & Drink

Considering its diverse geography and varied cultural influences it is fair to say that there is not one but several Slovenian cuisines. It can also broadly be said that continental Slovene cuisine is similar to Austrian cuisine but with different sausages. The best known Slovenian dishes are *kranjska klobasa* (Kranj sausages), *zrezek* (pork cutlets) and the inevitable *kislo zelje* (sauerkraut), once Carniola's best known export. There is also a local variety of goulash (*golaž*) and its less well-known cousin, *bograč*. The west of the country and the coastal areas are well known for Mediterranean fares such smoked ham (*kraški pršut*) that benefits from the cool sea air, polenta and *idrijski žlikrofi*, a regional specialty of potato dumplings similar to gnocchi with various fillings, from the mining town of Idrija.

Really traditional Slovenian dishes can be pretty rich, most being prepared with lard, bacon and plenty of dough. Two

Kranjska klobasa (Kranj sausages)

things that the locals invariably cherish are the *ajdovi žganci*, a buckwheat polenta, once the staple cuisine of Slovenian highlanders. Even more ubiquitous is *štruklji*, a sort of strudel from Dolenjska filled with anything from cottage cheese and potato to walnuts or tarragon and mentioned in cookbooks as early as 1589. Two dishes that perhaps best illustrate the mix of culinary tastes are winter specialty *jota*; a thick bean broth, sauerkraut, potatoes, pork ribs and lots of

Ajdovi žganci, a kind of polenta, is hugely popular in Slovenia

garlic; and *ričet* a thick porridge of whole wheat barley, dried meat, potatoes and any vegetables at hand.

The main meal of the day is lunch, usually taken in the early afternoon. No decent lunch starts without a soup (*juha*), usually beef (*goveja juha*). Don't miss traditional Slovenian **deserts** such as *potica*,

Prekmurska Gibanica

a rolled pastry with walnuts and spices, or *prekmurska gibanica*, a delicious cake with layers of apples, cheese, walnuts, raisins, all topped with cream.

The idyllic picture of the Slovenian Alps might make you think of Austria or Bavaria but unlike those beer swigging regions Slovenia is predominantly wine country. Union and Laško, the country's two major **breweries** (now under the same owner), produce reasonable lagers and a fine dark beer but not much more. There are also several micro-breweries, of which Human Fish, whose beer can be found on tap in several bars of the larger towns, stands out as one of the best. Slovenian **wines** are, on the other hand, not only of excellent quality but plentiful,

easily found and as varied as the country's landscapes. Try the renowned Teran, a dry red, or the white Rebula of the Karst region, Malvazija or Refošk if visiting the seaside, the light and sourly dry Cviček in Dolenjska or Ranina in the east. The best time to enjoy these wines is **Martinovanje** (St Martin's), November 11, when the season's new wine comes of age. On this day all the inns in Slovenia fill with merry crowds eager to try new wine together with the traditional goose roasted with *mlinci*, a thin dough. Note that wine is usually ordered and priced by the deciliter (*deci*). And finally, don't miss giving the local **spirits** (*žganje*), often distilled at home, a try. The most famous spirits are *slivovka*, a plum brandy, *medica* from honey and, best of all, the popular blueberry brandy *borovničevec*. The staple coffee in Slovenian cafés is espresso. On the other hand, in most homes you will still rather be served a strong Turkish coffee, a relic of Slovenia's time spent in union with its Balkan neighbours as part of Yugoslavia.

Slovene wines are plentiful and varied

Turkish-style coffee is still relatively common in Slovenia

specialties such as *pljeskavica* and *ćevapčići* (local varieties of hamburgers and kebabs). Of course, there are also plenty of pizzerias, sometimes so many you may want to double-check that you didn't accidentally cross the border into Italy.

Slovenian towns have some great restaurants on offer but even more wonderful than that are the numerous country inns (*gostilna*) scattered throughout the countryside. Though some might seem very plain they all dish up thoroughly decent, hearty food, often including otherwise hard to find regional specialties. For travellers on a tighter budget, many *gostilnas* and down to earth restaurants offer a fixed daily menu (*dnevno kosilo*), a reasonably priced three course lunch, usually for around €7.

Other phenomena from the Balkans that have found fertile ground in Slovenia include some **fast foods**, namely *burek*, a greasy pastry eaten either early in the morning or late at night, and grilled meat

Manners & Customs

Slovenes are a very friendly and hospitable people and, though at first they might sometimes appear somewhat reserved, they open up quickly upon becoming acquainted. This is especially true of their attitude towards foreigner visitors where there is always an element of curiosity.

Traditionally more or less a rural people, Slovenes are quite informal and direct in communication and have profoundly egalitarian manners. Although it is indeed possible to encounter real

Traditional costumes in Slovenia

impoliteness, you should not take it personally if addressed in an easy-going manner. More often than not, especially in the countryside, this is just a sign of friendliness and open-heartedness.

As elsewhere in Europe, formal etiquette is usually limited to communication between people who do not know each other and to formal occasions. Once better acquainted, communication can often become much more relaxed very quickly.

When meeting new people, a firm handshake and a straight look in the eyes is the norm. Of course, one should not exaggerate with strength, but it should nevertheless be born in mind that loose handshakes are considered impolite. A common phrase accompanying the handshake is *Me veseli* (Glad to meet you). Kisses – two or three on the cheeks – are usually exchanged only on special occasions such as birthdays or New Year's Eve.

If meeting people one is already acquainted with, one should shake hands and ask *Kako ste/si?* (How are you? – "ste" here is the plural, used in Slovenian as the formal form like *Vous* in French) or, more informally, *Kako gre?* (How's it going?). A good reply is *Dobro, hvala. Pa vi/ti?* (Well thanks and you?). Forms of address are *Gospod* (Mr.), *Gospa* (Mrs.) and *Gospodična* (Miss). These should be used unless the person in question is a good acquaintance or very young. The same goes with choosing between formal *Vi* (you, like the French *Vous*) and friendly and informal *Ti* (you).

A Slovene wedding

Common greetings are *Dober dan* (good day), *Dobro jutro* (good morning) and *Dober večer* (good evening). Friends and younger people most often say *Živjo* or *Zdravo* (hi or hello). At parting, *Nasvidenje* (goodbye) or the more informal *Adijo* are used.

Though formality may loosen up after getting acquainted the same does not usually apply to topics of conversation. Slovenes can be quite sensitive about private matters and these should be discussed only with people one knows well.

It is not at all unusual to be invited to someone's home for coffee, lunch or dinner and, as Slovenes take much pride in their hospitality, it might be quite a task to refuse. If you want to experience a more authentic side of Slovenia, and get a chance to try some home cooked food into the bargain, accepting such an invitation is definitely the best bet. By and large, Slovenes are very attached to their homes and families. They rarely move house and it is not uncommon for three generations of a family to live under one roof. Again, this is particularly true of, but not limited to, the countryside.

It is common to take your shoes off when visiting someone's home. Chances are the hosts will say it isn't necessary, which however does not mean that you shouldn't do it.

It is also not uncommon to get invited for a meal or a bigger social gathering as a lunch or a dinner party. In such a case it is appropriate to bring a small present – a bottle of wine, a box of chocolates or a bouquet of flowers.

There are no specifically Slovenian table manners and Slovenes are in general not too sensitive about them. Slovenes say *Dober tek* for "bon appetite", which is answered by *Hvala, enako* (thanks, same to you). When raising a toast, touch glasses, look everyone in the eye and say *Na zdravje!* (to your health!). Slovene for please is *prosim* or, more formally, *prosim Vas*. The Slovene for thank you is *hvala*.

When dining out or having drinks in company, it is customary for each person to pay for themselves, unless of course someone clearly expresses a wish to pay for everyone. In bars or pubs, paying for rounds of drinks is quite common, whereby it is also expected that everybody stands their round at some point.

In general one should not have any problems with basic communication in Slovenia, as a great majority of younger and middle-aged people either speak English well or have at the very least some rudimentary knowledge of English. The second most common foreign languages are German and Italian - the latter in the southwestern part of the country and the former everywhere else.

Due to their mutual relatedness, knowledge of any other Slavic language will also prove very useful. This applies especially to Serbo-Croatian, which is understood by most people old enough to remember Yugoslavia.

Landscape, Climate & Wildlife

On the lengthy list of varied attractions crammed into this small country, right up there is its geographical and natural diversity. Slovenia is where the Alps loom over the waters of the Mediterranean, where the Dinaric Alps of the Balkans reach their northernmost point and the vast Pannonian Plain comes to an end. The collision of these four very different environments is one of nature's greatest gifts to Slovenia.

It is thanks to its varied landscape that Slovenia is associated with hiking amongst mountain peaks, scenic walks through rolling hills, skiing the multitude of pistes and a host of other

An Ibex expertly negotiates the rocky landscape

Woods in Prekmurje

ALPINE SLOVENIA

When most people think of Slovenia they often think of the Alps, the "Sunny Side of the Alps", as an old tourist slogan would have it. The Alpine region is, however, only a small part of the country, covering just its northwest corner. The most impressive range is the **Julian Alps** stretching from Italy to the Sava River. This is awe inspiring country with dozens of mountain peaks soaring above 2500 meters, including the country's highest peak, Triglav. In their shade are deep valleys carved by long-gone glaciers, covered in dense woods. There are also many glacial lakes, deep blue and cold

outdoor pursuits. Many Slovenes are card carrying members of the National Mountain Association, an equal if not larger number enjoy skiing just about every weekend during the ski season. A less known fact is that Slovenia is the third most forested country in Europe! With 59% of its territory covered by woods, this is a country of fresh air, rare plants and rich woodland wildlife. Brown bears, wolves, boars, wildcats and even lynxes are just some of the animals that roam its forests while eagles, owls and hawks cruise its skies and trout, grayling, pike and carp swim in its streams and rivers.

Slovenes take a special pride in the natural beauty of their homeland and are serious about protecting it. There seems to be no corner of this small country that does not have its own fascinating, natural sight or ecologically protected area.

Kayaking the beautiful clear waters of the Soča

The Veli Badin rock shelters in Istria

Cows chilling on breathtaking Alpine meadows

even in midsummer, but utterly enchanting. Above the forests are alpine pastures, where herds of happy cows graze during the summers, and still higher meadows of iconic alpine flowers such as the gentian and edelweiss or the endemic "Triglav Rose" (a pink cinquefoil). With some luck, high up on its rocky cliffs you might see an ibex, a veritable trademark of the Alps

The Soča River flows through the heart of the Julian Alps. It starts as a fast stream flowing along the length of the Trenta valley, arguably the nicest of the glacial vales (see p. 128). Its bright emerald colour deepens as it grows, passing by small towns such as Bovec, Kobarid and Tolmin after which it enters a picturesque gorge to erupt in the sub-Mediterranean karst on the other side. In this marvellous river lives an equally marvellous fish – the Soča trout, found only in Slovenia.

On the other side of the Sava are two similar mountain ranges: the **Kamnik Alps** with their highest peak, Grintovec, reaching to 2559m and, forming the border with Austria, **Karavanke**, somewhat overlooked due to their comparatively lower and less steep peaks (the highest one being Stol at "only" 2239m).

Summers in the Alps are pleasant, though unpredictable, but the winters are bitterly cold. Due to the proximity of the Adriatic Sea, these mountains see a lot of rain and even more snow. The unforgiving climate and almost arid land that yields mostly potatoes has shaped the hardy men and women as diligent and thrifty. In search for more free land the villages have climbed up the mountain sides as high as 1,200m. Nowadays this is the most sparsely settled region in the country and in many of these mountain villages only the most elderly residents remain. However, the uncompromising nature of the Alps is part of what makes them so inviting for tourists.

Astounding Alpine vistas near Bovec

CENTRAL SLOVENIA

The administrative seat of Slovenia is, conveniently enough, also its geographical centre. From Bled the Sava River, now recognisable as the country's largest river, flows through a wide basin beyond Ljubljana. An occasional hill or two divide up the plain, keeping the scenery from becoming uninteresting. The land here is also rather unfertile but, surprisingly, this is country's most densely populated region.

The Ljubljansko Barje plain, much of which is a protected nature reserve

Apart from the capital and largest city, Ljubljana, the region is home to other sizable (at least in Slovenian terms!) towns like Kranj, Škofja Loka and Kamnik.

interesting to visitors are its streams and wetlands, home to a number of interesting bird species. A large chunk of the Barje is therefore protected as a nature reserve

The Velika Planina Alpine resort

The least hospitable area here is the **Ljubljansko Barje** ("Ljubljana Marshes") just south of the capital. Once an area of swamps and marshes, today it is partially farmland, though rather sodden farmland. More

MEDITERRANEAN SLOVENIA

Though only 43km long, the Slovenian coast is far from unattractive. First off it has a climate rather different to the rest of the country: it might be one of the northernmost points of the Mediterranean but it still enjoys pleasantly mild weather. The Mediterranean spring and autumn squeeze winter down to a month or two and even then snow is an unusual sight and does not last longer than it takes the puzzled locals to take a few photos. Lush Mediterranean vegetation, including delicious olives, almonds and figs, are proof enough of the weather's clemency.

The stunning coastline of the Strujan Nature Park

In the Middle Ages the towns of Koper and Izola were located on smaller islands but in time they were joined with the mainland. Today there are no islands (Slovenia's only one is on Lake Bled, 100km inland), but the coast is far from dull. The most picturesque of the three historic towns, Piran, spreads along an attractive cape and there are many nice sandy beaches, such as in the resort town of Portorož.

The Karst

Karst is a geological phenomenon where the easily porous limestone rocks are shaped by rains, creating a number of spongy surface features, letting water descend below to shape huge and intricate caverns (see p. 198). The Slovenian Karst includes the whole Southwest third of Slovenia, with the Dinaric Alps as its backbone. Karst in Slovenia is so prominent that many claim that its name comes from the Slovene word *kras*.

Distinctly Venetian architecture in Koper

A train takes visitors deep into the Postojna Cave

blowing from the land towards the sea. It is known across the eastern seaboard of the Adriatic, but it is exactly here that it is at its most devastating (see p. 127).

Further inland it seems that every hill and every village here has a cave of its own. Hundreds of smaller caves dot the landscape while dozens of the larger ones are open for visitors including the fascinating UNESCO protected caves in Škocjan, Pivka, Postojna. These caves are home to a unique amphibian, locally called the "human fish" (see p. 200), Another very peculiar Karst phenomenon is the disappearing Cerknica Lake (see p. 203) Not far from here lie vast, dark forests surrounding high mountains, with Snežnik (1796m) as their highest peak.

The whole eastern part of Dolenjska is also a karst region: streams disappear underground, not managing to form into rivers and its long fields have enough water only in during the spring rains. The region west of Novo Mesto used to be so short on

Written with a capital letter, the **Karst** is an area lying between Trieste and Gorizia. This is a land of stone, with no woods and only patches of dusty soil to which the hilltop villages preciously cling. Luckily, one of the few plants that thrives here is the grapevine. Beyond the Karst is the Vipava valley, open to warm Mediterranean air, with early springs and very hot summers, making it perfect for vineyards. The main drawback is the horrendous Burja wind,

One of the great caverns of Postojna Cave

The famous disappearing-reappearing lake at Cerknica

Pannonian Plain in the East. Flowing West to East, rivers such as the Krka, Sava, Drava and Mura leave mountains and ravines behind and enter wide plains. On their borders are pleasant low rolling hills, covered in orchards and vineyards, the largest and most bountiful in the whole country. Around and to the east of the River Mura the landscape becomes a vast plain, with hills on the horizons as distant reminders that you are still in a country famous for its mountains.

water that it got the name Suva Krajina – "Dry Land". The largest karst field is the one of **Kočevlje**, 700-800m tall and surrounded by virgin forests, protected since the 19th century. This has, since time immemorial, been one of the least populated areas in the country and thus also where wild animals found refuge. Your best chance to see one of Slovenia's 400 brown bears is here.

PANNONIAN SLOVENIA

No less than half of Slovenia opens up to the great

The gently rolling hills of Prekmurje

Visit some of Slovenia's stunning waterfalls on hiking trips organised by *Slotrips.si*

MORE MESMERIZING NUMBERS

+ Over 300 permanent waterfalls
+ Over 9000 caves
+ 36% of territory as protected areas
+ 10,000km of marked hiking paths

slotrips.si

Active Holidays

White-water rafting on the Soča River (see p. 128)

One of the great attractions of Slovenia is the variety and quality of active and adventure holidays on offer, enabling visitors to enjoy the country whatever the season. There is, in fact, so much on offer it could be the subject of a whole new guide. Rather than try to cover everything we decided on a quick overview to give you some ideas to help you take your experience of Slovenia that little bit further.

WATER SPORTS

Slovenia may only have a small coastline but this doesn't stop it from being one of Europe's top water sports destinations. Aside from traditional seaside sports such as water-skiing and sailing, the waters around Piran are excellent for diving. For more detailed information on diving and other seaside water sports, contact the Piran Tourist Information Centre, an offshoot of the Potorož Tourist Office (Tartinijev Trg 2, Piran 00386 5 673 44 40, *http://www.portoroz. si*).

Beyond the seaside, Slovenia's lakes and rivers also provide ample opportunity for fun and adventure. The Sava, Savinja and Krka rivers (see p. 69 & 229) are known for kayaking and canoeing opportunities, as are other rivers such as the Drava. The Soča river, with its emerald green waters and stunning scenery is also particularly good for canoeing. For help with organising water based active holidays, check out the Slovenian Tourist Board website (*www.slovenia.info*).

WINTER SPORTS

Though not recognised as such for a long time, Slovenia is now one of Europe's prime winter sports destinations and can comfortably be mentioned in the same breath as Austria, Switzerland or the French Alps. Beyond skiing, easily the most popular wintertime sport, Slovenia is also a top destination for snow-boarding, cross-country skiing and sledging.

Though the pistes of Kranjska Gora, Maribor Pohorje and, more recently, Cerkno are the most popular and well-known, there is a veritable multitude of other options with just about every town near a mountain having local skiing

Cerkno Ski-center-

Paragliding is an increasingly popular way to experience Slovenia's natural charms

tandem flights with an instructor, which are suitable for beginners. For the more experienced, solo paragliders, there are literally hundreds of clubs and even organised tours. The Slovenian Tourist Board is a great first port of call for more information (www.slovenia.info).

For those looking for a more sedate way to see Slovenia from the air, there are panoramic flights and hot air ballooning flights. Slovenia has a large number of small sports air fields that cater for visitors looking to soar but without the additional adrenalin kick of something like paragliding, the most popular of these are Lesce in Gorenjska, Skoke near Maribor and Rakičan near Murska Sobota. For more information on hot air ballooning, please see p 69.

facilities. Popular ski-centres include those at Kranj, Vogel and Kanin, while trails at Vršič, Velika Planina and on the Kamnik-Savinja Alps are popular for sledging.

▶ For a wealth of information on skiing, sledging, cross-country skiing and much, much more please visit the excellent website *slotrips.si* – through *slotrips.si* you can organise your own tours a perfect starting point around which to plan a winter holiday to Slovenia.

SLOVENIA FROM THE AIR

One of the best ways to experience Slovenia's breathtaking landscape is from the air. Luckily for all visitors, Slovenia abounds in opportunities to take to the skies and enjoy wonderful views in a unique and adventurous way.

A recent addition but now one of the most popular adventure sports in Slovenia is paragliding. There are many places to go paragliding throughout the country but amongst the best are in around Bovec, Krvavec and Tolmin. Most clubs offer

HIKING & CYCLING

In the hot summer months hiking and cycling take over from skiing and snowboarding as the recreation of choice. Slovene's have built up a rich culture of hiking, rambling and mountaineering as a great way to spend time away from towns and cities and explore the country's stunning landscape. Cycling trips to the countryside have also become a very popular pastime. Hiking and cycling are a fantastic way to get out and see the country if you are visiting during the warmer months and come with the additional benefit that excursions can be tailored to suit all ability levels. For more information on hiking of cycling trips please check out *www.slotrips.si*.

Biking the Walk of Peace, Kobarid (see p. 135)

Events & Festivals

The following list offers a selection of the yearly events that take place in Slovenia. For details check the internet pages suggested or look out for monthly reviews of what's on.

JANUARY

Golden Fox Trophy, Mt Pohorje (Maribor)
The world's best women skiers compete in slalom and giant slalom races in front of enthusiastic crowds.
www.goldenfox.org

The world's most prominent women's ski competition, the Golden Fox in Maribor

FEBRUARY

Kurentovanje, Ptuj
The most famous and most vibrant Shrovetide festivity, named after the famous kurent masks, which have become national symbols.
www.kurentovanje.net

The Kurentovanje Procession is perhaps Slovenia's most photogenic event

MARCH

World Ski Jumping Championships, Planica (Kranjska Gora)
One of the world's most famous ski jumping sites offers one of the most memorable experiences of the Slovenian Alps.
www.planica.si

Adrenalin pumping ski-jumps at Planica

APRIL

Spring Festival (Festival Pomladi), Ljubljana
Free open air concerts of the latest and most interesting acts from the world of electronic and experimental music.

MAY

Wild Flower Festival, Bohinj
An unusual science festival where visitors can learn about wild Alpine flowers in their natural habitat but can also enjoy local folk music and shop at a crafts market.
www.bohinj.si/alpskocvetje

The beauty of Slovenia's Alpine meadows comes to life

JUNE

Jazz Festival, Ljubljana
This selection of top musicians and performances over five summer days lives up to the impressive title of Europe's oldest jazz festival.
www.ljubljanajazz.si

Lent, Maribor
An outdoor festival where tons of music, street and theatre performances keep the city buzzing for two weeks.
www.festival-lent.si

International Street Theatre Festival "Ana Desetnica", Ljubljana and Maribor
Plays, contemporary dance, various performances, street musicians and circus performers visit the parks of Slovenia's major cities.

JULY

Rock Otočec, Otočec (Novo Mesto)
Paradise for hippies at heart, with rock gigs all night and chilling out in local forests, bathing in the Krka and mud-wrestling during the days.
www.rock-otocec.com

Otočec Rock Festival

Just one of the attractions of the Beer and Flowers festival in Laško

Beer and Flowers (*Pivo in cvetje*), Laško
Though the combination sounds unusual the beer tents, flower arrangements, brass marching bands and huge fireworks display attract large crowds.
www.pivo-cvetje.si

Great bands and great times at the Punk Rock Holiday festival

Punk Rock Holiday / Metaldays, Tolmin
Just two of several music festivals that take place in the great Alpine outdoors surrounding the townlet of Tolmin.
www.punkrockholiday.com
www.metaldays.net

AUGUST

Erazem's Medieval Tournament, Predjama Castle (Postojna)
Dueling knights, fair ladies, music and drinks to match, all in a genuine medieval setting.

Knights in shining armour at the Medieval Tournament by Predjama Castle

SEPTEMBER

Kravji bal, Bohinj
A celebration of the return of cattle from mountain pastures is the best opportunity to enjoy the customs and music of Alpine Slovenia.
http://kravjibal.bohinj-info.com

OCTOBER

Lipica Farm Day (*Dan kobilarne*), Lipica
Once a year this world-famous horse farm organizes an event where all can admire the skills and beauty of their horses as well as those of the many visiting troupes.

NOVEMBER

St Martin's Day, Maribor
Among the largest of events to take place in Slovenia, with plenty of old and new wines, food and music.

International Film Festival (LIFFE), Ljubljana
A cinematic frenzy grips the capital city as the cream of the crop of the year's movies are screened at its major theatres.
www.liffe.si

Slovenian Wine Festival, Ljubljana
The largest and the most exclusive gathering of wine and fine foods producers takes place at the Grand Union Hotel.
http://slovenskifestivalvin.si

Fine dining at the Slovene Wine Festival

DECEMBER

Christmas Market, Ljubljana
Wooden toys and seasonal treats are the most sought after traditional wares on sale at the stalls of this picturesque market.

SLOVENIA BY REGIONS

LJUBLJANA

A view of Ljubljana from Castle Hill

✦ Ljubljana, Slovenia's capital city, is a sublime blend of modern convenience and fascinating history and culture – and it's all pretty much within walking distance. It is a pretty, compact city that's easy to get around and with its great links to the rest of Slovenia it is perfect for a city break or as a base from which to explore the country's phenomenal natural beauty.

✦ Its colourful history has left its mark on the city in different ways, from the varied architecture to the small medieval streets and squares at the base of the Castle. History buffs will be thrilled with the excellent, accessible way the city's history is presented in the excellent museums, while other visitors can revel in the photogenic streets and relaxing pace of the city. Indeed, parts of Ljubljana can seem like an open air museum in their own right.

Don't let that fool you, however, as Ljubljana is still very much a living city, full of great cafes, restaurants, patisseries and with a colourful and lively nightlife. With accommodation ranging from inexpensive (but clean and welcoming) hostels to plush, grand hotels, Ljubljana is equally appealing to backpackers traversing Central Europe or the Balkans or to business visitors

looking for a calm, relaxing break away from the hustle and bustle of larger cities.

✦ For such a petite city Ljubljana still welcomes its visitors with a wide variety of activities (see p. 69) from excursions to areas of natural beauty just outside the city, to balloon rides with champagne, hiking in hills and mountains, canoeing on the Sava river and a whole lot more.

Ljubljana is as picturesque in the evenings as it is during the day

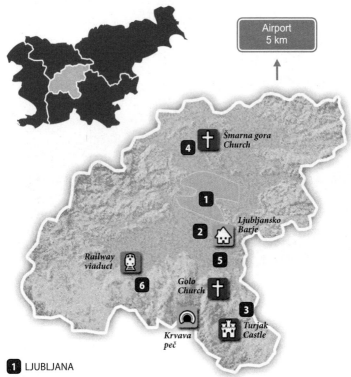

Airport
5 km

Šmarna gora
Church

Ljubljansko
Barje

Railway
viaduct

Golo
Church

Turjak
Castle

Krvava
peč

1 LJUBLJANA

2 ČRNA VAS

3 TURJAK CASTLE

4 ŠMARNA GORA

5 IŠKA GORGE

6 PEKEL

✦ One thing is certain, Ljubljana is an easy-going, comfortable city to visit but one that will keep you interested and active. Ideal either as a gateway to the rest of Slovenia or a city break destination.

Fairy tale Ljubljana decorated with Christmas lights

History of Ljubljana

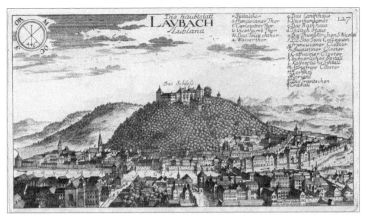

An engraving of medieval Ljubljana

Establishing their rule over the area around the year **15 BC**, the Romans built an encampment on the left bank of the Ljubljanica River, which from a pure military endeavour became a small thriving town named **Iulia Emona**. Its 5,000 inhabitants lived within strong walls in an orderly Roman city much alike many others around the Empire, with a rectangular street grid, a forum and all the other trappings of civilisation of the age. All of this came to an end soon afterwards as barbarians swept across the land. Anything that was left of Emona after the Goths and Langobards passed through was destroyed by Attila and his Huns in the middle of the 5th century.

A century later came the Slavs, who – in contrast to others before them – settled here permanently giving the river and the future town the names that remain to this day. By the 12th century, protected by the castle and the river, three adjacent hamlets developed, each with its own walls, earning the place the name "the town of Three Towns". Necessity forced the Hamlets to cooperate and they settled their problems in regular meetings that grew into a town council. In 1335 Ljubljana was acquired by the Habsburgs, under whose governance it would remain until 1918.

Medieval Ljubljana was constricted between Castle Hill and the Ljubljanica River, with Gradski Trg, Gornji Trg and Stari Trg forming a single street from which several short lanes branched off. Two bridges, Upper (today Cevljarski) and Lower (now Tromostovje), spanned the river. Across the first the new part of

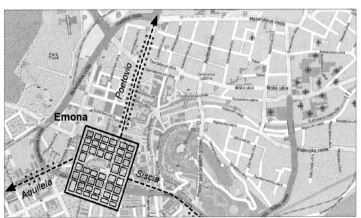

The location of Iulia Emona superimposed on modern-day Ljubljana

French rule during the Napoleonic Wars breathed new life into Ljubljana

broad streets were laid out to the west of the old town and, in the late 18th century a canal was constructed to siphon off surplus water from the Ljubljanica, to control seasonal flooding.

By the end of the century Ljubljana was a decent Hapsburg town of 10,000 people, with several schools and cultural societies. This culturally fertile ground made it possible for Valentin Vodnik and Anton Tomaž Linhardt to print their poems and dramas in Slovene, heralding a national awakening, further spurred by the short lived French rule (1809-13) that made Ljubljana the capital of the **Illyrian Provinces**. French rule opened equal prospects for people of all ranks and stimulated education and administration in the language of the majority. This brief respite from the rigid feudal system of Habsburg monarchy not only showed that things can work differently but also brought new architectural styles. Broad, tree-lined avenues modelled after those in Paris were cut through, with rational Classicism and Biedermeier replacing Baroque decoration. In 1821 Ljubljana came into the focus of European politics as the members of the Holly Alliance met here to discuss the suppression of revolutionary movements in Italy. The congress, which lasted three and a half months, was attended by the Austrian and Russian Emperors, as well as representatives of Prussia and Great Britain, and gave social life in the city a

the town, Novi Trg, developed. Centred around the seat of the Diet, town houses for the nobility sprung up while Jewish traders lived on the riverfront.

In 1461 the town became the seat of the bishop and renewed religious enthusiasm, combined with the traders' wish to get rid of the competition, led to the expulsion of the Jews. The town walls withstood their most important test in 1472 as a larger group of prowling Turks lay siege of the city, but collapsed along with most of the Medieval town in **1511** when Ljubljana was struck by the most disastrous of its recurrent earthquakes. Faced with the Turkish threat the town walls and castle were hastily rebuilt. This was also a time of religious upheaval: as the **Reformation** for a short period took hold in Slovene lands, Ljubljana became the centre of Slovene Protestantism, hosting Primož Trubar, author of the first book published in Slovene, and getting the first Slovene high school, library and printing press.

The **Counter-Reformation** soon struck back and in order to tighten the grip of Catholicism: in 1597 Jesuits came to the city, founding their gymnasium and bringing a **Baroque** aesthetic that remained predominant for two hundred years. Rid of the Turkish peril, the city demolished its walls and new,

The construction of the railway changed Ljubljana's fate, early locomotives can be seen at the Railway Museum (see page 64)

The Legend of Jason and the Argonauts
Searching for a legendary founder that would equal those of larger towns, Ljubljana's Renaissance historiographers came up with a legend to link their city with Ancient Greece. The story goes that after getting hold of the Golden Fleece, the heroic crew of the Argo, led by Jason, went off course and sailed up the Danube. They continued westwards along the Sava (up to this point the story tallies with the Greek legend) and then into the Ljubljanica. Heading for the source of the river at Vrhnika the ship was passing the marshes of Ljubljana when it was attacked by the dragon that inhabited them. The monster was slain by Jason, enabling the foundation of a new town. The Argonauts disassembled their ship in order to carry it to the Adriatic and continued their journey homewards.

whole new dimension. The arrival of the railway in 1849 stimulated the growth of industry and helped the late 19th century become a time of growth for both the middle and working classes. However, it was also a time of ethnic tensions between the German minority and Slovene majority that on several occasions turned violent.

In **1895** Ljubljana was struck by a devastating **earthquake**, however, luckily for the city, this was a time of economic prosperity and with the wise leadership of Mayor Ivan Hribar the disaster was turned to the city's benefit. Old streets were widened, new ones laid out, infrastructure improved, electricity introduced in 1898 and in 1901 the first tram service was introduced. The First World War left Ljubljana untouched and as the Habsburg Empire fell into ruin in **1918** the Slovenes joined the newly formed Kingdom of Serbs, Croats and Slovenes (renamed Yugoslavia in 1929). For the first time in its history Ljubljana became the **Slovene capital**. The city's rapid growth continued, boldly led by the ingenious architect Jože Plečnik (see p. 46).

In 1942 the Italians, the occupying power in Ljubljana during World War II, came to associate the hostile attitudes of Ljubljana's citizens with attacks on their troops stationed around Slovenia. In a bid to cut off the city they encircled it with 30km of barbed wire. In time, however, the fortifications proved to be nothing more than a monument to the defiance of the Slovenes.

In May 1945, after three and a half years as an open air prison, the city was liberated by the Partisans who once again made it the capital of Slovenia. Bent on industrialising the country, the communist authorities built new factories and residential estates for the growing number of workers. In time the unsophisticated socialist style become more refined and the city experienced a construction boom, acquiring modern hospitals, schools, cultural centres and residential complexes. When Slovenia became independent in 1991, Ljubljana revamped its somewhat neglected historical centre and continued to modernise in line with its European orientation, becoming a model European city.

Many of Ljubljana's winding lanes and streets retain their medieval feel

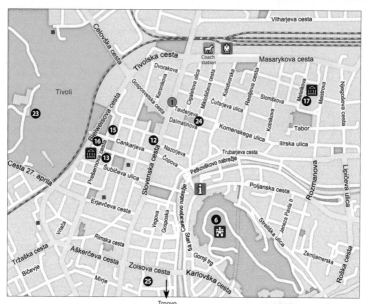

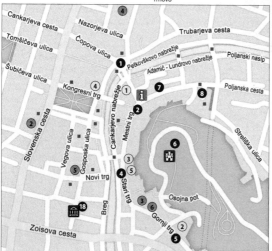

HOTELS:

1. Hostel Zeppelin
2. Hotel Cubo
3. Lesar hotel Angel
4. Grand Union Busines
5. Antiq Palace
6. Allegro hotel

RESTAURANTS:

1. Lolita
2. Spajza
3. Marley & Me
4. Kavarna Zvezda
5. Valvasor

1. Prešeren Square
2. Town Square
3. The Banks of the Ljubljanica
4. Old Square
5. Upper Square
6. The Castle
7. The Cathedral
8. Vodnik and Krek Squares
9. New Square
10. Congress Square
11. Republic Square
12. The Skyscraper
13. National Museum
14. Natural History Museum
15. National Gallery
16. Museum of Modern Art
17. Ethnographical Museum
18. City Museum
19. Museum of Architecture
20. Railway Museum
21. Brewery Museum
22. Tobacco Museum
23. Tivoli Park
24. Miklošič Road & Park
25. Krakovo & Trnovo

The dramatic statue of France Prešeren

On New Year's Eve Prešeren Square is transformed into a winter wonderland

1 Ljubljana

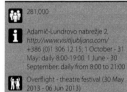

281,000

Adamič-Lundrovo nabrežje 2,
http://www.visitljubljana.com/
+386 (0)1 306 12 15; 1 October - 31
May: daily 8:00-19:00. 1 June - 30
September: daily from 8:00 to 21:00

Overflight - theatre festival (30 May
2013 - 06 Jun 2013)

Franja Marathon - recreational road
cycling competition (07 Jun 2013 -
09 Jun 2013)

Street theatre festival (03 Jul 2013
- 06 Jul 2013)

Locals love to meet or hang out on Prešeren Square

1 Prešeren Square *(Prešernov Trg)*

▶ Beyond doubt the city's most central
location, Prešeren Square has for centuries
been the main connection between the Old
Town across the river and the areas to the
north and west, where the new city centre
developed in the 19th century. One of the
liveliest places in Ljubljana, it is a favourite
meeting spot of both young and old and
a good place to sit and enjoy the buzz of
the city.

▶ The square is at the foot of the famous
Triple Bridge (*Tromostovje*) built
across the Ljubljanica in 1842. During
his reconstruction of the riverbanks in
1931, Jože Plečnik solved the problem
of broadening the busy bridge with
the inspired addition of two identical
pedestrian bridges on either side. Plečnik's
final touch was to arrange the three spans
in a radial pattern, spreading out onto the
broad Prešeren Square and focusing on
Stritareva Street on the other side, resulting
in another Ljubljana landmark.

▶ The central feature of
the square is the **Prešeren
Monument**, erected in 1905 in
memory of Slovenia's greatest
poet (see p. 97). The imposing
stone plinth with extracts
from Prešeren's poems was
designed by the famed architect
Max Fabiani while the statue
of Prešeren and the, for the
time scandalously nude, muse
holding a laurel wreath above
his head are the work of sculptor
Ivan Zajc. Prešeren gazes across

The Triple Bridge leading to Prešeren Square

The bust of Prešeren's unrequited love gazes across the square at his statue

the square to a house in Wolfova Street where a relief of his great love, Julia Primic, stands on the upper floor. Julia is portrayed looking back, considered by many to be a cruel reminder of Prešeren's unrequited love. In the days after its unveiling the monument became the gathering point of young Slovene nationalists who would gather here to give speeches and sing songs before setting off to harass the local German community. These days are long gone now and the monument is a favourite meeting point both of *Ljubljančani* and their visitors.

▶ To the left of the monument, at the corner with Miklošičeva Cesta, the eye is attracted to the ornate Art Nouveau façade of the **Centromerkur**, built in 1903 as the city's first department store. The edifice has recently been restored to its former glory and is once again a shining temple of consumerism, now under the name *Galerija Emporium*. Still, enjoying its ornate entrance or the central staircase, topped by an allegory of trade, is free for all.

▶ The focal point of Prešeren Square is the Church of the Annunciation, better known to all as the **Franciscan Church** (*Frančiškanska Cerkev*). The church and the adjoining monastery were originally built for Augustine monks, in place of its medieval predecessor that collapsed in a 1640s earthquake. Its cake-like pink façade is a typical, if not inspired, example of Jesuit Baroque. Inside (*open 10am-6pm*), you will see the high altar designed by Francesco Robba in the early 18th century; the frescoes covering much of the walls are a century and a half younger.

▶ The most unusual building in the square is the slender Hauptmann House, better known as the **Ura** ("The Clock") for the clock shop that operated here for a long

Ljubljana: A City Trademarked by Plečnik

Seldom will you find a city so influenced by a single architect as Ljubljana was by Jože Plečnik: it almost seems that he single-handedly sculpted the city in his own vision, from new streets, parks and quays to the tiniest of details on his buildings. Incredibly, this all happened over just two decades.

Time spent as a joiner in his father's workshop and then at carpentry school in Graz gave Plečnik the ability to understand architecture from a unique perspective. He went on to study architecture, first in Graz then as one of the best pupils of the great Otto Wagner in Vienna. In the 1910s he taught in Prague where he immensely influenced a group of students who would later lead the Czech cubist movement. In 1920 he was appointed by Czechoslovak President Masaryk to head a project to renovate Prague Castle and make it the focal point of the new state's ideals of democracy and freedom. Plečnik's work on the Castle, drawing inspiration from classical ideals but in keeping with its unique history, won him fame and critical acclaim.

In 1921 he became a Professor at the newly established Ljubljana University and, in parallel with work in Prague, started working on projects in his home town. His reputation and the backing of city officials enabled him to transform the city. In Plečnik's eyes, the young Slovene capital was to become a new Athens - democratic, open and Mediterranean in appearance. Over the next 20 years he put all his talent and energy into making this a reality, reinterpreting Ljubljana's appearance and self-perception at the rate of, on average, one project a year. A versed urbanist, he always had an eye on the big picture but paid equal attention to the smallest details, turning his every design into a work of art. His creations combined elements of classical architecture with Modernist tendencies, all wrapped up in his recognizable and highly original style.

After WWII the aged Plečnik, too conspicuous for his sound Catholicism and classical ideals, was slowly shunned, as were others connected with the old regime. As Slovene society turned its gaze in another direction his work fell into disregard only to be brought back into the spotlight during the 1986 exhibitions of his opus in Paris and Ljubljana, which coincided with a rise of Post-Modernism that came to regard him as one of its founding fathers.

The red façade of the Franciscan Church is the focal point of the square

time. This is the only house in the square that survived the 1895 earthquake that hit this area especially hard. Following the earthquake the façade had to be redecorated and it was done so superbly by Ciril-Metod Koch in a restrained geometrical style drawing its inspiration from folk embroideries that still makes it one of the most familiar sights in the city. Its bright colours also had a practical purpose as a sort of advertisement for Hauptmann who was a paint merchant.

❷ Town Square (*Mestni Trg*)

▶ This is one of three "squares" (actually marketplaces as "*trg*" is sometimes translated) of the Old Town, cramped in the narrow space between Castle Hill and the Ljubljanica. Until the end of the 19th century, the Town Square was the centre of Ljubljana's commerce, crowded with stalls, itinerant merchants and shops with the most fashionable goods. All of this changed with the introduction of the tram that ran the length of the three squares and the development of new districts that took on the role of the city centre.

The Town Square on a clear winter's evening

▶ Although it has lost its commercial dominance, the Town Square still retains its administrative importance with the **Town Hall** (*Mestna Hiša*) that dominates the square. Originally erected in 1484, its present-day appearance dates back to a major reconstruction by Gregor Maček in 1718. The architect decided on an uncommonly sober façade for the High Baroque age, its main decoration being the Palladian window with a balcony from which official proclamations were made. The reconstruction included the obligatory clock tower that not only keeps the time but also shows the phases of the moon. Feel free to step inside and admire the Gothic entrance hall adorned with a sculpture of Hercules and the Nemean Lion as well as the arcaded courtyard where the first theatrical performances in the city were held. In the corner of the courtyard you will notice another scene from classical antiquity - the 18th century fountain with Narcissus descending down to the rocks to admire his own image, by Robba. For those who want to learn more about the Town Hall and see spaces not open to the public such as the Grand Council chamber, banquet or wedding hall, there is a guided tour in English and Slovene available every Saturday at 1pm (*by prior appointment; €2 per person; organized group tours at prearranged times are also available*).

The grandiose but soberly decorated Town Hall

The courtyard of the Town Hall

The Robba Fountain on the Town Square

▶ Irreversibly connected with the image of the Town Hall is another of Ljubljana's landmarks, the adjacent **Robba Fountain** from 1751. The fountain's tall, serene obelisk is contrasted by the restless statues holding jugs from which water gushes, symbolizing the major rivers of Carniola – the Sava, Krka and Ljubljanica. This impressive fountain takes its name from its creator, sculptor Francesco Robba, a native Venetian who married in Ljubljana and stayed here for the next 35 years creating

its finest Baroque monuments. Although Robba evidently drew inspiration here from Bernini's Fountain of Four Rivers in Rome, his work is original and stands up well to that of his more famous counterpart. However, the money and effort he invested to make the fountain (thought to have taken eight years to finish) never paid off and four years later, shortly before his death, he left Ljubljana for Zagreb. The fountain you can see today is, unfortunately, merely a faithful copy of the original which was relocated for the safekeeping to the National Gallery (see p. 62), but don't let this spoil your enjoyment of this extraordinary work of art.

One of the houses of Carniolan aristocrats, the Souvan House

▶ After admiring the Town Hall and the fountain take some time to enjoy the beauty of the surrounding buildings, the houses of the most distinguished burghers and Carniolan aristocrats. Architecturally the most remarkable is the five-storey **Souvan House** opposite the Town Hall. Built at the end of the 17th century, it got two new storeys and a completely new Biedermeier front in 1827. The architect, Francesco Coconi, another Italian in Ljubljana, richly embellished the lower two floors while leaving the upper portion unornamented. Note the reliefs under the 2nd floor windows representing trade, art and agriculture.

❸ The Banks of the Ljubljanica

▶ The slow moving Ljubljanica is one of the essential components of the city without which it just wouldn't be the same. Weeping willows line the walkways stretching along its banks through the city center but by far the most interesting section is between Šentjakobski Bridge and Tromostovje where narrow façades in all styles and colors overlook the riverside walkways.

A view of the Castle from across the Cobbler's Bridge

Cafes spill out onto the street on summer evenings

The opening of café Maček ("The Cat") back in 1995 signaled the dawning of the new era for the area: since then a dozen or so new places have made this the centre of the city's

Cafes and art on the river banks

café culture. With the first rays of sun the pavements fill with chairs and tables and remain packed at most times of the day (and especially the evenings!) throughout the summer.

▶ The centre point of the area is the **Cobblers' Bridge** (Čevljarski Most). A bridge has spanned the river here since the 13th century, allowing the New Market to develop on the left bank. The old wooden construction was originally known as the Butchers' Bridge for the stalls of this guild that flanked it, but after the numerous complaints about the unbearable stench the butchers were moved out and other crafts took their place, the most numerous of which were the cobblers. A new bridge designed by Plečnik and similar to the Trnovo Bridge (see p. 68) was built here in 1932. Instead of a simple river crossing, Plečnik created a broad platform, a square above the river and, as he intended, many festivals and events take place on the bridge. Every Saturday from the beginning of May till the end of October the Cobblers' Bridge becomes the part of the **Arts and Crafts market** (9am-4pm), while on Sunday mornings the **antiques market** draws enthusiasts and passers-by.

▶ On the left (western) bank of the river, standing at the beginning of the quay that bears his name, you will see the **bust of Ivan Hribar**, a former major of Ljubljana (1896-1910) who was responsible for much of its renovation. The small lanes behind the bridge, once the Jewish quarter, are amongst the most charming in the city.

❹ Old Square (Stari Trg)

▶ The narrow street connecting the Town Square with Levstik Square has since the Middle Ages been known as the Old Market. Indeed, this was one of the main trading streets in Ljubljana, lined with the houses of prominent citizens, traders and nobles alike. Things have not changed much and this is still a prestigious shopping street with designer shops, cosy

Street cafes on the Old Square

cafés, quirky souvenirs behind old wooden shop windows and long passageways leading to shaded courtyards.

In the Middle Ages Town Square and Old Market were divided by a wall descending from Castle Hill to the Cobblers Bridge (see p. 49). At this demarcation point stood the city gallows and, at No. 2, the dungeon known as the **Tranča**.

Next to it, on **No. 4**, is a plaque stating that Johann Weikard Valvasor was born there in 1641. This is by no means an established fact, but since the house was at the time owned by his mother and Valvasor was christened in Ljubljana Cathedral it is a fair presumption.

▶ **Erberg House** (No. 9) has a Baroque frontage, while its neighbour at No. 11a, the **Schweiger House**, is a genuine Rococo masterpiece. The statue of Atlas holding the

The houses along the Old Square

central balcony has a finger raised to his lips recalling the name of the owner, which translates from German as "the silent one". A bust of Slovene poet Lili Novy (1885-1958), who spent the last part of her life here, stands by the entrance.

▶ The last house on Old Market, where it flows into Upper Square is **Stična Manor**, built in 1628-30 as the town residence of the Abbots of Stična Monastery, today housing the Music Academy. In front of it is a small **Hercules Fountain**, a recent copy of the 17th century original you can see in the Town Hall, depicting the antique hero slaying the Nemean lion.

The Hercules Fountain on the corner of the Old Square and Upper Square

5 Upper Square (*Gornji Trg*)

▶ It is hard to imagine that this picturesque corner of Ljubljana was once a major thoroughfare. The pretty Medieval and Baroque buildings lining it tell the story of its previous significance when all trade towards the Dolenjska region and to the South passed through here. After the broad Karlovška Cesta was constructed in the late 19th century the square sunk in to obscurity, and little has changed since. Nowadays, largely due to its well preserved Medieval appearance, Gornji Trg has revived its prestige with a mix of art galleries, antiques shops, boutique hotels and charming little restaurants.

Upper Square is pedestrianised and is a favourite meeting place

▶ Take a look at the group of **houses at Nos. 7-15**; these are the best preserved samples of the city's Medieval architecture built according to regulations that no house shall have more than three windows and

Well preserved medieval houses on Upper Square

that everyone had the same length of shop window. Behind their narrow façades run long courtyards with gardens climbing up the hill.

▶ In the times of torch lit streets and open fireplaces the area of Upper Square was recurrently damaged by fires. After one in 1660 that devastated twenty houses in Stari and Gornji Trg a **church dedicated to St. Florian**, the saint deemed to protect against fires, was constructed in 1672. This, however, didn't work out too well since the church was destroyed in a blaze a century later. Its present day appearance is

The Church of St. Florian on Upper Square

due largely to a reconstruction by Plečnik who added a new entrance with a stairway on the side street. The old entrance was transformed into a drinking well using elements from buildings pulled down at the time; in the same way Plečnik reused Robba's statue of St John of Nepomuk, that now adorns the face towards the Gornji Trg.

❻ The Castle (*Grad*)

www.ljubljanafestival.si; tel. 01/241 6000; open 1st May-30th Sept 9-23h, 1st Oct-30th Apr 9-21; admission free

▶ The Castle of Ljubljana is the heart of the city, the place where it all began. Jože Plečnik referred to it as the crown of Ljubljana; both visually and in terms of importance, a Slovene acropolis. With its hilltop position, it is visible from almost everywhere in the city and simply lures you to climb up and see what it's all about.

The towers of Ljubljana Castle

For the best part of its existence, the history of the castle was the history of Ljubljana (see p. 41). The core of what we see today dates from late 15th century when Habsburg Emperor Friedrich III thoroughly re-fortified the seat of the Duke of Carniola, but the earthquake of 1511 destroyed most of his efforts and extensive rebuilding took place throughout the next two centuries. After its last siege during the Napoleonic wars, the Castle lost its defensive role and was turned into a prison. The municipal authorities purchased it from the state in 1905 with ambitious plans but eventually turned it into a housing estate. The last

A panoramic view of the Castle from the air

The Ljubljana Castle, as seen from the streets below

residents of the Castle moved out in 1965 and meticulous restoration, completed only recently, made its halls and open-air stage popular for cultural events and weddings.

By far the best way to reach the Castle is **on foot** along one of the paths starting from the Old Town. There are three starting points from the Old Town: from the Church of St Florian in Upper Square along Ulica na Grad, from Stari Trg up the street called Reber and, thirdly, from Vodnikov Trg up the Študentova Street. From the eastern side you can climb up from Streliška Street taking the Na Stolbi path. As you climb upwards the houses shrink, the gardens meld into a forest and vistas over the whole of the town become more magnificent with every step. There are several side paths all of which are worth exploring. It would be fair to say that the ascent is at least half the fun of the Castle experience. Nevertheless, it is not an easy task so for those with doctors orders not to strain too much and for those who are feeling lazy there is a **funicular railway** (see p. 55) and **tourist train** from Prešeren Square which departs every hour on the hour from 9am to 9pm (*adults/ children €3/2*).

The ridge of Castle Hill is a pleasant promenade. Since 1974 the small vantage point on the side has been adorned by a monument to peasant rebels (by S. Batić), a Socialist counter-balance to the feudal castle.

Across the drawbridge you enter the Castle with its spacious courtyard where various concerts and performances take place in the summer months. On a usual day here you will find an open-air café, info point with a souvenir shop and an art-gallery housing temporary exhibitions. The main sight is the tall **lookout tower** (*razgledni stolp*), originally built of wood at the start of the 19th century for fire brigade watchmen and re-built in 1848. Inside is the **Virtual Museum** with a 20 minute 3D film that leads visitors through the history of Ljubljana. A flight of steps up and you're on top of the tower, at the highest point in Ljubljana, wherefrom panoramic views spread across the city all the way to the Alps (*combined ticket for the museum and the outlook platform: adults €3.50, children, students and groups over 15 people €2*).

▶ Adjoining the tower is the **chapel of St George**, the protector saint of the city. Gothic on the outside and baroque on the inside, its main features are the perfectly preserved wall paintings of coats-of-arms of Carniolan nobility that cover the upper portions of the walls and the ceiling.

The other sites of the Castle (such as its halls, some more frescoes and the artesian well) can be seen only on an hour-long **guided tour**, available from 1 June to 15 September at 10am, 11:30am, 2pm and 4pm and starting from the draw-bridge (*adults €5, students and pensioners €3.50*). The tour ticket is also valid for the Virtual Museum and the Lookout Tower.

A view of Gornji Trg from the climb up Castle Hill

❼ The Cathedral *(Stolnica)*

▶ Before reaching the small Pogačarjev Square surrounded with buildings linked to Ljubljana's cathedral, a visitor will notice the **colonnaded market** along the banks of the Ljubljanica. This extraordinary location in the very heart of the city was occupied by the wooden stalls of butchers and fruit and vegetable sellers until Jože Plečnik transformed it into one of Ljubljana's landmarks

The Cathedral seen from Castle Hill

The Butchers' Bridge is also famous for its 'love padlocks

in 1940. The down-to-earth market has been transformed into a work of art: the long line of small shops (still mostly butchers, but now also shops selling local specialties or organic food) have been set behind a graceful colonnade. Here the river is spanned by the brand new (2010) **Butchers' Bridge** ("Mesarski Most"), built in keeping with Plečnik's ideas. This unusual pedestrian bridge is one of several that are to be built in coming years to bring the Ljubljanica into the city's embrace. In homage to Plečnik's Trnovo Bridge (see p. 68), trees have been planted along its approaches and it also features glass paving on the side and golden sculptures of the wounded Prometheus, Adam and Eve, a satyr and other creatures by Jakov Brdar.

Market stalls spill out onto Pogačarjev Square

▶ From the lively market on Pogačarjev Square you have a good view to the north side of the **Cathedral**. The first church here was built in the mid 13th century by local fishermen and boatmen who dedicated it their patron saint, St Nicholas. Andrea Pozzo, a Jesuit, built the present day edifice in 1701-1707 modelling it on the Il Gezu in Rome, the main church of his order. Before you enter, take a look at the remarkable **bronze doors** added in 1996 to

Jakov Brdar's surreal sculptures on the Butchers' Bridge

commemorate the Papal visit; the west door (by Tone Demšar) celebrates 1250 years of Christianity in Slovenia, while the south door (by Mirsad Begić) depicts the six famous bishops of the city and the history of the bishopric.

The Cathedral's interior is a textbook example of Baroque lavishness with walls of white and pink marble, gilded capitols, with stucco work and numerous sculptures filling in the space between. The most impressive piece is the illusionist painted ceiling by Giulio Quaglio, but also note the angels on the main portal, statues of

The Cathedral's bronze doors commemorate the 1996 papal visit

Ljubljana bishops (by Angelo Pozzo) and the bishop's throne, by Plečnik.

▶ One of city's oldest buildings, the **Bishop's Palace** stands in front of Cathedral's west entrance. Built in 1512, it still retains some of its basic original features such as an arcaded central courtyard, though the façade has been altered several times. The roomy and well maintained palace has long been the lodging of choice for Ljubljana's most distinguished visitors, including prominent

The splendor of the Cathedral's Baroque interior

guests such as the Habsburg Emperors Leopold I and Charles VI, Napoleon, his marshals Bernadotte and Marmont – who governed the Illyrian Provinces from here - and, somewhat later, Russian Tsar Alexander I - who stayed here during the congress of the Holly Alliance (see p. 42). Pope John Paul II also spent the night here in 1996.

▶ On the other side of the square is the **Seminary** whose serene façade hides the fact that it was built in the age of High Baroque, between 1708 and 1772. Note the **south portal** from 1714 by Andrea Pozzo: the heavy gates are guarded by two stone Atlases over whom looms the dedication *Virtuti et Musis* ("To excellence and the arts"). Ljubljana's first public **library** opened here in 1725. Its main two-storey hall is a magnificent piece of Baroque art with oak panels and galleries, delicate stucco work and a ceiling painting by G. Quaglio depicting Theology giving birth to Fate, flanked by Hope and Love (*visits by prior arrangement with the Tourist Info Centre*).

The Bishop's Palace lies behind the Cathedral

❽ Vodnik and Krek Squares
(*Vodnikov Trg & Krekov Trg*)

▶ **Vodnik Square** is Ljubljana's **central green market**, one of the city's most picturesque sights full of colour, smells and tastes; it is a real treat if you're looking for fresh home-grown products ranging from berries to cheeses. Here you can also have a snack at one of the fast-food stalls or a proper lunch in one of the

The busy market on Vodnik Square

small restaurants, buy flowers or a more permanent souvenir. The market is at its liveliest on Saturdays but - except on Sundays when it's closed - is good to visit on any other day as well.

The area around the market was, until the earthquake of 1895, occupied by the city lyceum run by the Franciscans. Valentin Vodnik (1758-1819), a poet of the enlightenment period, attended the lyceum and later, having become a Franciscan monk, taught there. His bronze statue, (by Alojz Gangl) unveiled in 1889, still stands exactly as it did when the lyceum stood behind it.

The statue of poet Valentin Vodnik on the square dedicated to him

▶ Vodnik Square spills into **Krek Square**, named after former leader of the Christian-Socialist party, Janez Evangelist Krek. The building on the left that now houses, amongst other things, the central office of the Tourist Information Centre (TIC) of Ljubljana, previously housed the famous "Zum Österreichische Hof" Hotel whose patrons included field marshal Josef Radetzky and Prince Miloš Obrenović of Serbia while Prince Carlos, the Bourbon pretender to the Spanish and French thrones, was born here in 1848.

▶ On the other side of the square is the broad **Town Home** (*Mestni Dom*) built in 1899 to house various new municipal services such as the modernised fire brigade and the sewage, power and lightning departments. The upper floor has a hall which was used on ceremonial occasions and is today the stage of the "Šentjakobsko Gledališče" Theatre, the oldest amateur troupe in Slovenia, and the Puppet Theatre.

The Mestni Dom now houses a puppet theatre

▶ To its right is the lower station of the **castle funicular**, opened for service in 2007, whose glass gondola will take you 70m up the hill in just one minute, leaving you in front of the Castle (see p. 51, open 1st May – 30th Sept 9-23h, 1st Oct – 30th Apr 10-21; one way ticket/return €3/1.80).

▶ Looking away from Vodnik Square you will notice a strangely slim building between two streets, known to all as the **Peglezen** ("The Iron") due to its unique shape. Built by Plečnik in 1933 the building is as distinctive as is its name, with three storeys of different designs, each regressing further from the square.

▶ To the left of the Peglezen, Kopitarjeva Street leads straight to the **Dragon Bridge**, one of the most photographed symbols of the city. In 1896 mayor Hribar opened a tender for a new bridge; the winning design, with its reinforced concrete construction and secessionist decoration by Croatian sculptor Juraj Zaninović, a pupil of Otto Wagner, was state-of-the-art for the time. The bridge opened in 1901 and was named after Emperor Franz Joseph (hence the years 1848 and 1888 – his accession to the throne and the 40th anniversary thereof – on the sides of the bridge) but the name never caught on. Instead the bridge takes its name from its four dragon statues; according to a local joke, the dragons wag their tails every time a virgin crosses the bridge.

The Castle funicular railway departs from a station near Krek Square

❾ New Square *(Novi Trg)*

The New Square seen from across the Ljubljanica

▶ In the Middle Ages this was the first part of the town to extend over onto the left bank of the Ljubljanica River, hence the name. By the 17th century it became a favourite location for aristocrats looking to escape the confined streets of the Old Town. Here they could build on a larger scale and so they did, creating the New Square as it looks today. The last change came at the turn of the 20th century when the houses at its lower end were demolished opening it out on to the river.

The "Lontovž", home of the Slovenian Academy of Science

▶ The most notable building here is the "Lontovž", sitting at the upper end of the square (at no. 5). The name is a Slovenian deformation of German *Landhaus*, the seat of the provincial Diet of Carniola, which remained here until 1899 when it moved to the building in Congress Square (see p. 57). Rebuilt after a 16th century fire, the meeting place of provincial nobles got its fine baroque façade in 1780. In the 17th and 18th centuries this was the hub of theatrical life in the city as itinerant companies of Italian actors performed in its great hall and garden pavilion. Today the building is used by the Slovene Academy of Arts and Sciences established in 1938 to bring together the most distinguished

The Neptune Fountain on New Square

scientists of the country. Take a peek inside the Lontovž's garden and you will see the **Neptune Fountain**, a curious late renaissance venture, commissioned by the city council in 1675 to beautify the city for the visit of Emperor Leopold I and which stood in front of the Town Hall until it was replaced by the Robba Fountain. The Academy also uses the Koblenz House across the road (no. 4 on the Square) and the Lichtenberg House next to it, both fine examples of the Baroque style.

The monumental red-brick façade of the National Library

▶ Across Gospodska ("Gentlemen") Street is the **National and University Library**. The palace of Dukes Auersperg, one of the most opulent baroque edifices in town whose demolition was long lamented, stood here until an earthquake in 1895. Luckily in 1936-41 it got a worthy successor in what is considered to be the most important work by Plečnik in Ljubljana. The Library's exterior is monumental and reminiscent of a Renaissance palazzo with façades in red brick and rough stone blocks from various quarries in Slovenia. The façade is contrasted on its east and west side by the four-storey glass walls each guarded by a single typically Plečnik-like Ionian column.

❿ Congress Square
(*Kongresni Trg*)

▶ Central Ljubljana's largest square is surprisingly tranquil, taken up mostly by the leafy Zvezda ("Star") Park. Bordered by busy Slovenska Street and surrounded by many important buildings, the square is a melting pot of business people, students and tourists. From the early 17th century it was the site of the Capuchin monastery, which was, during Napoleonic rule, turned into barracks and stables, later demolished in 1817. The empty grounds were levelled and brought into order for the occasion of

Congress Square is one of central Ljubljana's main open spaces

Zvezda Park is an integral part of Congress Square

the Congress of Ljubljana in 1821 (see p. 42). In 1824, a Parisian-style park was laid featuring a central roundel and eight paths lined with trees branching from it – the shape that immediately earned it the name "The Star". On the southern side is a proper square designed by Plečnik, which was for a long time used as a car park but is now a square again with the cars moved underground. The park is also a prime location for important monuments. Today the best known monument in the park is the **Emonec** ("the Emonian"), representing a citizen of Roman Ljubljana of 4th century AD, which in time became one of the symbols

of the city. The statue stands on a stone column right about where it was excavated in 1836, in the grounds of a necropolis that spread north of Emona's defensive wall. Not far from it, on the north end of the park, there is a large **anchor**, placed here in 1954 on the 10th anniversary of the accession of Primorska province to Slovenia.

▶ The Square's most recognisable building is the stately **Seat of Ljubljana University**, which overlooks the south side of the square. Built in 1896-1902 for the Provincial Administration of Carniola, it was designed by architects V. Hrasky and J. Hudetz in a rich Neo-Renaissance style with many opulent details such as the gilded coats-of-arms of the fourteen towns of Carniola on the pilasters. On important occasions, such as after the liberation of the town in 1945, speeches to the people of Ljubljana were delivered from its large ceremonial balcony. Foundation of the first Slovene University was no easy task: pleas and demands to the Viennese Court for a higher education institution in Slovene lands fell on deaf ears and the University was not established until 1919. With over 40,000 students and numerous scientific institutes the University is today one of the drivers of Ljubljana's social and cultural life.

The Neo-Renaissance building of the University of Ljubljana

The Philharmonic Hall on Congress Square

Detail of the façade of the Philharmonic Hal

▶ The heading *Academia Philharmonicorum* on the building to the left of the University reveals it to be the **Philharmonic Hall**. Founded in 1701 as a branch of the city's learned society *Academia Operosorum*, the society staged concerts and operas and in 1794 evolved into the Philharmonic Society, amongst the first in the whole central Europe. Its honorary members included Haydn, Beethoven, Paganini and Brahms; tokens of gratitude they sent upon being bestowed the title, mostly manuscripts of their compositions, today present great value. The old Provincial Estates Theatre where all this, including the staging of the first Slovene-language play – Linhart's "Županova Micka" (1794) - took place disappeared in flames in 1887. The new concert hall was built in 1891 and soon became the seat of the Philharmonic Orchestra which regularly performs here to this day.

▶ Two buildings to the left (No. 8 on the Square) is the seat of **Slovenska Matica**. Founded in 1864 with the aim of publishing scientific and literary works in Slovene and is the oldest active scientific and cultural institution in the country.

▶ The bright red building facing the Primorska anchor was built in 1837 for the **Casino** (*Kazina*), a prime venue for cultured entertainment at the time, with a club, well stocked reading room and a ballroom inside its classicist premises. At the time of its founding its members included burghers of all languages but as nationalist tensions grew it became the meeting place for Ljubljana's Germans and in consequence a target for patriotic Slovene students who on several occasions threw stones at it.

▶ On the other side of the park the marvellous **Ursuline Monastery** with its **Church of Holy Trinity** stands tall, certainly the most interesting Baroque edifice in the city. The order of Ursuline sisters came to Ljubljana in early 17th century on the initiative of Johann Jakob Schell von Schellenburg, one of the richest people in Ljubljana at the time, who also financed the building of the whole monastic complex. For this he called in the Friulian architect Carlo Martinuzzi who in 1718-26 did an excellent job of combining different influences such as Palladio for the façade of strong columns and rows of windows and Borromini for the monumental top.

▶ In front of the church stands the **Holy Trinity Column**, brought here in 1927 as a part of Plečnik's reconstruction of the Square. The Column (by Francesco Robba) was erected in 1693 in gratitude to salvation from the plague. Contrasting the unornamented church interior is the high altar, also by Robba, made of African marble in several colours around a painting of Valentin Metzinger.

The Kazina building was once a meeting place for the local German community

The church of the Ursuline Monastery, one of Ljubljana's most distinct architectural works

⑪ Republic Square *(Trg Republike)*

▶ This is the area of downtown Ljubljana most affected by the urbanism of the socialist era. The Ursuline Convent and a whole block of old town villas, symbols of bourgeois wealth, were cleared in the 1960s to make space for the grandiose square envisioned as the new town centre and therefore populated with administrative, commercial and cultural buildings.

▶ The most important of these is the **Seat of the Parliament**, a largish square building (by V. Glanz, 1959) whose only decoration is a two-story high relief by Zdenko Kalin and Karel Putrih above the main entrance depicting work and workers, the two most hallowed ideals of the period. In the

The socialist-era Republic Square

park to the left of the Parliament lies the **Grave of National Heroes** in the shape of a Roman sarcophagus (by E. Mihevc & B. Kalin, 1949) where ten Partisan war heroes were reburied, later to be joined by other prominent communists. On 26 June 1991, a day after Slovenia's proclamation of independence, the flag of the newly independent country was first raised in an official ceremony, just in front of the Parliament building.

The square is dominated by two grey towers, one the seat of the Nova Ljubljanska Banka, the other, known just as TR3, houses many offices and some of the smaller embassies.

The Cankarijev Dom congress centre

The sculpture dedicated to workers at the entrance to the Parliament

▶ Behind them lies "Cankarjev Dom" *(open 8am-10pm)*, the largest and the most important concert and conference venue in Slovenia. Named after Ivan Cankar (1876-1918), considered to be one of the great writers of Slovene literature, this mammoth edifice most of which lies underground, was designed by Edvard Ravnikar and built in 1982-83, during which period the same architect also gave the final touches to the square. With no less than 14 halls of different sizes and purposes, the biggest one seating 2,000 and equipped with a grand concert organ, Cankarjev Dom remains the single biggest ever investment in culture in Slovenia.

The Monument to the Revolution

▶ In front of the entrance of the Centre is the cubic **monument to Cankar** (by S. Tihec, 1982), one of four monuments on the square, each related to the prevailing creed from the period. Next to the large car park is the wing-like **Monument to the Revolution** and by the greenery on the western side of the square is a **group of sculptures** representing Edvard Kardelj (1910-1979), Tito's presumed successor, discussing the problems of "self-management" with a group of workers. Behind Cankarjev Dom, facing Prešeren Street, is a **statue** (by Z. Kallin, 1959) **of Boris Kidrič** (1912-1953), another Slovene communist leader.

⑫ The Skyscraper
(*Nebotičnik*)

▶ The literal translation of the name of this building is "The Skytoucher", which is how the people of Ljubljana felt about it when in 1931-33 they got an opportunity to gape at the 13-storey building that rose up from Slovenska Cesta. It wasn't initially to everyone's liking though: some objected to its height surpassing the church spires, others mocked its unornamented façade. Not long after it was finished, however, the Nebotičnik became an icon, a symbol of Ljubljana striving to become a metropolis and a testament to the vigour and ability of

The Nebotičnik or, literally, Skytoucher

which you can enjoy stunning views over the rooftops of the city and all the way to the Alps (*open Sun-Wed 9am-1am, Thu-Sat 9am-2am*). While visiting the Nebotičnik, note that a lot of original details are still perfectly preserved. You might want to take the stairs as you descend, though the view down to the bottom of the spiral staircase is likely to make you dizzy. The covered passage connecting Štefanova and Cankarjeva Streets, the first in Ljubljana, is also an integral part of the Nebotičnik that should not be missed.

The Nebotičnik is perfect for an afternoon coffee with great views of the city

the young nation. At 70 metres tall, when it opened it was the ninth tallest building in Europe and the tallest in Yugoslavia and the rest of the Balkans. Funded by the Pensions & Insurance Fund and designed by architect Vladimir Šubic, the Skyscraper was a daring technical achievement, a genuine mega-structure of its day. The top floors are open to the public and feature a restaurant (10th floor), a club (11th) and a café-cum-club (12th) with a terrace from

▶ Also of interest are **Dukičevi Bloki** on Štefanova Street, a functionalist masterpiece by Jože Sivec from 1935. Rather than conventionally lining new buildings along a street in a closed block, the architect introduced new architectural principles and arranged them as free standing blocks around a park. The sole decoration of Sivec's blocks are the windows, protruding terraces and a lone sculpture. Combined, the concepts of the Skyscraper and free standing buildings, became staples of architectural creation in the later part of 20th century.

The Nebotičnik offers astounding views of Ljubljana

MUSEUMS AND GALLERIES

The four most important museums in Ljubljana are clustered together on the western edge of the city centre in an elegant, lush neighbourhood they share with many embassies.

The National Museum of Slovenia

13 Slovenia's oldest museum, the **National Museum** (*Narodni Muzej; Muzejska 1; www. narmuz-lj.si; tel. 01/24 14 400; open Thu 10am-8pm, all other days 10am-6pm; admission €3, students €2.50*) was founded in 1821 as the provincial museum of Carniola. Its present

Exhibits at the National Museum

day building facing the Parliament was constructed in 1888 by Viennese architect Wilhelm Rezori in neo-Renaissance style similar to that of the new museums in Vienna. A **monument to Johann Weichard Valvasor** (built in 1904), the most famous scientist of Carniola (see p. 181) stands in front of the museum.

Considering the museum's name you may be disappointed to learn that it contains very little on the history of the Slovenes themselves; the bulk of museum's collection consists of archaeological findings from the earliest civilizations to the late Middle Ages. Upon entering you will find yourself in a vestibule adored with a ceiling fresco of allegorical Carniola surrounded by its famous figures from the province's history. The permanent collection is displayed in rooms and corridors on the ground floor; of particular note are the **Vače situla**, a 6th century BC vessel with friezes depicting the daily life of the Illyrians; an Egyptian **mummy** and an early **Roman** *ascos* (a drinking vessel) adorned with Diana, the goddess of the hunt. The ground floor holds an exhibition on coinage from the Bronze Age to the present.

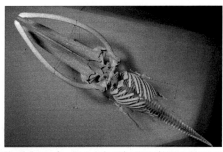

The skeleton of a white whale at the Natural History Museum

Zoisite, the mineral named in honour of the donor of the museum's collection

The monumental marble staircase takes you to the first floor; to the right are the museum's temporary exhibitions, often matching the quality of the permanent display.

14 A left turn from the stairs leads you to the exhibition rooms of the **Natural History Museum** (*Prirodoslovni Muzej; tel. 01/2 41 09 40; opening times as above; admission €3, students €2.50*) whose collection dates from 1821. Unfortunately, the presentation of exhibits has changed little since then and the rows and rows of stuffed animals, beetles, minerals or fossils can get a little boring. Nevertheless, there are many interesting exhibits, such as the skeletons of a white whale and a mammoth. The "human fish" (see p. 200) has its own section while the place of honour is taken by the mineral collection of Baron Zois, complete with a mineral named after him.

Lavishly decorated but small in size, the Ljubljana Opera House

The **Opera House**, just to the north of the museum building, seems like a shrunken version of one from some

The National Gallery building

larger Hapsburg town. Completed in 1892 after a few years of hasty work following the fire that destroyed the old theatre, it was designed by Czech duo Hrasky and Hruby in a rich Neo-Renaissance style so appropriate for theatres. The façade above the entrance is especially ornate with a group of muses in the tympanum; on the sides are allegories of tragedy and comedy.

In the beginning, the stage was shared by Slovene and German theatre groups, but in 1911 the Germans moved out to their new theatre. After the First World War the German theatre was reserved for dramatic works while the Slovene theatre was reserved for operas and ballet performances.

15 The third institution from the ensemble that enriches cultural life in Ljubljana, the **National Gallery**, lies to the right of the Opera House on Cankarjeva Cesta. This well-proportioned building was designed in 1893 by Czech architect František Skabrout as the *Narodni Dom*, the Slovene answer to the German Casino, a meeting place for the promotion of Slovene culture. Established in 1918, the National Gallery moved here in 1925. Since then its collection grew so much that two additional wings were added to the building and the main entrance is nowadays from Prešernova Street. The Gallery (*www.ng-slo.si; tel. 01/241 54 18;*

Matevž Langus' "Merchant Honn"

Kobilica's "Summer"

"The Sower" by Ivan Grohar

The Museum of Modern Art building was built in the late forties

open Tue-Sun 10am-6pm; admission for the permanent exhibition €7, discount €5, for temporary exhibitions €5, discount €3, free on every first Sunday of the month) has an extensive collection of artwork from Slovenia as well as works from every major European school.

Works of art from Slovenia from 13th to the start of the 20th century occupy the first floor (to the right of the entrance). Don't miss Matevž Langus' anthological "Merchant Hohn" with a view of Ljubljana; Ivan Kobilica's "Summer"; Juraj Šubic's "Gardener"; several excellent pointillist paintings by Ivan Grohar (including the "Sower" that made it on to the Slovene Euro coin); and Rihard Jakopič's bold experiments with colours and brush strokes. The collection ends with medieval art up to the 16th century featuring many anonymous artists and their religious art from the truly scary "Crucifixion" to a graceful pieta or "Mary with an infant Jesus".

The original of Robba's Fountain (see p. 48) stands in the hall connecting the old building with the new annex. The collection of **foreign works of art** is exhibited on the first floor of the new part and features an extensive overview of Italian art with several well-known names, a good collection of German, Dutch and Flemish masters, ending with 19th and 20th century artists from around Europe (look out for Jawlensky's fauvist "Flowers"). Next to it is a section on arts and crafts, with objects of applied arts, mostly of ecclesiastical origin, such as the intriguing 13th century reliquary allegedly containing the blood of St John the Baptist.

16 The **Museum of Modern Art** (*Cankarjeva Cesta 15; www.mg-lj.si; 01/241 6800; open Tue-Sun 10am-6pm; admission €5, students €2.50*) established immediately after WWII and housed in 1948 in a freshly finished functionalist building designed by Edvard "Edo" Ravnikar. The museum collection ranges from impressionists to modern installations and features regular exhibitions by contemporary artists. Its permanent collection offers an excellent insight into artistic movements over the last 60 years, not only in Slovenia but also from the other ex-Yugoslav republics, from socialist art (sculptures by Jakob Savinšek) to provocative works by the Neue Slowenische Kunst multimedia group.

OTHER MUSEUMS

17 **Ethnographical Museum** (*Etnografski Muzej*) Metelkova 2; www.etno-muzej.si; tel. 01/300 8700; open Tue-Sun 10am-6pm; admission adults €4.50, students €2.50.

The emphasis of this museum is the interaction of different cultures, of individuals with their environment, between the spiritual and physical and all of this through a wealth of creative exhibits, in line with its location in the Metelkova district.

The modern building of the Ethnographical Museum

18 **City Museum** (*Mestni Muzej*) Gosposka 15; www.mestnimuzej.si; tel. 01/241 25 00; open Tue-Sun 10-18h; admission €4, concessions €2.50, English language tours available every Sunday at 1pm.

Housed in the Auersperg Palace, one of the mansions of the Lords of Carniola, the museum's extensive and captivating collection offers an excellent insight into the history of Ljubljana. Don't miss the scale models of Plečnik's works that didn't see the light of day.

Plečnik's personal artifacts are just some of the exhibits at the City Museum

🔟9 Museum of Architecture and Design

(*Muzej za Arhitekturo in Oblikovanje*) Pot na Fužine 2: bus No. 20 from Slovenska Cesta or Levstikov Sq. (direction Fužine) to the last stop; www.aml.si; tel. 01/54 84 270; open Tue–Sun 10am–6pm; admission €3, concessions €1.50.

The museum, housed in a 16th c. castle on the Ljubljanica, named after a nearby ironworks (*fužine*), has a fine renaissance stone portal and a large arcaded courtyard. The permanent exhibition presents the opus of Jože Plečnik through plans, photos and models. The museum also has departments for industrial design, visual communications, photography and visual design as well as hosting related exhibitions.

🔟0 Railway Museum

(*Železniški Muzej*) Parmova 35; www.slo-zeleznice.si/en/company/about_us/railway_museum; tel. 01/29 12 641; open Tue–Sun 10am–6pm; admission adults €3.50, discounted €2.50.

The museum is located in two railway buildings in Bezigrad. In the first one you will see the locomotives, carriages and other vehicles that moved on tracks, while the other presents a stationmaster's office, equipment, railway uniforms and the history of the lines.

🔟1 Brewery Museum

(*Pivovarski Muzej*) Pivovarniška 2; www.pivo-union.si; tel. 01/471 73 40; open only on the first Tue of the month, 8am–1pm or by appointment; free admission.

Located to the back of the historical premises of the Union Brewery on Celovška Cesta, this comprehensive exhibition ripe with original items will lead you not only

A wealth of fascinating exhibits on display at the Architecture and Design Museum

through the history of beer making but will also give you insight into the coopers'

Original brewing equipment at the Union Brewery Museum

craft, inn-keeping and bottle and label design. After a visit to the museum you will be given a tour of the brewery and treated to a short movie.

㉒ Tobacco Museum (*Tobačni Muzej*) Tobačna 5; tel. 01/4 777 226; open only on first Wed and third Thu of the month 10am-6pm or by appointment; free admission.

Located on the premises of a closed down cigarette factory on the southern tip of Tivolska

The Railway Museum has a collection of vintage locomotives

Old fashioned cigar making at the Tobacco Museum

Cesta, the museum has exhibits on the history of smoking, the development of the tobacco industry in Ljubljana as well to the production processes of various tobacco goods that were made here. The best is saved for the last with a collection of pipes, tobacco boxes, and cigarette holders from different eras.

㉓ Tivoli Park

▶ Considering how green and woody Slovenia is it comes as no surprise that Ljubljana's largest park is just a stone's throw away from the city centre. Tivoli is the city's most popular park and a good place for those who did not go on a weekend excursion out of the city to enjoy a bit of nature. The park is open 24h a day and you are welcome to roam around or, as many people do, settle for a picnic on the grass. In summer there are several spots where you can rent a bicycle for free provided you leave some ID.

Conceived by French engineer Blanchard in 1813, but actually laid out by the Austrians in 1815, the park was named after the town in Italy famous for Hadrian's villa and renaissance gardens.

▶ The main **Promenade**, laid out by Plečnik in the early 1930s and lined with street lamps in a style typical for this period and panels for photo exhibitions, leads you up the gentle slope directly to **Tivoli**

One of the frequent outdoor exhibitions in Tivoli Park

Mansion (*Tivolski Grad*). This place has had quite some history: a tower that stood here since the 13th century was destroyed in 1442 when Ulrich II of Cilli (see p. 16) attacked Ljubljana; the ruins were replaced by a manor and then in the early 17th century by the present day building, owned by the Jesuit Order. In the mid 19th century the estate was bought by Emperor Franz Joseph who cleansed it of its Baroque decoration and then bestowed it to field marshal Josef Radetzky for his services to the dynasty. Today the Tivoli Mansion houses the **International Graphic Arts**

Centre (*www.mglc-lj.si; tel. 01/241 3800; open Wed-Sun 11-18h; admission €3.40, discounted €1.70*) with new exhibitions every third month.

▶ A short walk to the north will bring you to **Cekin Manor** (*Cekinov Grad*), a baroque edifice from 1752, home to the **Museum of Contemporary History** (*www.muzej-nz. si; tel. 01/300 96 10; open Tue-Sun 10-18h; admission €3.50, discounted €2.50*). The museum collection will lead you through the history of Slovenia in 20th century with its multitude of exhibits and

Tivoli Mansion, now home of the International Graphic Arts Centre

imaginative multimedia that will keep you intrigued. The centrally sited Knights' Hall, the Manor's ballroom is its only remaining original decoration. Next to Cekin Manor is the **Tivoli Sports Hall**, the most important sports venue in the city, with an Olympic swimming pool, basketball and hockey courts.

The National Museum of Contemporary History

▶ To the south of the main promenade you will find a large **children's playground** and just behind it the Tivoli **fishpond** and the **winter garden** with hundreds of Mediterranean plant species (*open Tue-Sun 10-17h; admission free*).

㉔ Miklošič Road & Park
(*Miklošičeva Cesta & Miklošičev Park*)

▶ The devastating earthquake of 1895 compelled the city major Ivan Hribar to reshape Ljubljana in line with contemporary town-planning principles. These efforts focused on an area north of the old city centre where new orderly streets and squares were laid out around the turn of the century. The streets were soon lined with buildings in fashionable styles, predominantly Art Nouveau, the best examples of which are to be found on Miklošič Road and around Miklošič Park.

▶ Starting from the Prešeren Square, the first of these is the **Grand Hotel Union**. When it opened its doors in 1905 it was not only one of the biggest hotels in this part of Europe but also one of the most luxurious, with central heating, an elevator and baths, to name just a few of its mod cons. Faithful to the modern spirit of the period, the Sarajevo based architect Josip Vancaš decorated its long shiny white façade with

Ljubljana's supremely luxurious Grand Union Hotel

Art Nouveau floral motives. During the First World War its luxurious premises were used by Austro-Hungarian generals in command of troops on the Isonzo Front. The Union's large glass-covered reception hall, once *the* place for high-class gatherings is now freshly refurbished, and is once more the most exclusive venue in the city.

▶ Facing the hotel is the **People's Loans Bank**, one of the most remarkable Art Nouveau edifices in Ljubljana. Commissioned in 1908 by Slovene bankers, it is another work by Vancaš who designed it in a bold new style in clear opposition to the historicism of German dominated state institutions. Step inside to see the impressive stained-glass panel from 1921.

The Art Nouveau People's Loans Bank

▶ Two buildings further along at no. 8, is Ivan Vurnik's **Cooperative Bank** of 1922. Its brightly coloured geometric patterns, drawing inspiration from folk costumes, represent what the architect saw as the basis for a new Slovene national style.

The colourful façade of the Cooperative Bank

▶ **Miklošič Park** was laid out in 1902 according to the plans of the influential Max Fabiani, a colleague of Otto Wagner and art consultant to the heir to the Hapsburg throne, the ill-fated Franz Ferdinand. In the park you will find the **monument to Fran Miklošič** (1813-1891), philologist and the main authority on Slavic languages of his age, praised for his campaign for the unification of Slovene lands in 1848. Miklošič's stone figure was put up in 1926 to replace a statue of Hapsburg Emperor Franz Joseph.

▶ On the north side of the square is the yellow **Krisper House**, on the corner of Tavčarjeva Street. Designed by Fabiani in 1901, with its three floors and an unusual corner tower, it was to serve as a model for all the corner edifices in the square. The closest that this idea came to fruition is the **Regali House** opposite, by Fran Berneker, a sculptor who designed the allegorical figures of day and night above the corner

entrance. Another expression of Fabiani's model is the **Čuden House** with its strange cupola, designed by Ciril-Metod Koch in 1901, standing tall on the opposite corner of the park. Koch also drew plans for the **Pogačnik House** immediately to the left (Cigaletova 1), executed that same year in a style reminiscent of Otto Wagner.

▶ If Ljubljana's Art Nouveau legacy interests you, take a walk along any of the streets protruding from the park where there are plenty more charming buildings to admire, in particular Trdinova no. 2, Dalmatinova 3 or Tavčarjeva 2.

▶ Two blocks further along Miklošič Road, at the corner with Trg Omladinske Fronte stands the **Sava Mutual Insurance Building**, another impressive work by Jože Plečnik. Built in 1928-30 for the second biggest insurance company in Yugoslavia, it features distinctive rows of brick columns giving it the monumental feel Plečnik looked for in a public building. The two friezes of human figures connected with ribbons, symbolise mutuality and solidarity.

The unusual architecture around Miklošič Park

㉕ Krakovo & Trnovo
(Krakovo in Trnovo)

The relaxing ambience of Trnovski Pristan

▶ Previously separate villages that have become suburbs of the city, Krakovo and Trnovo are two adjacent quarters with strong and unique identities, separated by Ljubljana's second river, the Gradaščica.

To the north of the river is **Krakovo**, once a fief of the Teutonic Knights who owned most of the land south of Ljubljana's city walls. The village has become famous for its market gardens. Vegetables from Krakovo – especially greens - gained such a reputation for quality that most families of Krakovo still maintain vegetable gardens. Strolling along Krakovska, Kladezna (Well), Rečna (River) or Vrtna (Garden) Street one can easily imagine being in an ordinary village, rather than a capital city! If you're lucky enough,

The twin spires of the Trnovo Church

you might even see one of the "Krakovo Salad Ladies" (*krakovske solatarice*), as they are colloquially known, pushing their old-fashioned barrows loaded with produce towards the central market (see p. 54).

▶ Unlike miniature Krakovo, **Trnovo** is larger; it spreads to the south as far as the local sense of pride carries its name. The heart of Trnovo is along the southern bank of Gradaščica where you will find the parish **Church of St John the Baptist**. Built in the early 18th century, the twin-spired church is best known as the place where poet France Prešeren first met Julia, the love of his life (see p. 97), which inspired him to write some of his best work.

▶ The **Trnovo Bridge**, the 1932 work of the quarter's most famous resident, the ubiquitous Jože Plečnik, is just in front of the church. As with many of his other works, Plečnik would not settle for a basic design: as the church was the heart of the

local community he decided to build a bridge wide enough to function as a small square. He also placed trees on the bridge, an unusual and original move even today, to say nothing of his time.

▶ Plečnik lived and worked for over 40 years in a house that lies just behind the church. Open to visitors as the **Plečnik Collection** (*Plečnikova Zbirka;Karunova 4; tel. 01/280 1600; open Tue-Thu 10am-6pm, Sat guided visits on the hour 10am-5pm, Mon & Fri open for groups booked in advance; admission €3*), it gives an insight in to the architect's modest private life, his inspiration and creations, including this house, remodelled in 1924, with lots of interesting details as well as nooks and crannies.

▶ Apart from the Prešeren Cultural Centre at 14, Karunova Street, the place where Trnovo comes to life is a group of bars along Gradaščica (Eipprova Street). In summer, much of the buzz transfers to **Trnovski Pristan** on the banks of Ljubljanica. Once docks where stone was unloaded from barges, after Plečnik's 1930s renovation, it became one of the most pleasant places in town. The gradually sloping terraces separated by grass and weeping willows bring the Ljubljanica close to the *Ljubljančani* and in summer this is where the young come to unwind, often with songs and acoustic guitars.

The Trnovo Bridge

Activities

BALLOONING

▶ **Tourist Info Centre Ljubljana** (see p. 45) organizes a 1hr flight over the city complete with tour guide (€80 adults, €40 children bellow 12 years). The tour starts and ends at their head office at Krekov Trg 10. After the flight you will enjoy a toast with sparkling wine. The whole tour takes about 3-4 hours. A minimum of two persons are needed for the tour.

▶ Another option is the **Balonarski Center Barje** (*Flandrova 1, tel. 01/51 29 22 0*), located on the outskirts of the city (take bus No. 7 or 7l from Slovenska Cesta in direction Pržan to the Andreja Bitenca stop) that offers one hour flights over the Ljubljana and Barje area (€105 for 1-3 persons, 4 or 5 persons €95, 6 or more €85). Please note, both of these tours take place only in clement weather and either in the morning or at dusk.

BOAT EXCURSIONS

▶ A one hour boat trip is available through **TIC Ljubljana** all year long. You can choose between a guided tour (*daily at 12pm and 4pm; adults/children bellow 12 years €10/5*) and an unguided one (*1ˢᵗ Nov-31ˢᵗ Mar at 1pm and 3pm daily, 1 Apr – 31 Oct at 10am, 11am, 5pm, 6pm, 7pm and 8pm; adults/kids below 12yrs €8/4*). The boat starts from the Riblji Trg pier just south of Tromostovje and will take you down the Ljubljanica to the Dragon Bridge and then up to Spica, past all the major sights. Tours may be cancelled due to bad weather.

CANOEING, KAYAKING & RAFTING

▶ The quiet Ljubljanica offers excellent conditions for canoeing and kayaking while the more sobering Sava is also nearby. There are several programs organized

Balonarski Center Barje provides balloon flights over Ljubljana

by **Skok sport** (*Marinovševa 8, www. skok-sport.si, tel. 01/512 44 02*) such as the canoe and kayak safari on the Ljubljanica that will take you on a 2-3 hour tour from Vrhnika down-river to Ljubljana. The organizers will pick you up and drop you at your place of accommodation. The same company organizes rafting on River Sava between Medvode and their centre several kilometres downstream at Ticno that takes 1½h (€24 per person).

The Sava by Ticno is also the location of an artificial kayaking route used for international competitions so that if you have some experience in kayaking you can rent equipment from Skok sport and head down to the rapids. Take bus No. 8 in the direction of Gameljine and get off at the Brod stop.

For a quiet, undemanding ride on the Ljubljanica you can rent a boat from Ljubljanica Rowing Club at the southern end of Trnovo pier (see opposite, Velika Colnarska 20)

HIKING

▶ A good way to see a less touristy Ljubljana, is the 33km long **Trail of Remembrance & Comradeship** (*Pot spomništva in tovarištva*, PST for short) that runs around the city following the line of barbed wire that surrounded Ljubljana between 1942 and 1945. Passing through fields and suburbs, across the Golovec Hill and around Rožnik this walkway is marked with 102 memorial

Kayaking on the Sava near Ljubljana

stones, six monuments and some remnants from the time of the wire, such as Italian bunkers. Perhaps too demanding to cover fully on foot it is a most interesting cycling route. Popular with joggers and cyclists in summer and cross-country skiers in winter, the Trail is at its liveliest during the traditional recreational march (8-10 May).

CITY WALKING TOURS

▶ The Tourist Info Centre offers a number of scheduled walking tours of Ljubljana. The classic one is a 2 hour tour of central Ljubljana starting every day at 11am in front of the Town Hall and ending on Castle Hill (*adults €10, children €5 + €1.80 for the*

The Trail of Remembrance and Comradeship takes in the Church of the Visitation of Mary in Rožnik

Visit Plečnik's house as part of the city walking tour

ride on funicular and €1 for the entry to the Lookout Tower).

A similar tour starts from the same spot at 5pm with the difference that here the Castle Hill is reached by tourist train (*adults €10, children €5 + €2 for the train ticket*).

To learn more about architect Jože Plečnik and his huge impact on Ljubljana take the 2h walking tour that starts in front of the Town Hall every Saturday at noon; the tour takes you past many of his masterpieces and ends with a half-hour visit to Plečnik's house (*adults €10*).

Getting Around

Due to its compact size and well organised traffic, Ljubljana is easy to navigate. The main sights in the city centre are within walking distance from one another and, if you have the time, a relaxing half an hour to 45min walk will take you to most of the parts of the town.

TO AND FROM THE AIRPORT

▶ The cheapest way to reach the city from the airport is to take bus No. 64 to the bus terminal. On weekdays it departs from the airport every hour on the hour between 5am and 8pm. From the city the buses

Ljubljana Jože Pučnik Airport

depart at ten minutes past the hour. On weekends these buses operate every two hours. The ride takes roughly 50min and costs €4.10.

A quicker option (about 30mins) is the shuttle bus from/to the bus terminal for €5 or to a number of locations in the town for €9.

Taking a metered taxi to or from the airport will set you back some €30-40, depending on the company. Ask around and compare prices before getting into a taxi.

TO AND FROM THE TRAIN STATION AND BUS TERMINAL

▶ Ljubljana's only train station and bus terminal are located next to one another. The train station (Železniška Postaja) is a stately old building with all the facilities you could need, including a tourist info centre, ATM, exchange office and coin operated lockers. The bus terminal, on the other hand, is merely an open-air bus park in front of the railway station with nothing

Ljubljana Train Station

but ticket counters, a small internet café and car rental. If you're staying in the city centre it is probably easiest to walk there, if not, choose between getting a city bus or a hailing a cab from the taxi rank.

You can rent bikes in Ljubljana with your Urbana Card

CYCLING

▶ Most people agree that the best way to move around the city is by **bike**. Except for Castle Hill and Rožnik the rest of Ljubljana is as flat as a pancake so even an inexperienced cyclist on an ordinary bike will do fine. It is also the favourite means of transport for locals - be they families or hipsters - and on any given day cyclists take over the streets. Once you're on a bike nothing is out of reach and in an hour at most you can traverse from one end of Ljubljana to the other. Most major streets have bicycle lanes and when there are none the drivers are careful enough. Beware that some of the streets, like the downtown thoroughfare Slovenska Cesta, are closed for cycling. On the other hand, downtown Ljubljana is by and large pedestrianised so that the fastest and the most dangerous thing around are other cyclists.

In the warmer months of the year (April through October), Ljubljana has a municipal bike rental scheme available at a eight locations scattered around the broader city centre, the most convenient ones being

the Tourist Office at Krekov Trg, the new part of hotel Union on Miklošičeva 3, Hotel Antiq on Gornji Trg or Hostel Celica. To hire one you will need valid ID and €1 for up to 2hrs or €5 for the whole day (*June-Sep 8-21h, Apr, May & Oct 8-19*). At Krekov Trg you can use your Urbana Card and get one for 4hrs. The bicycles are simple one-speeders (that come with a small basket and a lock). The scheme is quite popular and on a nice day you could easily have a problem finding available bikes. If this is the case you can rent one from a number of private bike rentals with similar prices. Be aware that bike theft is common so don't leave your bike unattended or unlocked.

Cycling in Ljubljana can be a fun and stylish way to get around

BUSES

▶ Ljubljana public transport consists of 22 **bus** lines operated by the LPP (*Ljubljanski Potniški Promet*) public utility company. The buses are clean and the network covers most of the city Mon-Sat 5-22.30h, on Sundays from 6am. The only problem is that some lines are not too frequent (up to 15min between buses). At bus stops you will find the frequency of departures, not the exact schedule. You can check the schedule of the next three buses online at *http://bus.talktrack.com*.

▶ The only way to pay for your ride is by **Urbana Card** (*Kartica Urbana*). The

Ljubljana city buses are white and green

The Urbana Card is widely available and easy to use

cards can be purchased at most kiosks, post offices, tourist info centres, some supermarkets and at LPP ticket offices. There are two types – yellow and green, the difference being that the latter is not transferable. A refundable deposit of €2 is payable for the yellow cards (*oranžna*). *Eno prenosno kartico Urbana, prosim!* (One transferable Urbana Card, please). You can top it up at the place you bought it or at some 30-odd easily recognisable, bright green "Urbanomats" scattered around, by cash or debit/credit card (between €1 and €50); just follow the on screen instructions. A single fare is €0.80 and entitles you to a **90 minute ride** with unlimited transfers. To pay for the ride touch in with your card on one of the green readers on entering the bus. If you want to pay for more than one person entering the bus you must point that out to the bus driver and then touch in twice in line with his instructions. Children up to 6 years of age travel free of charge. Dogs must be leashed and muzzled.

Between 10.30pm and 5am the only means of public transport are **night lines**, marked with N1 to N6. The procedure and fees at these buses are the same as on the day lines.

For some locations further from Ljubljana you will need to take one of the **BUS lines** that depart from the central bus terminal. To pay for your ride can either obtain a card similar to Urbana at the terminal or at the head office on Dunajska 56 or go for the slightly higher fare and pay with cash when entering the bus.

TAXIS

▶ Taxis in Ljubljana are clean and reliable. They are all metered but the rates vary considerably depending on a taxi company or the time of the day with start being usually €0.80-1.50 and the fare per km €0.70-1.70. These are considerably lower if you order a taxi by phone. Since the calls with 080 prefix are free, you can also call from any public phone. Try to order one where the driver speaks English. Even better, ask the operator or the driver to estimate the price of the journey. Make sure that the meter is on. If you think you're being overcharged ask for the bill so you can make a complaint: *Račun, prosim!* (Bill, please!). Tips are not obligatory - tip only if you're satisfied with the service.

Beware of "sharks" – especially around Train station – since they have ridiculously high prices. They are distinguished by not having taxi company logos on their cars but only a "taxi" sign on the roof.

CAR & PARKING

▶ Driving around Ljubljana is no problem but parking, especially on workdays might be. There are two **Park & Ride** facilities, but the only way to pay is by Urbana Card which is also available at these parking lots. Both facilities lie on the ring road: **Dolgi Most** when coming from the seaside (E 70) and **Stožice** on the northern section of the ring. Parking costs a mere €1 at Dolgi Most and €3 at Stožice for that day (expiring at midnight) and comes with two single fare credits that will get you to and from the centre of the city.

There are several clearly marked public **car parks and garages** around central Ljubljana. They are all divided into four categories depending on their location, charging between €0.60 and €4.80 per hour. Apart from public car parks there are also some private ones.

The whole of central Ljubljana is a **short-term parking zone** allowing you to leave your car between 30 and 120 minutes; when you find a place to park (or should we say *if* since it can be a real feat), buy a ticket at the nearest meter and display it in your windscreen. The parking meter does not give change so ensure you have the exact amount on you.

If your car is illegally parked you will be clamped or towed away.

Laguna 080 11 17
Metro 080 11 90
Intertours 080 311 311

TAXI

Around Ljubljana

1	LJUBLJANA
2	ČRNA VAS
3	TURJAK CASTLE
4	ŠMARNA GORA
5	IŠKA GORGE
6	PEKEL

2 Črna Vas

The village of Črna Vas (literally "Black Village") lies in the region of Barje ("Marshes") that spreads to the south and southwest of Ljubljana. The area can be as inhospitable as it sounds and though labelled as a Regional Park it remains of little interest to all but marshland birdwatchers. The village of Črna Vas, however, hides a valuable cultural monument, the **Church of St Michael**, one of Jože Plečnik's best and most interesting works.

Črna Vas is easy to reach since it lies a mere 6km from the city centre

Plečnik's impressive and unusual church is a real gem for architecture lovers

along Ižanska Cesta, which starts at the Botanical Gardens; take the right at the first intersection after passing over the highway; the church is the among the first things you will see in the village. If coming by public transport, take the No. 19 bus from Slovenska Cesta; it will leave you at the intersection, a 3min walk from the church.

It was Plečnik's nephew Karel Matkovič, a parish priest in the Barje region, who had the idea to build a new church. Funding was scarce and the black marshy soil problematic for construction, even so the whole project was finished

Plečnik's 'house of God'

The interior of the church

between 1937 and 1940 – showing what one can do with not much money and a bit of originality.

If it wasn't for the tall, flat belfry overgrown with ivy, from the street the church would simply look like an unusual house. This is not far from the truth as the ground floor is reserved for the living quarters of the priest and the whole idea behind the project was to build a "house of God". The church proper is on the upper floor, reached by a staircase that with its three arches reminds one of a bridge. As the whole structure stands on pylons stuck in the marshy ground the interior is made almost completely out of wood, to make it lighter.

The church hall contains lots of imaginative details such as scales hanging from the cross on the candelabra or the colourful geometric patterns on the pillars which are actually made out of old drainage pipes!

To see the interior of the church you will have to arrange a visit with the parish office of Barje on 01/427 22 18.

3 Turjak Castle

Turjak is one of the most formidable castles of Slovenia, lying in countryside equally rich in natural sights, historical heritage and folk legends. The castle is 24km south of Ljubljana along Route 106 leading to Kočevlje, the continuation of Dolenjska Cesta that starts in central Ljubljana. The turn for Turjak village, by a "Mercator" supermarket and pizzeria "Rozamunda", is easy to spot.

One of the towers of Turjak Castle

The castle was built by the Auersperg family, who moved here from Swabia in the 11th century. The first castle lay

The heraldic symbol, the *Tur*, after which the Castle is named

somewhat lower, controlling the road but already in 1338 the new castle is mentioned parallel with the old one. Both perished in 1511 earthquake after which the Auerspergs started building the present day fortification. Its massive walls and three bastions reflect the power that this family enjoyed in Carniola at the time, earned by wealth in land and fame in battles against the Turks. The death of Herbert Auersperg in 1575 was celebrated in far-away Istanbul, but in 1593 his relative Andreas led the army to a decisive victory over the Ottomans at Sisak, Croatia. In the 16th century the Counts of Auersperg also supported the Reformation and it was here that the famous Jurij Dalmatin translated the Bible into Slovene for the first time. As the castle slowly fell into disuse its venerable walls produced no more history but legends; it was here that France Prešeren set the stage for his poem "Turjaška Rozamunda" the story of the fate of beautiful Rozamunda. In 1943 the castle was the sight of one of the Slovene Partisans' largest victories. After a week long siege the Partisans managed to capture the castle and almost 700 Slovene White Guards and royalists. Sadly, this victory was celebrated by setting the castle on fire and leaving it in ruins for many years.

The castle is still under reconstruction but is open to the public (*open Sat 12am-7pm, Sun 11am-7pm; admission adults €3, schoolchildren & students €2; guided tour available by arrangement on 01/788 1006*). Before entering take a walk around its walls to the

The interior of the Dalmatin Chapel

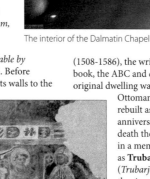
The fresco of the Three Wise Men

western bastion of renaissance features, decorated with the heraldic image of an Aurochs (*Tur*), an extinct species of wild bull from which the castle takes its name and which features on the Auersperg coat-of-arms. One of the trees in the nearby row of Lindens is very large, old and broken in half by age – the same tree was mentioned as being very old in Valvasor's "Glory of the Dutchy of Carniola", written 300 years ago!

Inside the castle grounds the most interesting sight is the **Dalmatin chapel** lying just to the left of the entrance and named after the famous writer and translator that worked and preached here. This is the oldest preserved part of the castle and has nice Gothic cross-vault construction, but the main sight here are the preserved fragments of frescoes depicting the Three Wise Men (left of the entrance) and the crucifixion (to the right).

To the right of the entrance is the **Knights' Hall**, a large stone room used for receptions. In the renovated wing of the castle you can see the **exhibition** on Andreas von Auersperg as well as several temporary exhibitions.

Just 2km down the 106 lies Rascia, known as the birthplace of Primož Trubar

(1508-1586), the writer of the first Slovene book, the ABC and catechesis (1550). The original dwelling was burned down in an Ottoman raid but was later rebuilt as a mill. On the 400th anniversary of the Trubar's death the complex was turned in a memorial centre known as **Trubar's Homestead** (*Trubarjeva Domačija*); follow the signs with this inscription from the main road.

Rašica was where the Auerspergs had their mills, sawmills, ironworks and even a dormouse farm used to produce furs exported to Venice. In the lower floor of Temk's Mill (*Temkov Mlin*) you will learn about milling and life in the village, while above it you can see the exhibition on Trubar's life and works, set in a broader frame of the time of restoration (*tel. 01/788 1006*). The smaller house in front of the mill today houses a gallery with temporary exhibitions

Temkov Mlin

DON'T MISS!

Čot, Kočevska Cesta 140, Pijava Gorica;
tel. 01/366 12 02; open Wed-Sun 9am-11pm

On the Ljubljana-Kočevlje road in Pijava Gorica, this large, well-frequented inn offers a wide range of delicious Slovene dishes. The weekly breakfast and lunch set menus lean towards international cuisine but are excellent value.

and an inn whose outdoor tables by the stream would be a good place to relax if it wasn't for the many school excursions flocking here to see the birthplace of this icon of Slovene culture; if visiting anytime between September and June consider yourself very lucky if there are no school kids around.

4 Šmarna Gora

One of the most popular excursions out of Ljubljana is to a lone mountain with twin peaks (Šmarna Gora 669m and Grmada 676m) and with out of this world views across Ljubljana. Triglav can also be seen on a clear day. On weekends and holidays, the mountain is crammed with day-trippers so if your idea of an escape into nature includes a little seclusion, this may not be the best place to go.

To reach Šmarna Gora (20km from centre of Ljubljana) by car get on the ring-road and head for Kranj. After some 10km take exit No. 12 (Ljubljana Šmartno). If coming by public transport take bus No. 8 from the city centre, direction Gameljne and get off at Tacen or Šmartno station.

Although you can drive to the top, if you want to do it the Slovene way you should park your car in one of the villages surrounding Šmarna Gora like Tacen, Šmartno or Vikrče. From there you should

The twin peaks of Šmarna Gora as seen from Ljubljana

follow marked paths that will take you on a 20min-1hr hike through dense woods to the peak of Šmarna Gora. Most of the hiking routes are not challenging, but the last section is quite steep. The route climbing the western side from Pirniče, is demanding with several places where you need to climb rocks (though with metal ladders). There are many side roads, so if you're not in a hurry, take your time and roam around and learn about the local environment from the information boards.

On top of Šmarna Gora you will find the **Mother of God Church**, an airy 18th century edifice set behind medieval walls. The biggest attraction here is the **belfry** that you will hear ringing all day long. The bell is rung so frequently because it is believed that ringing the bell once makes a wish come true. In front of the complex is the pretty "Ledinek" inn, which serves refreshments and some Slovene specialties like *ričet* (a barley stew) or *miške* (a fried dough snack).

The bell tower of the church at Šmarna Gora

5 Iška Gorge

It is hard to believe that the deep, unspoiled ravine of the Iška River (*Iški Vintgar*) is less than a half an hour drive from the Slovene capital. Slovenes, accustomed to having the natural beauty of their homeland within easy reach, use this convenience to its full potential. Therefore the Iška Gorge is a favourite daytrip destination for *Ljubljančani*, especially in the summer months when they come here in numbers looking to escape the heat in its shady woods and cool waters.

To reach it, just head south across the Barje to the village of Ig which gave the river its name (Iška means simply "of Ig"). In the centre of the village turn right and then left at the fork; pass the Iška Vas hamlet with its many weekend homes and head on deeper into the mountains to the car park in front of the local mountain cabin where the road ends. The cabin (open

The Iška River

The picturesque Ljubljansko Barje

1st April – 31st Oct) has a large terrace and a dining hall and offers snacks and refreshments.

If coming by public transport, bus lines No. 40 and 41 will take you to Iška Vas wherefrom it's an enjoyable 10 minute walk to the mountain cabin.

Flowing between the dolomite sides of mountains Krim (1107m) and Mokerc (1059m), the Iška has carved out a 4 kilometre gorge covered in deep lush greenery. Its waters are always cold and have a green colour similar to that of the Soča River (See page 128). The abundance of river crabs, trout and grayling is testament to the cleanliness of the water and provides excellent conditions for angling and especially for fly fishing (*daily permit €1, inquire at the Ljubljana tourist office*). To organize a picnic here you should announce it to the wardens at the mountain cabin.

▶ The beaten path here is to follow the road that follows the noisy river pass to **Vrbica**, the confluence of the Iška and its largest tributary, the Zala. On this road you will see the Votli Kamen, a rock through which the river has carved a tunnel while at the confluence is at the high rock called Sklani Mož ("Rock Man"). The walk (*allow 2½ to 3h there and back*) is not demanding at all and can easily be covered by all. Continuing for an hour more from Vrbica, and now climbing a bit higher, you will reach the rocks of **Krvava Peč** ("Bloody Cave") from where one can enjoy a view back across the gorge. The shortest, but also the steepest walk from the mountain hut is to **Krvavica** and its well hidden Partisan hospital active in 1942-43. Since here you are already at a height of 600m you might want to proceed for an 1½ more to the top of **Krim**, one of the best viewpoints across the Barje.

▶ If you want to spice up this excursion with some culture, return to Ig and then

The Volti Kamen carved out by the Vrbica river

follow the signs for Kureščak that will take you uphill through villages of Škrilje and Golo. Make a stop at **Golo** whose large but unassuming **church of St Margaret** contains the altar and pulpit from the famous Kostanjevica monastery (see p. 140). Continue by taking the first left and then right pass the mountain cabin to the very summit of **Kureščak** (825m) and the **Church of the Nativity**. The church was destroyed in WWII but rebuilt

Krim rises above the Barje

in 1992 as it is an important pilgrimage site. Needless to say, glorious views abound. Head back and at take the right at the first intersection to reach **Visoko** village and its **Church of St Nicholas**. On the outer wall of this old church there is a painting with a rarely found theme: a devil dragging a bound, naked woman, representing impurity, to hell.

The Church of St. Margaret in Golo

6 Pekel

With lush forests and numerous waterfalls the Pekel Gorge (*Soteska Pekel*) is arguably the most interesting natural sight near Ljubljana.

To get there by car head south across the Barje to the village of Ig then westwards, following the curvy road that clings to the foot of Mt Krim. On your way you will pass the village of **Jezero** named after a round lake with clear blue waters, a popular place to cool off in summer. Continue further

The destroyed viaduct in Borovnica

to **Borovnica** ("Blueberry",), the village closest to the Pekel Gorge. Borovnica was once famous for a railway viaduct built in 1850-56 that cut across its valley. This fascinating sight was damaged in 1941 and then finished off by Allied bombs in 1944. All that now remains is one of the columns preserved in the village centre.

The best way to reach Borovnica by public transport is to take one of about 20 trains that depart daily towards Sežana and will leave you at Borovnica train station after a 15-20min ride. On work days you can also reach Borovnica by bus line No. 45

The Carniolian Primula is unique to Slovenia and can be seen in the Pekel Gorge (last departure from Ljubljana at 3:30pm), but the last bus taking you back to Ljubljana (No. 46) leaves at 2:20pm.

Proceed to the south taking the first right after the new viaduct towards the hamlet of Ohonica. The woody hillsides quickly draw nearer and by the time you've reached the car park in front of Pekel, the valley has been reduced to a meadow by the Borovniščica brook.

▶ The **Pekel Gorge** is created by a stream of the Otavščica that cuts through the dolomite rocks exiting on the other side as the Borovniščica. The curious name of the gorge, "Hell Gorge", comes from its mysterious, dark, inhospitable woods always cold and wet, which fired up the imagination of the locals. The ravine is home to many plants and animals; on a rainy day you're bound to see salamanders while in springtime you will notice the Carniolan Primula, an attractive bright rose flower found only in the moist ground of south-central Slovenia. Today, due to

One of the waterfalls of the Pekel Gorge

the marked path, ladders and ropes it is possible to follow the stream and enjoy views of its five waterfalls. Though this hike is from time to time quite demanding, well prepared walkers will be able to make it to the top, 300m above the starting point (*allow 1½ to 2hrs*).

The pathway through Pekel is well appointed and maintained

▶ The **walk** starts by the information board facing the renovated mill. Not far from this you are greeted by a wooden statue of the devil. Pass the two wooden bridges and you arrive at the succession of the first three waterfalls, 5m, 16m and 18m tall respectively. After this the path splits into two. The left route continues along the stream to the fourth fall (17m) that plunges into a deep stone pool popular with bathers in the summer, and to the fifth fall (20m), beyond a steep climb through the narrowest part of the gorge. The right fork takes you above the stream to Hudičev Zob ("Devil's Tooth"), a rock with good vistas over the forest; and on to the fifth waterfall.

DON'T MISS!

Pekel, Ohonica 22, Borovnica (Perek Gorge car park), tel. 01/754 61 24, open Wed-Sat 12-22h, Sun 12-18

This small restaurant cooled by the waters of Borovniščica brook and surrounded by deep forests is the best place near Ljubljana to try freshwater trout (postrva) or crayfish (potočni raki) but you won't be disappointed if you order any other dish. The restaurant is especially pleasant in fair weather when the terrace is open.

Due to the abundance and diversity of accommodation available in Ljubljana – not to mention the difficulty of keeping printed listings current – we chose to provide just a quick overview. For full up-to-date listings of hotels, hostels and other accommodation we recommend you go online. You also can get accommodation advice and bookings from *Slotrips.si*.

Ljubljana – Hotels – ★ ★ ★ ★ ★			
Name	**Address**	**Website**	**Tel.**
Hotel Lev	Vošnjakova ulica 1	www.hotel-lev.si	+386 1 433 21 55

Ljubljana – Hotels – ★ ★ ★ ★			
Name	**Address**	**Website**	**Tel.**
Hotel Cubo	Slovenska cesta 15	www.hotelcubo.com	+386 1 425 60 00
Lesar Hotel Angel	Gornji Trg 7	www.angelhotel.si	+386 59 11 96 80
Grand Hotel Union Business	Miklosiceva 3	www.gh-union.si	+386 1 308 12 70
Antiq Palace	Gosposka 10	www.antiqpalace.com	+386 838 96 700
Allegro Hotel	Gornji trg 6	www.allegrohotel.si	+386 5 911 96 20
B&B Dvor Tacen	Pot sodarjev 2	http://dvortacen.si	+386 8 205 56 11
Best Western Premier Hotel Slon	Slovenska cesta 34	www.hotelslon.com	+386 1 470 11 00
Antiq Hotel	Gornji Trg 3	www.antiqhotel.eu	+386 1 4213560
Central Hotel	Miklošičeva 9	www.centralhotel.si	+386 1 308 43 00
Apartments Trnulja	Črna vas 265	N/A	+386 1 427 19 03

Ljubljana – Hotels – ★ ★ ★			
Name	**Address**	**Website**	**Tel.**
Adora Hotel	Rožna ulica 7	www.adorahotel.si	+386 820 57 240
Meščanka	Ključavničarska 4	www.mescanka.si	+386 51 88 00 44
Galeria Rooms	Župančičeva ulica 11	galeriarooms.com	+386 40 476 756
Penzion Tavcar	Cesta v Šmartno 7	www.penzion-tavcar.si	+386 1 546 69 70
B&B Slamic	Kersnikova 1	www.slamic.si	+386 1 433 82 33
Hotel Meksiko	Njegoševa 6K	N/A	+386 1 200 90 90
Penzion Kmečki Hram	Tomačevska cesta 50	www.kmeckihram.si	+386 1 560 70 00
City Hotel	Dalmatinova 15	www.cityhotel.si	+386 1 239 00 00
Macek Rooms	Krojaška ulica 5	www.sobe-macek.si	+386 4 050 20 29

Hotel Katrca 1905	Rožna dolina Cesta I/ 26 a	www.katrca.si/gb	+386 1 422 88 40
M Hotel	Derceva 4	www.m-hotel.si	+386 1 513 70 00
Hotel Park	Tabor 9	www.hotelpark.si	+386 1 300 25 00

Ljubljana – Apartmans i guesthouses			
Name	Address	Website	Email
Penzion Pod Lipo	Borštnikov trg 3	www.penzion-podlipo.com	+386 31 809 893
Hotel Center	Slovenska cesta 51	www.hotelcenter.si	+386 1 5200 640
Guesthouse Stari Tišler	Kolodvorska ulica 8	www.stari-tisler.com	+386 1 430 33 70

Ljubljana – Hotsels			
Name	Address	Website	Email
Bit Center Hostel	Litijska 57	www.bit-center.net	+386 1 54 800 55
H2O Hostel	Petkovškovo nabrežje 47	www.h2ohostel.com	+386 41 662 266
Alibi M14 Hostel	Cankarjevo nabrežje 27	www.alibi.si	+386 1 25 11 244
Fluxus Hostel	Tomšičeva ulica 4	www. fluxus-hostel.com	+386 41 849 680

Lolita   *Cankarjevo Nabrežje 1, Ljubljana*

Relax in this downright sexy and chic cake shop right by the river and enjoy decadent but affordable desserts and amazing coffee. Wonderful, welcoming service and a cool ambience.

Manna   *Eipprova Ulica 1a, Ljubljana 1000, Slovenia* ☎ 00386 5 99 22 308

Famous for its local specialties with a modern twist as well as its amiable staff, Manna also offers a choice of over 300 types of wine served by the glass.

Spajza   *Gornji trg 28, Ljubljana 1000, Slovenia* ☎ 01 425 3094

Relaxing and cosy, like being in a living room, and with good food and great wine.

Marley & Me   *Stari Trg 9, Ljubljana* ☎ 0038640564188

A relaxed restaurant right in the centre of Ljubljana, good food, friendly staff but be prepared to spend a little more.

Kavarna Zvezda   *Wolfova Ulica 14, Ljubljana* ☎ +386 1 421 90 90

One of the most popular meeting places for Ljubljana locals. Treat yourself with a legendary Zvezda cake or just take a coffee break from sightseeing.

Valvasor   *Stari trg 7, Ljubljana* ☎ 386 4 1 381 561

If you are looking for good food, great service and a fine dining ambience and are willing to spend a little more then Valvasor is the place to visit.

Restavracija Nebotičnik   *Stefanova 1, Ljubljana*

Located at the top of the Nebotičnik (see p. 60), with stunning views over the whole city, this classy cafe is the perfect place for coffee and cake on a Sunday afternoon.

Julija   *Stari Trg 9, Ljubljana* ☎ +386 1 425 6463

A cosy typically Slovenian restaurant, where you will find great food at an agreeable price. Good for families.

Cacao   *Petkovskovo Nabrežje 3, Ljubljana*

Amazing range of fresh ice cream, tasty cakes and smoothies at a beautiful location. On the pricey side.

Pizzerija Trta   *Grudnovo nabrežje 21, Ljubljana*

Amazing large pizza (easily enough for two) and half a litre of wine in a nice setting for fifteen euros. The choice and quality of the pizzas is excellent.

Falafel   *Trubarjeva 40, Ljubljana*

One of the few places in Ljubljana that caters for vegans or for Middle Eastern cuisine aficionados. It only opens in the evenings but is excellent for a late night snack.

Gostilnica XXI   *Rimska 21, Ljubljana* ☎ 0038612565654

The menu changes daily, the dishes are innovative and freshly prepared from fresh ingredients. Great atmosphere, reasonable prices but slightly slow service.

Bar Konoba   *Stari Trg 19, Ljubljana,*

One of the best fish restaurants in Ljubljana, excellent Greek food and reasonably priced drinks.

Dubočica   *Zaloška Cesta 31, Ljubljana* ☎ 01 542 37 77

A bit outside the centre, but still worth a visit. Super professional staff, great Serbian food, and pleasant ambiance.

Osterija Pr'Noni   *Gorice 1, Ljubljana 1000* ☎ +386-1-242-582

Italian cuisine in an authentic ambience, with excellent outdoor (garden and deck) seating available. Great for Sunday lunch or a romantic dinner but a little expensive.

Govinda's vegetarijanska restavracija   *Žibertova 23, Ljubljana* ☎ 00386(0)59058381

A relaxed vegetarian/vegan restaurant with self service and a variety of tasty dishes. Choose a plate that suits how hungry you are and top it up yourself.

Most   *Petkovskovo Nabrežje 21, Ljubljana* ☎ +386 1 232 81 83

Lovely setting, good food, friendly staff. Large choice of Slovenian/Italian cuisine at affordable prices.

Picerija Foculus   *Gregorčičeva Ulica 3, Ljubljana*

some of the best Pizzas in Ljubljana. Popular with the locals thanks to large portions at good prices.

Dabuda   *Subičeva 1, Ljubljana* ☎ +386 (0)1 425 30 60

Decent Thai/Asian food, large portions at reasonable prices. Worth stopping by if you want a change of culinary pace!

Pri Vitezu   *20 Breg, Ljubljana,* 01 426 6058

Very good food and good service. Come before 4pm for a very affordable lunch menu or choose the pricier but larger evening dishes.

Čompa   *40 Trubarjeva Cesta,* ☎ +386 (0) 40 799 334

A warm, welcoming Slovenian cuisine restaurant that is so good we hesitated to include it for fear of flooding its local feel with tourist diners. Great service, great food and affordable too!

GORENJSKA

The Julian Alps

✛ Everywhere you look in Gorenjska mountains loom over and around you and their silouettes dominate the skyline. If it's mountain air and Alpine scenery you're after, there is no finer place than Gorenjska. The region occupies the North West corner of Slovenia and, being close to Ljubljana, is easily accessible and equally popular during winter and summer.

✛ If you arrive in Slovenia by air, and if you are lucky to have clear weather as you arrive, you will be treated to a view of Gorenjska's mountain ridges and deep valleys. If you arrive by road or rail, chances are you will have to cross the alpine passes or take a tunnel under one of the country's three mountain chains, the Julian Alps, the Karavanke Alps and the Kamnik-Savinja Alps. Slovenia's mountains may not be impressive in terms of height (the highest being Triglav at 2,864 metres) but what they lack in altitude they make up in charm and beauty.

✛ Undoubtedly one of the best ways to appreciate Gorenjska is to get outdoors and get involved in one of the many outdoor activities on offer. There is plenty to do, both for adrenaline junkies and for those seeking more gentle pleasures. Walking is especially popular with plenty of challenging mountain hikes available together with more gentle, level walks,

along gorges and around lakes. It's from the mountain tops that you really get a sense of the landscape, the valleys and the forests and of course you can usually enjoy some delicious hearty mountain food in one of the many mountain cabins and take-in the views.

✛ In many of the rural areas, a traditional way of life still endures with people living and working their farms, often as a family. In the summer, many herdsmen take their cows, goats and sheep to graze in the mountain pastures. One of the notable features of this rural lifestyle are brightly painted beehives typical for this region. Gorenjska was home to the first hives in the country and thanks to isolation provided by the mountains, it is a good area for successful queen bee mating. Further evidence of this can be found in the Museum of Apiculture (see p. 100).

Traditional *kozolci* in the Bohinj region

1 KAMNIK

2 ŠKOFJA LOKA

3 KRANJ

4 KROPA

5 RADOVLJICA

6 BEGUNJE

7 BLED

8 BOHINJ

9 TRIGLAV NATIONAL PARK

10 KRANJSKA GORA

Vršič pass

Winter in Gorenjska

+ Unique Slovenian haystacks (*kozolci*) used for drying and storing hay are found throughout most of the country. Their design differs according to the region and you will certainly see plenty whilst travelling around Gorenjska. Here they are usually a long single rack covered with a roof but other variations such as the two-storey 'toplar' are found too, particularly in the Bohinj region.

+ Because of the harsh mountain climate, forging a living here has historically been challenging and Gorenjska folk have developed a reputation for being rather on the 'tight' side and are the butt of a fair few jokes amongst other Slovenes. As a visitor however you won't be aware of this and will find people friendly, helpful and welcoming.

+ Tourism in Gorenjska is well-developed and the major towns, Škofja Loka, Kamnik, Kranj, Jesenice and Tržič, are full of Gothic, Renaissance and Baroque art and architecture. Meanwhile, Bled and Bohinj attract visitors with the stunning natural beauty of their lakes and mountain vistas.

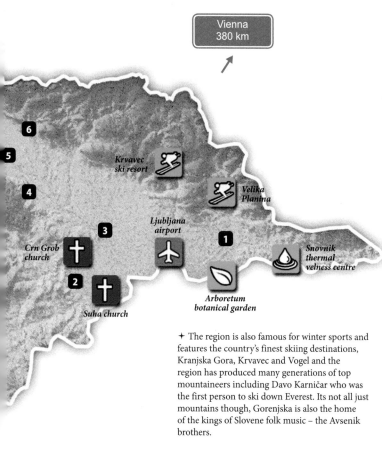

Vienna
380 km

Krvavec
ski resort

Velika
Planina

Ljubljana
airport

Crn Grob
church

Snovnik
thermal
velness centre

Arboretum
botanical garden

Suha church

✝ The region is also famous for winter sports and features the country's finest skiing destinations, Kranjska Gora, Krvavec and Vogel and the region has produced many generations of top mountaineers including Davo Karničar who was the first person to ski down Everest. Its not all just mountains though, Gorenjska is also the home of the kings of Slovene folk music – the Avsenik brothers.

The Julian Alps in Winter

1 Kamnik

13.400

Glavni trg 2,
www.kamnik-tourism.si
018 318250, Open Mon-Sat
10am-6pm, Sun 10am-2pm

Medieval Days (June);
National Costumes Day
(September)

First mentioned in written records as early as 1061, Kamnik is one of the oldest towns in Slovenia. Owing to Turkish invasions, an earthquake and numerous fires, however, many of the town's most famous buildings were destroyed and nowadays only the ruins of Mali and Stari Grad (*Little and Old Castle*) remain. Kamnik developed rapidly during the 19th and 20th centuries, especially after a railway line from Ljubljana was built in 1890. Due to its good location, favourable climate and picturesque scenery, the city and its surroundings have established a reputation for recreation, tourism and wellness.

▶ A stroll through the compact old town, along **Šutna Street**, the medieval high street, and the central square **Glavni trg**, is a great opportunity to wander through the narrow streets, visit the historical sights and take in the surrounding Alps from one of the many cafes that spill out onto the street.

1 Mali grad
2 Zaprice Castle
3 Sadnikar's Museum
4 Franciscan Monastery
5 Old Castle

HOTELS:

1 Malograjski dvor hotel
2 Hostel pod Skalo

RESTAURANTS:

1 Gostilna Marjanca
2 Kavarna Majolka
3 Gostinstvo Zdenka Zajc

Kamnik old town

A view of Kamnik

▶ The **Museum of Kamnik** is situated in the **Zaprice Castle** (*Muzejska pot 3, www.muzej-kamnik-on.net, 018 317647, open Tues-Fri 8am-1pm & 4pm-7pm, Sat 10am-1pm & 4pm-6pm, Sun 10am-1pm, entrance fee €2.10 adults, €1.25 children*). It was built in the 16th century and later restored in the Baroque style. The museum houses permanent and temporary exhibitions, including the open-air museum weapons, sacral objects, period furniture, porcelain, coloured and cut glass, paintings, statues and other art works, books, needlework, national costumes, clocks, lamps, painted beehive panels, and the skeleton of a cave bear. The museum is still managed by Sadnikar's son, Niko, who (*by arrangement*) is happy to guide visitors through this very personal collection.

Zaprice Castle

▶ The **Franciscan Monastery** (*Frančiškanski trg 2*), dating from 1492, has a library containing rich collections of philosophical and scientific manuscripts and incunabula from the 15th century. Its most prized possession is Dalmatin's Bible, the first Slovenian translation of the Bible from 1584. The library can be visited by prior arrangement through the Kamnik Tourist Office.

of granaries from the Tuhinj Valley, a collection of 'bentwood' furniture from a nearby workshop and an exhibition displaying the rich history of Kamnik and its inhabitants from the 18th and 19th centuries.

▶ **Sadnikar's Museum** (*Šutna 33, 018 391 362*), established in 1893 by Josip Nikolaj Sadnikar was the first private museum in Slovenia. Today it houses a mishmash of over 1500 specimens including medieval

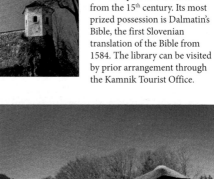

The open air museum at Zaprice Castle

Mali Grad

► The **Little Castle** (*Mali grad*) is on a small hill at the end of the main square (*Glavni trg*) and is one of the greatest attractions in Kamnik. The two-storey Romanesque **chapel** is the only remains of the medieval castle, thought to have been built in the 11th Century. The chapel, renovated in the Baroque style, contains 15th frescoes and paintings by Janez Potočnik while the upper part has late gothic frescoes with images of saints.

► A favourite local excursion is to the **Old Castle** (*Stari grad*) located on Bergantova Gora on the eastern side of the town. The castle can be reached in around 30 minutes via a marked footpath from **Maistrova ulica** or via a paved road which leads to the top. The history of Stari Grad reaches back to the beginning of the 13th Century, when it was owned by the Andechs Counts. It had many owners until 1576, when the last owner's daughter was killed by lightning and the castle abandoned. Today the castle itself is in ruins but it has beautiful views over the entire Ljubljana basin.

► Away from the centre, **Budnar's House Museum** (*Budnarjeva hiša, 031 528 747, open Sat & Sun from 2pm to 5pm*) is located in a settlement above Kamnik in the village of **Zgornje Palovče**. At over 350 years old, it is one of the oldest homes in the area and has been reconstructed, protected as cultural heritage and converted into a museum. The main attraction of the house is the black kitchen, where you can get a sense of how past generations lived and cooked. The lower floor of Budnar's Museum houses a number of exhibitions and traditional events including traditional bonfire-making and the making of advent wreaths.

Budnar's House Museum

AROUND KAMNIK

► The **Arboretum** in the nearby village of **Volčji potok** (*4km south of Kamnik, www.arboretum-vp.si, 018 312345, open Apr-Aug 8am-8pm, Mar&Oct 8am-6pm, Sept 8am-7pm, entrance fee €5.50 adults,€3.30 children, €13.50 family*) is the most visited botanical garden in Slovenia.

The Kamnik-Savinja alps

In the last few years the garden has became famous for the Spring Flower Show. Visitors from all over the country and from further abroad come to see the millions of daffodils, tulips and other spring flowers. Today the park contains more than 3000 varieties of trees and shrubs, produces plants in its own nurseries, runs a garden centre, employs a group of landscape architects and works on practical landscaping all over Slovenia. The Arboretum

The beneficiaries of Velika Planina's alpine pastures

can be reached from the Ljubljana – Celje motorway taking the turn off for Radomlje from where it is signposted. Alternatively buses run from Ljubljana and from Kamnik and stop directly outside.

▶ The village of Tunjice (northeast of Kamnik) houses the **Tunjice Natural Healing Park** (*www.zdravilnigaj.si, Park 018 317085, open daily 10am – 5pm*). The Resort is located in a large dense forest near the picturesque baroque **church of St. Ana**. Research carried out in Tunjice pointed to several energy-rich springs with special healing effects on various parts of body and many people come here to re-energise, rest and recuperate.

▶ The **Snovik Thermal Wellness Centre** (*Terme Snovik, www.terme-snovik.si, 018 344100*) is set in an idyllic green valley

Breathtaking mountain views near Kamniska Bistrica

between Kamnik and Vransko, on the doorstep of the Kamnik-Savinja Alps. The main feature of the spa are its indoor and outdoor thermal pools where the water is rich in calcium and magnesium is good for ailments of the bones, skin and digestive system. The centre also offers saunas, massage and other wellness services, the Potočka restaurant and a 4 star apartment village.

▶ Kamnik is also a great starting point for trips into the **Kamnik-Savinja Alps**, so called because Kamnik lies on the south and the river Savinja on the north. The valley of the river **Kamniška Bistrica** is one of the many starting points for hikes into the mountains.

▶ One of the most popular trips is to **Velika Planina** (1660m) (*www.velikaplanina.si*) which has beautiful alpine pastures and grassy meadows where farmers graze their cattle in the summer months. It is the largest and one of the oldest pastures in Slovenia and is ideal for hiking and climbing and is also a popular destination for downhill and cross-country skiing (6km of slopes), tobogganing and, snowshoeing. A good road leads to Kamniška Bistrica (13km from Kamnik), first to the lower station of the cable car and then onwards, a further 3km, to the head of the valley. If you are looking for an easier hike or just want to enjoy the scenery, take a ride in the cable-car. It operates year-round and travels to a height of 1407m. Once on the Planina, there are numerous well-marked paths including those to the mountain cabins Dom na Veliki Planini (1534m) and Dom na Mali Planini (1526m) where refreshments and accommodation are available. More challenging hikes, such as to Grintovec (2558m), Planjava (2394m) and Kamniško sedlo (1884m), start from the car park at Dom v Kamniški Bistrici.

▶ The Church of **Ss. Primus & Felician** occupies a prominent position on the southern side of Velika Planina. It is about an hour's walk from the village of **Stahovica**. The church is one of the best

The Kamniška Bistrica Valley

known and best preserved Gothic monuments in Slovenia. The interior of the church is decorated by frescoes, which are among the highest quality paintings from the Middle Ages in Slovenia. Directly above it is the simple medieval church of **St Peter**, which is covered with a shingled roof.

2 Škofja Loka

12,300

Mestni trg 7,
www.skofjaloka.info
045 120 268

Paths of Venus
(Venerina Pot) (June)

In 973 Roman Emperor Otto gifted the Bavarian Bishops of Freising land along the Poljanska Sora and Selška Sora rivers and a town called

The rooftops of Škofja Loka

Stara Loka sprang up. The Bishops later renamed it Škofja Loka, meaning 'Bishops' Meadow'. Through the ages, the town encountered many periods of tragedy. First, in 1457 an army of the Counts of Celje burnt the town to the ground and then two decades later, the Ottomans attacked. Further misfortune followed when in 1511 an earthquake struck the town and in the 17th century it was again destroyed by fire. Today, however, Škofja Loka is most notable for its historical town centre which has miraculously preserved its medieval form.

▶ The best place from which to start a tour of the town is the 14th century **Capuchin Bridge** (*Kapucinski most*). Legend has it that Bishop Leopold, who commissioned the bridge, drowned when his horse bolted and he plunged into the raging water below. The stone bridge features a statue of St. John Nepomuk, the patron saint of bridges, and the pedestal bears the Loka coat of arms. After crossing the bridge you reach the site of the five gateways which previously regulated entry in the medieval defensive

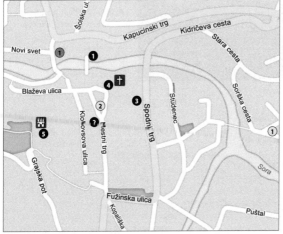

1 Capuchin Bridge
2 Town Square
3 Lower Square
4 St Jacobs Church
5 Loka Castle

HOTELS:
1 Hotel Garni Pale

RESTAURANTS:
1 Felix
2 Homan

The Capuchin Bridge

The statue of St. John Nepomuk

walls. The walls have been removed on all but the south side.

▶ The town consists of two main squares, the Town Square (*Mestni trg*) and the Lower Square (*Spodnji trg*) The **Town Square**, used to be the centre of business and social life and still has a number of buildings and monuments of historical and architectural importance. The three-storey houses are all colourful and ornately adorned with features such as stone window-frames, painted facades and pretty courtyards. One of the houses, **Martin House** leans against part of the old town wall and has a late Gothic portal and vaulted entrance hall. Another, **Homan House**, is composed of three buildings and features frescoes of St. Christopher and a soldier which were only discovered during renovation works

The Town Square

in 1970. The **former Town Hall** is the most prominent building in the square. It is decorated with baroque frescoes and has a three-storey Gothic-style arcaded courtyard. Standing in the centre of the square the **Plague Pillar** was erected in 1751 as a mark of gratitude for protection from plague and fire.

▶ The town's second square, the **Lower Square** runs parallel to the Town Square. Here the houses are more modest and far simpler as this is where the less well-off town folk lived. The 16th century **Granary** (No. 2) once held all the town's grain stores which were collected in the form of taxes. These days it houses a pub, wine-cellar and **gallery** displaying the work of the painter Franc Mihelič

Frescoes of St. Christopher on Homan House

Skofja Loka old town

(*045 124300, open daily 12pm–5pm, entrance fee €1.50 adults, €1 children, guided tours only*). The 18th century Baroque **Spital Church** is simple but has a richly decorated interior and is connected to the **Spital Almhouses** which were established in the mid-16th century to provide shelter and food for the old, poor and frail.

▶ **St. Jacobs Church** (*Cerkev Sv. Jakob*) in Cankarjev trg dates from 1471 and was built on the foundations of a previous church, at least 200 years older than the present one. Parts of the church, including the modern lamps and baptismal font, were renovated in accordance with the plans of architect Jože Plečnik. Its mighty bell tower was constructed in 1532 and the church contains unusual black marble Renaissance altars from 1694.

▶ **Loka Castle** (*Loški grad, Grajska pot 13*) is set on a small hill west of Mestni trg. The castle was built in the 13th century but after the earthquake in 1511 it was completely renovated. Since 1959, Loka Castle has also housed the **Loka Museum** (*www.loksi-muzej.si, 045 170400, open Apr-Oct 9am-6pm daily except Monday, Nov-Mar Sat & Sun 9am-5pm, entrance fee €4 adults, €2.50 children*) which is responsible for the natural and cultural heritage of the Škofja Loka area. It has seven permanent collections and a gallery encompassing archaeology, recent history, cultural history, arts, ethnology, natural history and one of the richest ethnographical collections in Slovenia. The Castle Chapel exhibits the spectacular golden altars which were removed from St. Lucy's Church in the village of Dražgoše after it was destroyed by fire.

AROUND ŠKOFJA LOKA

The hills surrounding Škofja Loka together with the Poljanska and Selška valleys,

The Church of St Jacob in Cankarjev trg

make the area an ideal place for **walking and cycling**. There is a network of well marked hiking and cycling trails. The 300km long Loka Cycling Trail is divided into 12 stages. Whist a mountain bike is required for some of the longer and more demanding stages, some of the easier ones can be completed on any type of bike in just a few hours. A copy of the 1:50,000 map "Škofja Loka and Cerkno Hills" is available from the **Blegoš tourist office** (*Kidričeva 1, www.lto-blegos.si,*

Loka Castle

Cycling the hills around Skofja Loka

045 170600) together with a leaflet detailing the 12 cycling routes while the tourist office website describes some alternative cycling and walking routes in more detail. Bikes can be rented for €8 for a full day and €5 for a half-day. A popular destination for a walk is **Lubnik**, a mountain which can be reached in around 2 hours ascending via Loka Castle. Near the summit the small mountain cabin Dom na Lubniku offers refreshments (*open daily Apr–Dec, weekends only Jan–Mar*).

▶ The village of **Suha** (2.5km from Skofja Loka) is famous for its **Church of St. John the Baptist** and is popular amongst art admirers. It has a beautiful presbytery which is adorned with 15th century paintings and well-preserved frescoes depicting scenes from the life of Christ which were painted by well-known local master Jernej from Škofja Loka.

▶ The village of **Crngrob** (5km north of Škofja Loka) meaning 'black grave' is renowned for the **Church of Annunciation** (*Cerjev Marijino Oznanjenje*) an architectural masterpiece which dominates the village. Built in the 13th century and extended over time, it was used as a place of pilgrimage rather than just a parish church which is why seems rather out of proportion considering the size of the village. The bell tower dates from 1666 and the most recent addition was the neo-Gothic porch in 1858. It boasts some of the most valuable frescoes in Slovenia, some of which are painted on the exterior walls. Highlights inside the church include a large gilt altar dating from 1652, the Baroque style side altars, a spectacular organ, the lavishly painted presbytery and an extremely narrow stone staircase leading to the rafters. If the church is not open, the key can be obtained from the nearby house (number 10).

▶ The **Stari vrh Ski Resort** (19kms from Škofja Loka) (*www.starivrh.si*) is a popular choice due to its proximity to Ljubljana. It lies at an altitude of 1210-580m and offers 10kms of slopes (1km difficult, 5kms medium, 4kms easy) together with a snowboard park, night skiing, a toboggan run and a children's snow playground.

Fortifications on Blegoš hill

A view over the rooftops of Kranj

3 Kranj

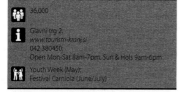

36,000

Glavni trg 2,
www.tourism-kranj.si
042 380450;
Open Mon-Sat 8am-7pm, Sun & Hols 9am-6pm

Youth Week (May);
Festival Carniola (June/July)

A statue of France Prešeren in Kranj

Kranj is the largest town in the Gorenjska region and the fourth largest town in Slovenia. The historical region of Carniola (in Slovene *Kranjska*) was named after the town, which was its provincial capital in the Early Middle ages. It stands above the **Kokra River** at the confluence with the Sava River. It is well served by bus and train connections and is only 7km from Ljubljana International Airport.

The old town centre was largely designed by one of the most renowned Slovene architects, Joze Plečnik and around the town there is much evidence of his work including the entrance to the town with its fountain and arcades. In 1983 the authorities declared the old town centre of Kranj a 'historical and cultural monument.' The poet France Prešeren is another figure synonymous with Kranj and all around the town you will find links to him. These include **Prešeren's Grove** (*Prešernov gaj*), the small parish cemetery where he is laid to rest, **Prešeren Theatre** (*Glavni trg 6*) with its Joze Plečnik designed bronze **Prešeren Monument** and **Prešeren Street** (*Prešernova ulica*) with its Gothic and Baroque townhouses. At No.7 Prešeren Street we find **Prešeren House** (*Prešernova hiša*) where the poet spent the latter years of his life. The house is now a museum in his memory (*042 013 983, open Tues – Sun 10am – 6pm, entrance fee €2.30 adults, €1.70 children and pensioners*).

▶ The **Main Square** (*Glavni trg*) is, as its name suggests, the most important part of the old town with its grand Gothic and

Renaissance buildings and beautiful arcaded courtyards. The former **Town Hall** (*Mestna hiša, Glavni trg 4*) is a complex edifice created from an 16th century corner house and a 17th century nobleman's manor in a renaissance style. It houses the **Gorenjska Museum** (*www. gorenjski-muzej.si, 042 013950, open Tues – Sun 10am-6pm, entrance fee €2.30 adults, €1.70 children & pensioners*), which has a gallery and exhibition rooms with three permanent collections featuring the work of the sculptor Loize Dolinar (1883-1970), an ethnological collection of folk art from the Gorenjska region and an archaeological exhibition entitled 'Iron Thread' displaying findings from the Iron Age.

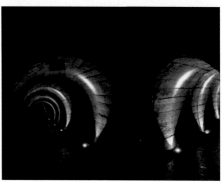

The Kranj Tunnels

▶ The **Kranj Tunnels**, a complex of manmade tunnels under Kranj, were built at the start of World War II to provide shelter for civilians and expanded in 1944 when the danger of air raids by the allies increased. Although never properly completed, the bunkers were nevertheless frequently used by local people.. The most interesting is the 1,300m long city bunker and the Tourist Board of Kranj, who are now responsible for the tunnels and their contents, organise guided sightseeing tours of the tunnels and the town (*by prior arrangement*).

▶ In 2008, Slovenia hosted the European Union Presidency for six months, an honour for a nation so young and so recently accepted into the EU. The majority of the events and sessions were held at **Brdo** (5km north of Kranj, *www.brdo.si*), Slovenia's

The poet **France Prešeren**, born in 1800 in the village of Vrba, is one of Slovenia's most prominent literary figures. His father was a farmer and his intentions were that his first son would continue the family farming tradition. His ambitious, educated mother had other ideas, however, and wanted her sons to become priests. She taught them to read and write and then sent them away to live with uncles who served as priests in different parishes. Prešeren left the family home aged eight, only returning home for holidays. After his school days, he realised he could not follow his mother's wishes and moved to Vienna to study law. It was here, in 1824 that he first started to write poetry. His initial work was more by way of a joke; *Zarjovena d'vičica* (A Rusty Virgin) written for one of his friends who was unhappily in love. More serious compositions such as *Povodni Mož* (The River Man) and *Dekletom* (To Girls) appeared in print in 1827. After graduating as a Doctor of Law he went on to work as a lawyer's clerk and met Julija Primic, the daughter of a wealthy merchant. He was instantly smitten, though his feelings were not reciprocated and several of his works from this period reflected these emotions. In 1835, Julija got engaged, Prešeren's best friend drowned and for a short period he sank into depression and his works from this period reflect this. In 1837 he met Ana Jelovšek with whom he had three children, out of wedlock. When in 1841 he fell in love again another poetically productive period followed. In 1846 *The Poems of Dr. France Prešeren* was printed, a key work of Slovene literature. In 1849 Prešeren died from cirrhosis of the liver after having found solace in the bottle during the turbulent periods of his life. It was only posthumously that he received the accolades and recognition that he deserved. At his burial, a committee was formed to organise a memorial in his memory and the date of his death was later declared a national holiday. In 1992, when Slovenia became independent, his face was printed on the 1,000 tolar banknote and in 1994 his work *Zdravljica* (A Toast) became the National Anthem.

The Renaissance Brdo Castle

regular home for official state visits and VIP's. The renaissance **Brdo Castle** was built in the early 16th century and is characterised by its four dominant corner towers. Under the ownership of the Zois family (1753-1929) the orangerie and manor house were built and the Baroque park was planted. By 1929 however, the castle was in dire need of renovation. Art-lover Prince Pavle Karadjordjević bought and transformed the castle into one of the most beautiful residences in the former Yugoslavia. Further renovations and new additions were made to the castle in the 1960's during Tito's rule to change it from a summer residence to a venue suitable for protocol activities. After Tito's death, the Republic of Slovenia took over of the property and these days it is primarily used for holding summits and high-level congresses, celebrations and even weddings for the more well-to-do citizens. Several prominent guests have visited or stayed at Brdo, including Britain's King Edward VII, Pope John Paul II and, most recently, in 2001 George W. Bush and Vladimir Putin held a summit here, the first official meeting between the two leaders. *NB: The castle is not currently open to the public though this situation is expected to change and it may be possible to arrange small group visits if arranged in advance via email; brdo.recepcija.gov.si or 042 601 000.* The Brdo Estate covers nearly 500 hectares, includes 11 lakes and is classified as an ecologically significant area. To date, over 1140 plant special and 1165 animal species have been found on the Estate including 26 animal species that are listed on Slovenia's endangered species list. The **Brdo Park** is open to the public (*entrance fee €2.50, children under 7 free*) and is a pleasant destination for a walk. As well as enjoying the Park's impeccable gardens, visitors can also see the Park's collection of sculptures. Most of the sculptures were designed in 1947 for the external decoration of Vila Bled (see p. 105)

▶ The **Krvavec ski resort** (*www.rtc-krvavec.si*) is close to Kranj and just 8km from Ljubljana airport making it the closest ski resort to an international airport in Europe. It is situated on a peak at the edge of the Kalška mountain range and does not require a deep blanket of snow to create ideal skiing conditions. Artificial snow machines assist nature to cover 90 percent of the trails and the ski season normally lasts 150 days. Krvavec, regularly voted Slovenia's best ski resort, lies at a height of 1450m and is accessed by cable-car. It has 35km of ski slopes, 7km easy, 15km medium, 8km demanding and its facilities include 10 chair lifts, a ski school, ski rental, a dedicated beginners area and several hotels and guests houses including an Igloo Village (*www.eskimska-vas.si*) where you can stay overnight in the Igloo Hotel.

DON'T MISS!

Kranjska klobasa (Carniolan sausage) – a speciality of the region dating back to 1896 and the best known Slovenian foodstuff in the world. Its recipe was first published in the Slovene cookbook, *Slovenska kuharica*, in 1912. The sausage must contain 95% meat with the other 5% containing water, salt, garlic and pepper, no other ingredients are permitted. In Gorenjska, they usually come served simply with mustard and elsewhere with ketchup or both.

The Krvavec Ski Resort

▶ The resort is also open throughout the summer when you can take the hourly cable-car to enjoy scenic walks, mountain-biking and paragliding (*cable car operates Mon-Fri 7am-5pm, weekends & hols 8am – 6pm*). A pleasant hike starts at the top cable-car station and continues to the

Chapel of Mary of the Snows (*kapelica Marije Snežne*) in the village of Ambrož pod Krvavcem. The chapel, designed by Joze Plečnik was built in 1927 in an alpine style resembling the traditional stone built shepherds' huts.

4 Kropa

850

Kropa 3,
tdkropa@gmail.com
041 839 951;

Blacksmith's Festival: First
weekend in July

The village of Kropa

The village of Kropa is nested snugly into a corner at the foot of the Jelovica mountain plateau. It can be reached from three directions: from Radovljica past Lacovo in the north, from Kranj past Podnart in the east and from Dražgoše past the village of Jamnik in the south. Kropa is famous for its blacksmiths who produced a range of ironwork. Houses in the village are ornamented with iron features and almost without exception adorned with flowers. A definite sense of local pride eminates from the village.

Exhibits at the Blacksmiths Museum

▶ On entering the village from the north (the most accessible and easiest approach), you are initially greeted by a former metal works, however just a couple of hundred metres on you reach the heart of the village and its beauty and charm quickly become apparent. The most notable feature of the village is the fast flowing **Kroparica** mountain stream which flows in amongst the village houses. It is ironic therefore that the outstanding

The Church of Our Lady of Kropa nestled in woods above the village

feature of the village is also a thorn in its side. The fast flowing stream leaves the village vulnerable to flooding, most recently in 2007. At times the water flows with such ferocity it is like water boiling in a pot, 'krop' originally meant boiling water.

▶ The **Kropa Blacksmith's Museum** (*Kropa 10; 045 337200; open Tue–Sun 10am-6pm from May to October and selected times off-season; entrance fee €2 children, €2.50 adults, €7 family, www.muzeji-radovljica.si*) is housed in a 17th century building on the east side of the village. Its exhibits document the technical and historical development of iron mongering, the cultural development of Kropa and the neighbouring ironworking areas from the 15th century until the decline of the ironworks in the 19th century.

5 Radovljica

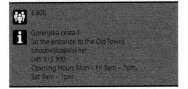

5.800

Gorenjska cesta 1
(at the entrance to the Old Town),
tdradovljica@siol.net
045 315 300;
Opening Hours Mon – Fri 9am – 7pm,
Sat 9am – 1pm

Radovljica is just 7kms from the popular tourist town of Bled. The Radovljica plain was formed when, during the last Ice Age, a glacier moved down the Sava Bohinkja valley from the Triglav mountain chain and ended at Radovljica. As the glacier retreated, it carved a series of terraces into the landscape. Radovljica is situated on the highest terrace, 75 metres above the river where the opposing flows of the rivers Sava Dolinka and Sava Bohinjka meet, and it is from this position that the town is afforded its magnificent views over the river, the valley and the mountains.

The Kropa Tourist Association together with **UKO** is in charge of preserving the cultural and historical tradition of Kropa and at the headquarters of UKO (Kropa 7a) there is a shop selling various products and souvenirs made of wrought-iron.

▶ Kropa has two churches: the **Church of St. Leonard** which was built in 1481 and features interior paintings by the baroque artist Janez Potočnik (1749-1834), and the **Church of Our Lady of Kropa**, built in 1713 on the hill to the south of the village. A special feature of this church is its two bell-towers, one very tall whilst the other much smaller. It is the small one that is known as 'the death bell' and is traditionally rung to offer luck to those who set off to deliver nails.

▶ The old town centre of Radovljica has many well-preserved late Gothic and Renaissance buildings and monuments. The largest of these buildings is the **Graščina**, which houses the Music School, the Town Museum (*Mestni muzej*) and the Museum of Apiculture (*www.muzeji-radovljica. si*). The **Town Museum** has collections displaying the history of Radovljica and its surrounding areas together with a collection of the work of Anton Tomaž Linhart. Radovljica was the birthplace and home of Linhart, one of Slovenia's most celebrated 18th century playwrights and memorials to him are found throughout the town. The **Museum of Apiculture** (*Čebelarski muzej*), one of the most popular museums in Slovenia, was founded in 1957 and records Slovene beekeeping traditions throughout the centuries. The museum (*045 320520, open daily except Mon in summer and on selected days off-season,*

Radovljica old town

entrance fee €2 children, €2.50 adults, €7 family) houses over 200 hives, depicting Slovene folk art shown in a gallery style, the oldest dating from 1758. Slovenia has a long and rich tradition of beekeeping. Its trade in honey and beeswax has been documented since the 15th century and Slovene beekeepers became famous for their queen bees in the 19th century. In the 20th century the Carniolan bee was exported all over the world and it became the leading bee in several countries as it is prized for its calmness and honey yield. Every August the Graščina also hosts the very popular annual Radovljica Festival of Music, which features a variety of Slovene musicians performing a range of music styles. (*www.festival-radovljica.si*).

▶ Next door to the Graščina is the **Lectar Inn and Gingerbread Workshop**. The workshop, which originally opened in 1766, now operates as a museum you can visit to witness the old original process of gingerbread making and purchase unique gifts and souvenirs (*045 374800, open daily except Tue, from 12 – 10pm, www.lectar.com*). Whilst here you can also sample traditional home-made Slovene cuisine, served by staff in traditional dress at the 500 year old Lectar Inn.

▶ Still within the confines of the old town, you will find several other historic buildings such as Šivčeva Hiša and Magušarjeva Hiša. **Šivčeva**

hiša (*open Tue-Sun, hours vary according to the season; €1.50 children, €2 adults, €7 families*) is a listed architectural building from the mid-16th century which ranks amongst the most important examples of Late Gothic buildings in the whole of Slovenia. Inside, the gallery holds regular displays and exhibitions. **Magušarjeva hiša** (*045 315167, open daily 10am – 6pm, www.magusarjevahisa.si*) is an ancestral house where, within the Late Gothic arcaded atrium, there is a ceramic museum and workshop containing one of the biggest and most diverse private collections in Slovenia.

▶ At the far end of the old town stands the **Church of St. Peter** which was originally built over 750 years ago and was rebuilt and enlarged in the mid-15th century in the Gothic style. The interior is covered by a high vaulted embellished ceiling, below which are ornamental sculptures and altars whilst paintings, including one of its builder, further enrich the interior.

The Gothic Šivčeva Hiša

▶ Heading away from the old town, there is still much to see and do in Radovljica. Passing through the small but pleasant **Town Park** will lead you to the town's main thoroughfare, Gorenjska cesta, where **Linhart's Hall** (*Linhartova dvorana, www.ld-radovljica. si, 045 372900*) hosts a variety of films, concerts and plays throughout the year.

Watch films and plays at Linhart's Hall

DON'T MISS!

At the entrance to the old town you will find the wine bar **Vinoteka Sodček** where you can sample some delicious Slovene produced wine at great prices to match. The owner will be happy to guide you around his wine cellar to make recommendations and prepare some Slovene pršut and cheese to complement your drinks too.

▶ Radovljica offers many **scenic walks and activities** including rafting on the Sava River, walking the suspension bridge and numerous walks in the surrounding area at Fuxova Brv, the nature trail at Gozdna Učna Pot and more. More information about these can be obtained at the tourist office.

6 Begunje

| 980 |
| Avsenik Festival, August |

Begunje is just 5km North of Radovljica and contains many hidden and important historic sites for such a small town.

▶ When entering the town from the south side, the first point of note is the **Avsenik Restaurant, Gallery & Museum** (*www. avsenik.com*). This is the birthplace of famous folk-musician brothers, Slavko and Vilko Avsenik, who made the traditional music of Gorenjska famous. These days, the Avsenik House Ensemble still perform in Slovenia but also internationally. Regular performances together with music workshops take place at the adjoining music school and every year the Avsenik Festival attracts over 6,000 people from far and wide. The Gallery and Museum display artistic works by national and international artists together with a permanent museum collection dedicated to the Avseniks' music. The restaurant, **Pri Jožovcu** dates from 1865. Whilst modernized, the traditional feel of the original house has been preserved, as have many of the original recipes, this

The ruins of Kamen Castle

combined with the Avsenik musical talent, makes this venue unique

▶ Continuing through the town, you reach the **Church of St. Ulrich,** built at the end of the 14th century and renovated in the baroque style. Opposite stands the site of the 14th century **Begunje Castle**, most of which now houses a mental hospital whilst the remainder is occupied by the **Museum of Hostages** (*045 333790; closed Jan/Feb, otherwise open with varying hours,* see www.muzeji-radovljica.si for further details; entrance €1.5 children, €2 adults, €7 families). During Austro-Hungarian Empire days it also housed a women's prison and was transformed into a Gestapo prison during World War II. The museum exhibitions show original prison cells with messages from the prisoners recording their suffering. It is thought that around 12,000 people passed through the prison before being moved on to concentration camps and it is known that 849 were killed and are buried in the castle grounds.

The Avsenik Restaurant and Gallery in Begunje

The 14th C. Church of St. Ulrich in Begunje

▶ On a hill to the northwest of the village stands **St. Peter's Church**, locally considered a favourite walking destination. Signs lead to the parking area at the Krpin Recreation Centre where a path leads up to the church and also beyond for stunning views over the valley

and Lake Bled. Also from the parking area, a path runs in the opposite direction towards the Draga Valley and behind **Kamen Castle** (approx. 30 mins away on foot). The castle, which is now largely in ruins, dates from the 12th century. It was altered and extended several times but from the 18th century it began to decline. Enrty to the castle ruins is free, however, care should be taken around the old and crumbling structures.

▶ The road through the **Draga Valley** also has further monuments and a cemetery in remembrance of the hostages. At the end of the valley is a car park from which several popular hiking destinations in the Karavanke Alps start. A local favourite is the hike to the mountain cabin **Roblek dom** which takes approximately 2½ hours (one-way). The cabin is open daily during the summer months and is weekends only off-season.

7 Bled

5,300

Cesta svobode 11
www.bled.si
045 741 122; Opening Hours July & August, Mon – Sat 8am–9pm, Sun & Hols 9am–5pm (remaining months open daily, hours vary)

Bled Days & Nights (July); Okarina Ethno Festival (August); The Legend of the Sunken Bell (December)

The fairytale-like scenery of Lake Bled has made it a favourite holiday destination since the 19th century and it remains Slovenia's most popular tourist attraction. The splendour of the lake attracts people from all over the world and has been written about countless times, not least by Slovenia's greatest poet, France Prešeren who called it a "second Eden, full of charm and grace."

A view of the Bled lake

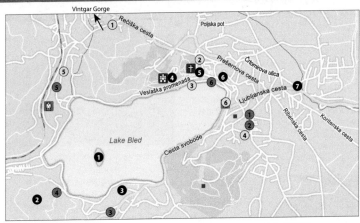

1 Blejski otok

2 Osojnica

3 Vila Bled

4 Bled Castle

5 Church of St Martin

6 Bled Festival Hall

7 Triglav National Park info centre

HOTELS:

1 Hotel Golf

2 Hotel Savica

3 Hotel Vila Bled

4 Pension Bomi

5 Hotel Triglav Bled

6 Hotel Villa prešeren

RESTAURANTS:

1 Vila Mangart

2 Pizzeria Pustica

3 Grajska Plaza

4 Promenada

5 "1906" restaurant

6 Okarina

Bled's international renown is in large part due to the work of Swiss hydropathist Arnold Rikli, who lived and worked in Bled for more than fifty years. He recognized the lake's potential due to the springs feeding the lake, its warm waters and clean mountain air. In the early 20th century he founded the sanatorium which quickly became the finest health resort in the Austrian Empire and attracted many members of the aristocracy. These days the town still commemorates him with

Bled Island

the annual summer Rikli Sport Days – a weekend of activities incorporating a walk along the pathways he used for his healing methods and an opportunity to sample some of his exercise methods (*www.bled-si*).

▶ In the middle of the lake the Church of St. Mary stands on **Bled Island** (*Blejski otok*), which can be reached only by boat (*the church entrance fee is €3*). The stairway leading up from the lake to the island has 99 steps and dates from 1655. It is a tradition at weddings for the groom to carry his bride up the steps (with varying degrees of success!). The church, a popular pilgrimage site, was originally built in 8th century on the site of a Slavic pagan temple and has been modified many times with most of what a visitor could see today dating from the Gothic and Baroque renovations in the 15th and 18th centuries. The original Late Gothic bell tower is 54m high and contains three bells together with the 'wishing-bell'; ring it and supposedly your wishes will come true!

▶ It is not possible to drive around the lake so the most popular way to explore and appreciate its beauty is to walk the 6km trail. Alternative methods of taking in the whole lake are by **boat**, either rent your own or go by one of the traditional Bled 'Pletna' boats with oarsmen who row visitors to Bled Island (*€12 per person return trip*), the tourist train (*operates daily in good weather every 45 minutes from 10am–6pm, €3 adults, €2 children*) or the Bled 'fijakers' who take tourists around the lake by horse and carriage (*www.fijaker-bled.si*).

Traditional Pletna boats by the lakeside

▶ For those with a desire for a slightly longer walk, the climb up above the lake to **Osojnica** (756m) which consists of three small hills, is worthy of its effort. The path starts at the bend of the road on the south-west side, approximately fifty metres before the start of the boardwalk (when walking in a clockwise direction). The route is on a marked path but is quite steep and rocky in places and at one point, a section of steel

A view of Bled Lake at night

cable provides a handrail, followed by a steep steel staircase, with 88 steps, climbing 20m up to the viewpoint.

▶ At the south end of the lake stands **Vila Bled**, now a luxury hotel but once the summer home of former President Tito. It was built when the region was part of Imperial Austria and from 1920 until the start of World War II, it served as a summer residence to the Yugoslav Royal Family. After the war, the villa was rebuilt into a presidential residence for Marshal Tito where he hosted many important events and in 1984 it re-opened as a hotel and has now joined the prestigious hotel association, Relais & Chateaux.

▶ Above the lake on the Northwest side stands the imposing **Bled Castle** (*Blejski grad*; 045 729782; *open May-Oct 8am-8pm, Nov-Apr 8am-5pm; entrance fee €7 adults, €3.50 children; www.blejskigrad.si*) which is, according to written sources, the oldest castle in Slovenia. It was first mentioned in 1011 and stands 130 meters above the lake forming a dramatic backdrop to the lake whilst providing spectacular views

across to the island and the surrounding mountains. Renovation work lasting ten years began in 1952 and give the castle a slightly more modern appearance as well as making it more accessible for tourists. In 2008 The Bled Culture Institute renovated the museum wing of the castle where exhibits show the eventful history of Bled in eight thematic units including Landscape, Water and Fire. The 16th century chapel, dedicated to the Bishops St. Albuin and St. Ingenuin, is adorned with Baroque frescoes. The castle also features a wine cellar, restaurant, printing workshop and gallery and hosts events and performances such as the Medieval Festival produced by its own theatre group.

▶ Beneath the castle is the Neo-Gothic parish **Church of St. Martin.** The present church was built in 1905 on the site of the previous 15th century church. It is adorned with splendid frescoes, the work of painter

Bled Castle perched on a rock high above the lake

The view from Bled Castle

including thermal baths, saunas and a beauty centre. Alternative wellness centres include those at hotels Kompas, Park and Toplice.

▶ The **Bled Festival Hall** (*www.kongresni-center-bled.si*) situated close to the lakeshore hosts the annual **Bled Festival** along with numerous other concerts, theatrical events, festivals and exhibitions throughout the year.

Slavko Pengov between 1932 and 1937. In front of the church there is a pillar which was designed by the great Slovenian architect, Jože Plečnik (1872-1957), in the years before World War II. The well-preserved walls from the 15th century were built as protection from Ottoman invasions.

Bled has a variety of facilities and services including a small shopping centre, a casino, an ice-rink, a well-appointed 18 hole golf course (*www.golfbled.com*), and is also a great base for trips to the surrounding mountains. The **Triglav National Park Information Centre** (*Ljubljanska cesta 27, triglavski-narodni-park@tnp.gov.si; 045 780200*) is the ideal place to find out more information about Slovenia's only National Park. The centre provides visitors with basic information on the park and its cultural heritage, has an auditorium and souvenir shop with typical National Park products and also hosts both permanent and occasional exhibitions

A number of hotels in Bled have **wellness centres**. The largest and best amongst them (as well as being very child-friendly) is the Živa Wellness Centre at the Golf Hotel. It has a variety of facilities

▶ A stone's throw from the centre of Bled lies **Straža**, in winter a small ski complex which operates a toboggan run in the summer. Straža is 1.2km in length, 634m

The Church of St Martin nestled beneath Bled Castle

at its highest point and is equipped with a double chair-lift and snow cannon. Whilst small and somewhat limited, Straža certainly offers good value, the cheapest skiing in the country together with the marvelous views over Lake Bled. Ski passes range from €5-8 for children and from €8-14 for adults. Alternatively, a **ski bus** operates in winter (*€10 per person return*) and transports skiers from various Bled hotels to the ski resorts of Krvavec (see p. 98), Kobla or Vogel (see p. 110).

DON'T MISS!

Kremšnita

For those with a sweet tooth, try as slice of **Kremšnita** – a traditional cake made in Bled from with vanilla and sweet cream. It has been made since the end of World War II and is a local speciality. Kremšnita is available in many cafes, cakes shops and hotels in Bled

The causeways along Vintgar gorge

▶ Whilst Bled is well served with bus routes and connections with Ljubljana and elsewhere, the train station is situated a couple of kilometres from the town centre and is not on the main rail line. Trains stopping at Bled run only from/to Villach (Austria) and Nova Gorica. The nearest alternative station therefore is Lesce, 4km away, where connections can be caught for Jesenice, Ljubljana, Villach, Belgrade and beyond. For rail enthusiasts, a steam-train

Rapids storm through the gorge

runs along the picturesque **Bohinj line** departing from Jesenice, stopping at Bled and Bohinjska Bistrica and ending at Most na Soči. The train runs on selected dates only and tickets must be booked in advance (*www.abc-tourism.si*).

AROUND BLED

▶ **Vintgar Gorge** is without a doubt an unmissable sight in Slovenia. The gorge is just 4km from Bled and makes a pleasant day walk from Bled or you can drive from Bled via the village of Gorje to the parking area at the entrance to the gorge. Buses also run from the main bus station in Bled to Vintgar during the summer months. Either way some walking will be involved

as a 1600m wooden boardwalk, originally constructed in 1893, hugs the rock-face along the entire length of the gorge hugging the rocks. The walk is spectacular with the raging waters flowing ferociously beneath your feet (particularly after heavy rain) as you cross the bridges. Be warned, however, it can be a little wet and slippery at times and the temperature in the gorge is significantly lower so be prepared!

The gorge was stumbled upon accidentally in 1891 by the then Mayor of Gorje, Jakob Zumer, and the cartographer and photographer Benedikt Lergetporer who were exploring the area. It was formed by the Radovna River which flows east towards its confluence with the Sava Dolinka. The end of the gorge is marked by the 16m high Šum waterfall and here there is also a kiosk where refreshments are available. Refreshments can also be obtained from the kiosk at the main entrance to the gorge where the entrance fee is paid (*open daily May to October, 8am – 7pm; entrance fee €4.00 adults, €0.80 children 0-6 years, €2 children 6-16 years*).

The emerald waters of the Vintgar Gorge

8 Bohinj

5,300

Ribčev Laz 48
www.bohinj-info.com
045 726 010; Open July &
August Mon-Sat 8am-8pm,
Sun 9am-7pm, other
months Mon-Sat 8am-7pm,
Sun 9am-3pm

Cow Ball (September);
International Wild Flower
Festival (May/June)

Bohinj Lake at sunrise

The name Bohinj translates (roughly) as 'Gods land' and on catching your first glimpse of the valley and glacial lake, you will surely understand why. There can be no doubt Bohinj is one of the most outstanding beauty spots in the country. The lake is the largest of Slovenia's lakes (4100m long, 1200m wide and 527m above sea level) and is free-flowing: the river Savica flows into it and the river Sava Bohinja flows out of it. In summer water temperatures reach around 20 degrees and the lakeshore it is popular place for sunbathing, picnicking and taking a refreshing dip.

the attraction for visitors. In Bohinj you can really take a break from the grind of modern life - you won't find any shopping centres, motorways or nightclubs here, only stunning scenery, friendly people and an undeniable charm.

Bohinj can easily be reached by road from Bled. Buses run from Bled and Ljubljana to Ribčev Laz and Ukanc whilst the nearest train station is in Bohinjska Bistrica on the Jesenice to Nova Gorica line.

Haystacks in the Bohinj area

▶ There is a small tourist centre in **Ribčev Laz**, the village at the east end of the lake. The village also features hotels and apartments, a small supermarket, a climbing centre and a handful of companies offering outdoor activities such as parachuting, canoeing and climbing. The bridge at Ribčev Laz provides a spectacular view across the lake and to the mountains encircling the valley.

▶ The valley is dotted with villages, predominantly farming settlements surrounded by fields, meadows and the double hay racks typical for this area. More than two thirds of the Bohinj area lies within the **Triglav National Park** which has contributed to the preservation of a more traditional way of life. Historically, life hasn't been easily for people living in these parts due to the area's relative isolation and harsh winters. Subsequently there is a saying amongst people from other parts of Gorenjska that Bohinj is '100 years behind the rest of the world'. On the other hand, this is certainly part of

▶ Next to the bridge is the **Church of St. John the Baptist**, a patron saint of the area to whom old churches beside lakes or on the banks of rivers are often dedicated. The Gothic presbytery was built around 1440;

The church of St John in Ribčev Laz

Canoes at the ready in Ribicev Laz

its walls and ceilings are covered with well-preserved 15th and 16th century frescoes; the bell-tower is Baroque and the altars 17th century. The church also features beautiful exterior wall paintings, such as the one on the southern wall depicting St. Christopher, that have recently been restored.

▶ One of the best ways to get acquainted with the area is on foot and with over 280km of marked paths, you are totally spoilt for choice. The tourist office in Bohinj has a free leaflet recommending some of the walks. Many visitors like to start

with a tour of the lake itself. A casual walker should allow at least 3 hours for the 12km circuit. Walking away from the bridge at Ribčev Laz in the direction of Ukanc is the **statue of Zlatorog**, the golden-horned ibex (*see box*). After a further 100m on the left is the climbing centre and from here, you have the option of either walking the path adjacent to the road or following the sign for hotel "Zlatorog" in Ukanc, and the head of the Bohinj Valley. This path climbs gently into the forest so whilst a little more effort is required, it is also delightfully shady. At Ukanc you will cross a bridge over the Savica, where the water sparkles with such a startling shade of green it almost looks artificial. Just after the bridge, a signpost directs you again to the path on the opposite side of the lake and to Ribčev Laz.

▶ An alternative way of seeing the lake is to take the electric **tourist boat** (outboard motors are prohibited to preserve the calm) which runs from Ribčev Laz to Ukanc. You can choose a one-way or return trip and

Canoeing on Bohinj Lake

The legend of Zlatorog, the mythical ibex with golden horns who lived on Mt. Triglav, is told in many forms and was first recorded in 1868.

Zlatorog roamed the valley and helped humans whenever he found them in need. An inn-keeper's daughter in the Soča Valley had been given jewels by a wealthy Venetian merchant but the girl's mother demanded that her daughter's lover, a hunter, matched the treasure with Zlatorog's gold which was hidden under Mount Bogatin or, if not, at least to bring back a bunch of pink Triglav roses to prove his fidelity (an impossible task during the winter snow cover.) The lover set off in search of these prizes and when he at last spotted Zlatorog, he shot him. The blood gushing from Zlatorog's wound melted the snow and up sprang a magical Triglav rose. Zlatorog ate a few petals and instantly regained his strength and sprung to his feet. As he leapt away, roses sprang up from under his hooves thus luring the hunter higher and higher. As they climbed the hunter was suddenly blinded when the sun caught Zlatorog's shiny horns and, losing his footing on the trecherous rocks, plunged to his death. These days the symbol of Zlatorog is used widely throughout the country, not least on the label of one of the two Slovene beers produced by the Laško factory (see p. 241)

Bohinj Lake at sunset

during the journey a guide will explain points of interest. Weather permitting, the tourist boat runs from April to September. The timetable, prices and further information is available on the website (*www.agencijafibula.com*).

▶ On arriving at the Ukanc end of the lake, a road bears left towards the **Vogel Gondola** and **Vogel Ski Centre** *(www.vogel.si)*. The cable car carries you to a height of 1,537m where wonderful panoramic views down over the lake and valley beckon. At the top there are numerous marked walking paths ideal for enjoying the peace, flora and fauna of the high mountains, a hotel, an Alpine village and restaurants including the mountain hut Merjasec. Vogel is one of the highest ski resorts in Slovenia meaning that it has reliable natural snow conditions and offers terrain suitable for skiers of all levels with a total of 17km of tracks.

▶ If, instead of turning left as above, you follow the road directly ahead in an upwards direction, you reach the parking area for the **Savica waterfall** (*slap Savica*). This beautiful double waterfall drops down an angled gully and then continues to fall

Outboard motors may be prohibited but people still enjoy boating on the calm waters

forming a 78 metre high fall and a smaller 25 metre fall. From the parking area it is approximately 20 minutes walk to the waterfall following the signs to the entrance kiosk (*entrance fee €2.40 adults, €1.20 children and pensioners*)

▶ The village of **Stara Fužina** (meaning 'old forge') is also at the east end of the lake. The **Museum of Alpine Dairy Farming** (*Stara Fužina 181; www.gorenjski-muzej.si; 045 770156; open Jul & Aug daily 11am-7pm, remaining months 10-12am and 4-6pm, closed Mondays year-round; entrance fee €2.50 adults, €2.00 children*) is located in the former village dairy where cheese was made until 1967. It displays dairy

Skiing on some of Slovenia's highest slopes at the Vogel Ski Resort

The Vogel Ski resort abounds in stunning views of the Alps

equipment, cheese making cauldrons and presses and an original furnished Alpine shepherd's hut. The village is also the starting point for visiting the **Mostnica Gorge** where you will see the **Devil's Bridge** (*Hudičev most*) and the **Mostnica Waterfall** at the head of the **Voje Valley**. The gorge, which has carved its way into the limestone strata, is about 2km long, up to 20m deep and in the narrowest parts, barely a metre wide.

A roadside shrine near Studor

▶ The small **village of Studor** (2km from Stara Fužina) is notable for its traditional

double haystacks, which are unique to this area and have been declared architectural

The clear waters running through Mostnica Gorge

The view from the Devil's Bridge

The Oplen House

the village, beside the small supermarket, is the lime tree which is a regular gathering place and the venue of the free summer music concerts, performed by the local men's choir, folkdance group and guest performers, which take place every Monday evening in July and August. Unusually for a village of its size, it also boasts three good quality restaurants which are often frequented by people returning from a day of skiing at Vogel and by holidaymakers in the Bohinj area.

▶ **Bohinjska Bistrica** (5km south of Bohinj) is the largest village in the Bohinj area and is the administrative and economic centre. The village has numerous facilities, shops and services, a tourist office (*Trg*

monuments. The very popular Mrcina Ranch with its Icelandic horses can also be found here (*www.ranc-mrcina.com, open year-round*). The ranch offers riding for adults and children in the surrounding countryside with 18 different tours ranging from 1 hour tours to full day and multi-day tours.

▶ The **Oplen House** (*Oplenova hiša, Studor 16, 045 723522, details as per Stara Fužina*) is a museum presenting the way of life in the early 20th century. The entire building contains the original furniture of its previous owners and combines its residential function with farming facilities including an open-hearth kitchen, an attic where tools, produce and clothing were kept and the farm outbuildings where the farming tools are on display.

The Julian Alps

▶ The village of **Srednja Vas** (3km from the lake) features the **Parish Church of St. Martin.** The church was first mentioned in 1493 and rebuilt in the 18th century in the Baroque style. Its paintings and frescoes by the well-known Slovene painters Franc Jelovšek, Matija Koželj, and Matevž Langus are especially interesting. In the centre of

svobode 3a) as well as bus and train stations. In addition, the **car train** (*avtovlak*) runs from here to Most na Soči and is the easiest way to get from the Gorenjska side of the Julian Alps to the Primorska side without the need to drive over Soriška Planina (1277m). The car train carries motorbikes, cars, campers and is also useful to cyclists not wishing to make the difficult climb.

▶ The Bohinj area is also ideal for exploring by bike though many of the trails are quite demanding and a mountain bike is required. The 16km **Bohinj Bike Trail** is also suitable for family trips. It starts at the bridge over the Sava Bohinjska river, just before the petrol station in Bohinjska Bistrica and follows the right bank of the river through the villages of Savica, Kamnje, Polje and Laški Rovt ending at Ribčev Laz. You can return via the same route or make a circular route by continuing onwards to the villages of Stara Fužina and Sredna Vas before returning to Bohinjska Bistrica downhill.

DON'T MISS!

If you are staying in the Bohinj area for at least two nights, the **Bohinj Guest Card** offers visitors additional benefits, such as discounts on food and drink or boat rental as well as free parking. Ask at your hotel or apartment for your free Guest Card.

Beautiful scenery in the Bohinj region

❾ Triglav National Park

The Triglav National Park (TNP), named after the country's highest mountain, Triglav, is the only national park in Slovenia. The Park extends along the Italian border in the north-west of Slovenia and covers 880 square kilometres, more than three percent of the territory of Slovenia.

The plant life is rich and varied and there are many species unique to the Park. In contrast, fauna within the park is limited due to the difficult climate and poorly regulated hunting. The most prominent species are wild ibex and alpine marmots, the occasional lynx and brown bears are also occasional visitors to the park but they are not known to reside within it. The Park is especially rich with birdlife: over eighty species of birds are known to nest within the park including peregrines, golden eagles and wild black grouse. During the summer local herdsmen drive their cattle into the park and spend the summer in the highlands producing cheese and sour milk (*kislo mleko*), a kind of thick yoghurt.

Hiking opportunities abound within the TNP and designated mountain cabins are available for multi-day hikes. Further information about the Park, walking, accommodation and access can be found at the TNP website (*www.tnp.si*) or by visiting one of the information centres.

▶ **Triglav** (2864m) is Slovenia's highest mountain and it is an unwritten rule that every Slovene should visit it at least once in their lifetime. When talking to Slovenes about the mountains, especially those from Gorenjska, the first thing you will be asked is 'Have you climbed Triglav yet?' The first recorded climb to the peak was in 1777,

The Triglav National Park

The three 'heads' of Triglav!

cold weather whatever the season.

Triglav can be approached from several directions, most often from Pokljuka, Vrata, Bohinj or Trenta. Ascents from the southern side are considered to be the easier routes however there are, as such, no 'easy routes' to the summit. There are five mountain hostels surrounding the approaches whose overnight accommodation and food services will be necessary as the acknowledged and preferred method of reaching Triglav is to spend the night in a hostel before making the ascent to the peak in early morning.

eight years before the first recorded ascent of Mont Blanc. The shape of Triglav gave the mountain its name meaning 'three heads' as from the south side at least, the mountain appears to have three peaks resembling three heads.

If you wish to say you've climbed the highest mountain and you don't mind the idea of sharing it, then Triglav certainly makes for an adventurous 2 to 3 day trip. In summer, however, there can be queues of people waiting to ascend to the summit and many prefer to head for the quieter mountain areas instead. Should you decide to make the trip to Triglav you must certainly be prepared. Be cautious, be equipped for all possibilities and, if possible, go with a guide from the Mountain Association of Slovenia *(www. pzs.si)* Even at the height of summer there is partial snow-cover and patches of ice can linger on. The weather can be very unpredictable and summer thunder storms are a common occurrence. Average temperatures at the peak range from -8˚C in winter to +6˚C in summer so dress for

Climbing Triglav

▶ The beautiful **Radovna Valley** lies within the boundaries of Triglav National Park. It is a haven of peace, tranquility and Alpine views. The valley begins where the valleys of Kot and Krma end and cuts deep into the north-eastern part of the Julian Alps. It is embraced on either side by the Pokljuka (see below) and Mežakla plateaus. The valley can be reached by passing through

The TNP in winter

the village of Gorje and by taking the right fork in the road, signposted for Krnica, just before the road starts to climb up towards Pokljuka. The valley is best explored by bike and a 16km cycle path has been created for that purpose. The road surface is gravel and therefore not ideally suited for cars which can throw up dust and make conditions unpleasant for cyclists.

The view from Triglav

▶ The **Radovna Cycle Route** is the first cycle route that has been prepared in Triglav National Park and was the concept of the Youth Tourist Club and the Primary School in Gorje. The route was designed to best showcase the natural and cultural landscape and attractions in the valley in an environmentally friendly way. It runs from Krnica to the Pocar Farm Museum at Zgornja Radovna and can be cycled in approximately 2-3 hours including stopping at the twelve information boards placed along the route. Points of interest

seasons. There is an abundance of walking routes, a ski centre and it is also the home of the Annual Winter World Biathlon Championships which will take place at the new Pokljuka Sport Centre at Rudno Polje (opened winter 2009).

▶ A good way to acquaint yourself with the area, and for those looking for a less strenuous walk, is **the Pokljuka Trail.** It is 7.5km long, can be walked in approximately 3 hours but can also be tailored for shorter trips and is suitable for families and individuals of all ages. The trail is marked with Triglav National Park information boards which mark interesting or important sites. A brochure about the trail is also available from the TNP office in Bled.

Winter conditions on Triglav

▶ The climbs to Debela Peč (2014m), Brda (2009m) & Lipanski Vrk (1975m) offer breathtaking views, however beware, snow can still be a hazard here, even in the summer so proper mountain walking equipment and footwear is a must. There are several mountain cabins on Pokljuka. **Blejska Koča** (1630m) offers an ideal stopping point en-route up or down to the peaks and is open throughout the

include The Napoleon Stone, The Pocar Farmhouse, The Psnak Mill and Sawmill and the Burnout ruins of Radovna. According to tradition, Napoleon's army marched through the valley at the beginning of the 19th century and one of his soldiers was said to have carved the initials of his Emperor into the stone hence The Napoleon Stone. A brochure describing the entire route can be found at the TNP office in Bled.

▶ **Pokljuka** is the largest forest plateau in the Julian Alps and spans almost 20km both in length and width.
  Pokljuka is a haven for outdoor sport lovers in all

Hiking in the Triglav National Park

Cross country skiing across the TNP

prove invaluable in helping to plan your route.

Pokljuka can be reached by car from Bled, passing through the village of Gorje before reaching the long winding road which climbs up to the plateau. It can also be reached from the south from Bohinjska Bistrica via the villages of Koprivnik and Gorjuse. In July and August there is one bus a day to Pokljuka from Bled (check the times at the bus station) however for the remainder of the year, there is no public transport available to/from Pokljuka.

year (one of the few Slovene mountain cabins that are open year-round). A particularly pleasant route starts near the Sport Hotel, continues on level ground through the mountain highland Planina Javornik before starting the ascent towards Blejska Koča. A copy of the 1:30,000 or 1:50,000 Triglav National Park map will

Please remember that the TNP is a protected area and that special rules and regulations must be observed whilst visiting the Park. Picking flowers, lighting open fires and camping outside of designated areas are all strictly prohibited.

8 Kranjska Gora

1,500

Ticarjeva 2
www.kranjska-gora.si
045 809 440; Open Mon–Fri
8am–7pm, Sun & Hols 9am–1pm
(high season)

Planica World Ski Jumping (March);
Kekec Festival (June)

Hiking above the Vrsic Pass

Kranjska Gora is situated in the upper Sava Valley region bordering Austria and Italy, making it a popular destination for foreign visitors and also a convenient place from which to visit other locations. It is probably most famous for its world renowned ski resort but its surroundings offer ample sights and activities for visitors during winter and summer.

▶ The original settlement dates back to the 14th century on the road connecting Gorenjska with Tarvisio in Italy and close to the Koren pass (*Korensko sedlo*), the lowest pass between the Drava and Sava valleys.

Kranjska Gora in all its glory

Thanks to its location the town was able to achieve rapid and sustained growth. It became particularly significant during World War I when Russian prisoners of war constructed the **Vršič Pass**, originally a military road and now one of only 2 roads connecting the Sava and Soča Valleys. The town became a tourist destination when the Ljubljana to Tarvisio railway was constructed in 1870. Sadly this railway line was abandoned in 1966 so that Kranjska Gora is

Hiking in the Julian Alps

now accessible only by car or bus. There is, however, a paved path running the length of the railway line from Mojstrana to Rateče (and onwards into Italy) which is very popular for cycling, skating and walking.

Kranjska Gora is also synonymous with nearby **Planica** *(www.planica.si)*, the world famous home of ski jumping and where the World Ski Jumping Cup takes place every March.

Just one of the pistes of Kranjska Gora

▶ In winter, **skiing** is the big draw with a wide array of options comprising ski runs totalling 20km (10km easy, 8km medium, 2km advanced), 18 drag lifts and 5 chair lifts, over 40kms of cross-country skiing, night skiing, ski schools, ski rental and sledging. Other winter highlights include ice climbing and dog sledding. The resort is also known for easy access to the slopes – you can almost step right out of bed onto them.

▶ During the summer months, **hiking** opportunities in the surrounding mountains abound. There is a well marked network of numbered paths, details of which can be found on the 1:30,000 Kranjska Gora map, available at the tourist office. The areas surrounding Kranjska Gora offer over 150km of cycling tracks and a brochure entitled 'Bike Trips Kranjska Gora' is also available from the tourist

The Legend of Ajdovska Deklica

Ajdovska deklica was a girl with a good heart. She lived below the walls of the mountain Prisojnik and led travelers through the snow across the Vrsic pass to Trenta. When the travelers returned, she provided food and drink for them so they would never be hungry or thirsty. She also advised farmers about when to sow and harvest their crops as well as predicting their fates. One day she visited a young mother and her newborn in Trenta. Whilst the mother was sleeping, Ajdovska deklica silently approached the child and prophesized that he would become a hunter and would shoot Zlatorog (see p. 109) and from his horns would achieve fabulous wealth. The prophecy of Zlatorog's death angered the other Ajdovska women and so they punished her by turning her into stone. Her face is still clearly visible in the wall of the north face of Prisojnik above the Vršič Pass.

Lake Jasna

office. Additionally, for those seeking more adventurous adrenaline-filled activities, Kranjska Gora also has its own Bike Park (*www.bikepark.si*) and a 1,500m summer toboggan run (*www.kr-gora.si*).

The chapel commemorating Russian PoWs

AROUND KRANJSKA GORA

▶ Just 1km south of Kranjska Gora is **Lake Jasna**, a beautiful lake which lives up to its name – 'jasen' meaning 'clear' in Slovene. The **Vršič mountain pass** (1611m) starts just past the lake. The road winds round 50 hairpin bends, 24 on the ascent from Kranjska Gora and 26 on the descent towards Trenta and each bend is marked with a post showing its number and height. Between bends 6 & 7 lies the **Russian Chapel** *(Ruska kapelica),* built in memory to Russian PoWs who died here when they were engulfed by an avalanche in 1916 by whilst building the road. The chapel has two small towers built in traditional Russian style. Close to bend 17 the face of the legendary maiden Ajdovsa Deklica is clearly visible in the wall of the north face of Prisojnik (see p. 117). There are five mountain cabins on the pass, all located within a short distance of each other offering rest and refreshment to visitors.

▶ Heading west from Kranjska Gora is the quaint village of **Podkoren**, a peaceful haven from the tourist hustle and bustle of Kranjska Gora, while still within walking distance of all its amenities. The village flourished due to its proximity to the **Korensko Sedlo** pass to Austria. Sir Humphrey Davy, the British inventor of the miner's safety lamp, lived in Podkoren and there is a plaque in his memory on the house at Podkoren 63.

A view of the mountains around Vršič Pass

▶ Travelling from Kranjska Gora towards Rateče and the Italian Border, the **Zelenici Pools** are formed from the waters of the Nadiža waterfall in the Tamar Valley which together with other streams flow downwards towards the Planica valley. When these waters reach their lowest level, they strike upon a moraine deposit and gush to the surface in a multitude of springs. The underground water, which is saturated with carbonate, begins to release limestone and owing to the calmness of the lake, the limestone settles at the bottom. The springs, which bubble up from the porous bottom, can be clearly seen through the crystal clear emerald green water bubbling from the ground. The temperature of the water is a permanent 5-6°C year round and never freezes, regardless of the

The Zelenci Pools

The stunning scenery of the Zelenci Pools

air temperature. The area surrounding the pools is a nature reserve with a viewing tower and walkways. Entrance to the reserve is free and it is a lovely place to linger, take in the stunning landscapes and observe the local flora and fauna.

▶ Further west, the pretty village of **Rateče** stands at the border with Italy. Though the border-post itself no longer functions, it still remains together with a still running duty free shop. **Kajžnokova hiša** (*Rateče 43, 045 876148, open Tue-Sat 10am-6pm, entrance fee €2.50 adults, €1.70 children*) was bought by the local community in 1995 after having sustained damage in a fire and was gradually restored and opened to the public in 2004. It exhibitions include an ethnologic collection with emphasis on the presentation of Rateče folk costume, an authentically equipped black kitchen and pantry and an exhibition of local history. The entrance is made of stone and the façade is adorned with frescoes of St. Florian and a sun-dial. Rateče is also the

start point for the walk to **Tromeja** (also locally known as Peč) meaning 'three borders'. It is at this location that Slovenia, Italy and Austria meet and in it was here that in 2004 Slovenia was officially accepted into the EU. From the central square in Rateče, the path is well marked, first ascending by road then climbing gently through the forest. The peak can be reached in around two hours on foot and you will be rewarded with extensive views of the Julian Alps and across Austria to Lake Worthensee (near Klagenfurt).

▶ The **Slap Martjulek** waterfalls are another very popular attraction in this area and comprise the lower and upper falls. The Martjulek stream cascades in three stages down a 110 metre cliff face forming the Upper fall then continues its path a further 500 metres before dropping again over a 50 metre cliff forming the Lower fall. Access to the falls is from the Kranjska Gora to Jesenice road, and on reaching the village of Gozd Martjulek there is a small parking area and information board.

The Slap Martjulek waterfall

Due to the abundance and diversity of accommodation
available in Gorenjska – not to mention the difficulty of
keeping printed listings current – we chose to provide just
a quick overview. For full up-to-date listings of hotels,
hostels and other accommodation we recommend you
go online. You also can get accommodation advice and
bookings from **Slotrips.si**.

Kamnik

	Name	Website	Address	Tel.
★★★★	Terme Snovik	terme-snovik.si	Snovik 7	+386 1 834 41 00
★★★	Malograjski Dvor	www.hotelkamnik.si	Maistrova ulica 13	+386 1 830 31 00
Hostel	Hostel pod Skalo	www. youth-hostel.si	Maistrova ulica 32	+386 1 839 12 33

Kranj

	Name	Website	Address	Tel.
★★★	Hotel Bellevue	www.bellevue.si	Šmarjetna gora 6	+386 4 270 00 00
★★★	Hotel Azul	www.hotel-azul.si	Suceva 26	+386 8 200 03 00
★★★	Hotel Creina	www.hotelcreina.si	Koroška cesta 5	+386 4 281 75 00

Bled

	Name	Website	adresa	Tel.
★★★★★	Grand Hotel Toplice	www.sava-hotels-resorts.com	Cesta svobode 12	+386 4 579 10 00
★★★★	Hotel Golf	www.sava-hotels-resorts.com	Cankarjeva 4	+386 4 579 17 00
★★★★	Hotel Vila Bled	www.vila-bled.si	Cesta svobode 26	+386 4 575 37 10
★★★★	Hotel Triglav Bled	www. hoteltriglavbled.si	Kolodvorska cesta 33	+386 4 575 26 10
★★★★	Hotel Villa Prešeren	www.villa-preseren. com	Veslaška promenada 14	+386 4 575 25 10
★★★	Hotel Savica	www.sava-hotels-resorts.com	Cankarjeva cesta 6	+386 4 579 19 00
★★★	Hotel Jelovica	www.hotol-jelovica.si	Cesta svobode 8	+386 4 5796 000
Hostel	Castle Hostel	hostel1004.com	Grajska cesta 22	+386 70 732 799
Hostel	Hostel Bledec	www.youth-hostel.si	Grajska 17	+386 4 574 52 50
Apart.	Pension Bomi	www.vir.si	Kidričeva 12	+386 4 574 35 94

Škofja Loka

	Name	Website	Address	Tel.
★ ★ ★ ★	Turizem B&B	www.loka.si	Stara Loka 8a	+386 4 515 09 86
★ ★ ★	Hotel Garni Paleta	www.hotel-skofjaloka.si	Kapucinski trg 17	+386 4 512 64 00
Apart.	Apartment Nejc	N/A	Partizanska 35	+386 4 513 31 80

Radovljica

	Name	Website	Address	Tel.
★ ★ ★	Sport Hotel Manca	www.manca-sp.si	Gradnikova cesta 2	+386 4 531 40 51
Guest-house	Guesthouse Kunstelj	www.kunstelj.net	Gorenjska cesta 9	+386 4 531 51 78

Bohinj

	Name	Website	Address	Tel.
★ ★ ★ ★	Hotel Zlatorog	hoteli-bohinj.si	Ribčev Laz 65	+386 4 572 33 81
★ ★ ★	Penzion Vila Bistrica	www.penzion-vilabistrica.si	Mencingerjeva 24	+386 8 38 30 852
★ ★ ★	Hotel Center	www.hotelcenterbohinj.si	Ribčev Laz 50	+386 4 572 31 70
★ ★	Penzion Bohinj	www.bohinj.si	Stara Fužina 12	+386 4 572 34 81
Hostel	Hostel pod Voglom	www.youth-hostel.si	Ribčev Laz 60	+386 4 572 34 61
Hostel	Hostel Studor13	www. studor13.si	Studor v Bohinju 13	+386 31 466 707

Kranjska Gora

	Name	Website	Address	Tel.
★ ★ ★ ★	Grand Hotel Prisank	www.hitholidays-kg.si	Borovška cesta 93	+386 4 589 20 73
★ ★ ★ ★	Hotel Kotnik	www.kranjska-gora.si	Borovška cesta 75	+386 4 588 15 64
Hostel	Alpine hostel Tamar	www.kranjska-gora.si	Rateče 12	+386 4 587 60 55
Hostel	Aljažev dom	www.mojstrana.com	Savska cesta 1	+ 386 4 589 51 00

Kamnik

Gostilna Repnik   *Vrhpolje 186, Kamnik* ☎ 01/839 12 93

Great local food at a reasonable price. If you're a real Slovene dining experience, this is by far the best option in the region!

Kitajska restavracija Hong Kong   *Groharjeva ulica 6, Kamnik* ☎ 01/831 46 98

Good prices, good location, good Chinese food - what more can you ask for?

Radovljica

Gostilna Lectar   *Linhartov 2, Radovljica* ☎ 04/531 56 42

Good range of authentic Slovenian cuisine in a restaurant favoured by locals. Generous portions, good value.

Gostilna Augustin   *Linhartov Trg 15, Radovljica* ☎ 04/531 41 63

With great views over Alpine meadows or the town square this is a great place to eat or just enjoy a beer. Book in advance!

Bohihnjsko Jezero

Gostilna Rupa   *Srednja Vas 87, Bohinjsko Jezero* ☎ 04/572 34 01

Excellent local food for those who are prepared to pay a little more. very good local food. Booking in advance very much recommended.

Gostilna Mihovc   *Stara Fuzina 118, Bohinjsko Jezero,*

Authentic local restaurant with a traditional style interior. Good food at good prices and with a range of vegetarian dishes.

Gostilna Erlah   *Ukanc 67, Bohinjsko Jezero*

Traditional dishes from the whole of former Yugoslavia at reasonable prices served in a friendly, welcoming atmosphere.

Kranjska gora

Gostilna Pri Martinu   *Borovska 61, Kranjska Gora*

Huge portions of hearty food at great prices. Unsurprisingly booking in advance is recommended.

Restaurant Kotnik   *Borovska cesta 75, Kranjska Gora*

A little bit of everything on offer here at one of the best Kranjska Gora restaurants. Reasonable prices and a good outdoor seating area.

Kranj

Kot   *Maistrov trg 4, Kranj*

Good food and great local beer at this welcoming, tourist friendly restaurant.

Gostilna Kristof   *Predoslje 22, Kranj*

An interesting mix of the modern and traditional in both cuisine and ambiance. Worth a visit but a little on the pricey side.

Kruhkerija Gorjanc   *Hotemaze, Kranj*

Gorgeous bread rolls (kruhki) with a myriad of different toppings.

Das Ist Valter   *Cesta 1. maja 1A, Kranj*

The best Balkan restaurant in Kranj. Reasonably priced and very popular.

Brioni   *Koroška cesta 10, Kranj,*

Amazing cakes and ice creams - easily the best in Kranj.

Bled

Vila Mangart   *Kolodvorska cesta 2, Bled* ☎ 05/993 26 12

A real gem of a restaurant, family owned and very welcoming. A little on the pricey side, however.

Pizzeria Rustika   *Riklijeva Cesta 13, Bled* ☎ 04/76 89 00

Really great pizza place, enormous portions of good pizza at very affordable prices.

Grajska Plaza   *Veslaska promenada 11, Bled* ☎ 03/181 38 86

Unpretentious haute cuisine, sublime views over the lake - what more could one ask for in a dining experience?

Restavracija Promenada   *Cankarjeva cesta 6, Bled* ☎ 04/579 16 40

Wonderful French cuisine and even better wine at this artisan restaurant. Be ready for slightly higher prices.

A la Carte Restaurant 1906 Bled   *Kolodvorska cesta 33, Bled* ☎ 04/575 26 10

Local cuisine with a modern twist, local wines and a view of the lake - all at reasonable prices.

Ostarija Peglez'n   *Cesta Svobode 19a, Bled*

Lovely little restaurant with antique plates, teapots and other knick-knacks on the walls. Good food and friendly service.

Mayer Penzion   *Želeška cesta 7, Bled*

There is a real Alpine feel to this cosy restaurant serving good local food.

Okarina   *Ljubljanska cesta 8, Bled*

Who would think that Bled would be a good place for Indian food. Enjoy the great food and excellent service at this unusual little gem of a restaurant.

Castle Restaurant *Grajska cesta 25, Bled*

Work up an appetite by walking to Bled's highest restaurant and you'll enjoy the artistically presented food even more. At the pricey end of the spectrum.

PRIMORSKA & WESTERN SLOVENIA

The emerald waters of the Soča River

✛ The Primorska region forms the western part of Slovenia stretching from the Iulian Alps in the north, across the vineyard covered hills to the Adriatic coast in the south. It combines the northern tip of Istria peninsula and the eastern part of the

Skiing at the top of the world on Slovenia's highest peists

historical province of Gorizia and Gradisca, the western part of which is now in Italy. Primorska one of the most visited regions of Slovenia, with tourists drawn by the coastal resorts and the Soča Valley.

✛ Primorska's area is large and very diverse, from the mountains and rivers of Upper Primorska, the rolling hills and Karst of Central Primorska and the warm Adriatic waters at the Coast.

✛ With such an extensive territory, there is no shortage of things to do in Primorska. From

skiing at Slovenia's highest ski resort; hiking in the Kanin mountain range; white water rafting in the Soča Valley; sun-bathing and exploring the quaint coastal towns; wine-tasting around the Vipava Valley and Brda Hills near Nova Gorica; exploring the karst caves and castles or hiking in the Cerkno and Idrija hills - the Primorska region is an entire destination in itself.

✛ **Upper Primorska** is located in the westernmost part of the Julian Alps and famed for the emerald green Soča River that runs along its length. The major tourist hubs here are Bovec, the "adventure capital" of the valley where you will be able to try all the outdoor sports your heart desires and historic Kobarid, scene of the great mountain battle of the Isonzo that was witnessed by a young Earnest Hemmingway.

A view of the Bovec basin

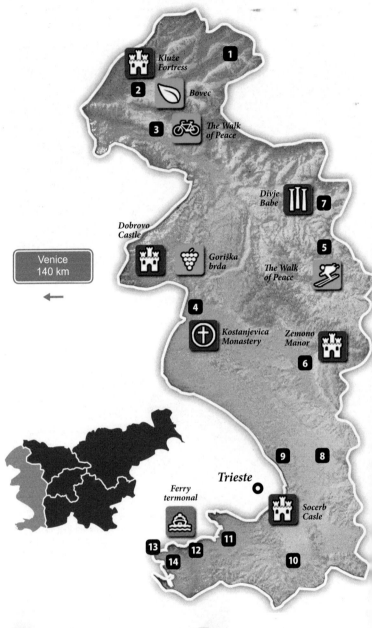

Kluže
Fortress

Bovec

The Walk
of Peace

Divje
Babe

Dobrovo
Castle

Goriška
brda

The Walk
of Peace

Kostanjevica
Monastery

Zemono
Manor

Venice
140 km

Trieste

Ferry
termonal

Socerb
Casle

1 THE TRENTA VALLEY

2 BOVEC

3 KOBARID

4 NOVA GORICA

5 IDRIJA

6 THE VIPAVA VALLEY

7 CERKNO

8 ŠKOCJAN CAVES

9 LIPICA

10 HRASTOVLJE

11 KOPER

12 IZOLA

13 PIRAN

14 PORTOROŽ

The Cerkno Hills

✦ **Central Primorska** is dominated by the Cerkno and Idrija hills. The major towns are Idrija, a medieval mining town known for its mercury and lace, Cerkno, a great base for hiking and skiing in the Cerkno Hills, and Nova Gorica, a socialist new town built after the war but now reunited with its twin to form a genuine Berlin of the Mediterranean. Central Primorska is also home to Slovenia's main wine growing areas in the Vipaska and Goriška Brda valleys. To the south of Central Primorska is the Karst, a limestone plateau of caves, potholes and springs. Here you will find the fascinating Škocjan Caves, listed by UNESCO as a World Heritage Site in 1986.

✦ **The Coast,** in Slovene *Pri Morju*, or "by the sea", which gives the region its name, is small but beautiful. Slovenia's 46km stretch of Adriatic coastline separates Italy from Croatia is packed with interesting seaside destinations. The highlight of the coastal area has to be the charming Venetian town of Piran. But check out Portorož, home of Riviera-style glitz and glamour, Izola, a small fishing town and Koper, Slovenia's only port and the seat of its third university.

A view of the coastal town of Piran

Burja, the Slovene Hurricane!
Named after Boreas, the Ancient Greek god of the north wind the northeast *Burja* wind blows across the eastern Adriatic shore in winter. In Slovenia the *Burja* blows powerfully across the Karst plateaus towards the coast, with gusts reaching up to 200km an hour. A local Burja can blow forcibly for an hour or two but sometimes this wicked wind can last as long as a week or more. It frequently causes significant damage and closes roads and has a strong influence throughout the region from the way houses are built to the way trees grow bowed to the south. The *Burja* is a hindrance residents have adapted to by living in areas which are sheltered from the wind, building houses whose fronts face to the south and that have stones on their roofs to prevent the wind snatching away roof tiles. When driving around this area, you will notice roadsigns displaying the current wind speed and it is not uncommon to find sections of the motorway closed to high-sided vehicles. In the end, *Burja* is a dry wind bringing fair weather but it is also thought to make people moody and bad tempered.

❶ Trenta valley

 114

Located at the heart of Triglav National Park, the isolated Trenta Valley comprises no more than three villages, Trenta, Lepena and Soča. Carved by a glacier, the valley floor is covered with forest, mainly beech, whilst the landscape is a mixture of steep slopes, deep-cut valleys and gorges formed by the Soča river.

The Soča carves its way through the landscape

▶ The first written mention of Trenta dates back to 1326. It is not known exactly when iron ore was first found in the valley, or indeed who discovered it, however in 1576 iron forges were erected and soon the valley was swarming with army deserters, prison fugitives and free-spirited people, most of them from South Tirol and Trento after whom the valley was eventually named. Due to the high costs and the poor quality of the ore, the mine was unable to remain competitive and was closed down in 1778. The end of the iron industry marked the start of a period of poverty and slow development for the valley. Some of the workers and their families did stay, however, making their living breeding cattle, harvesting timber and hunting. After World War Two, Trenta's decline hastened, mainly as a result of depopulation and the abandonment of cattle grazing in the mountains. Cultivated land fell from 28% to a mere 1% and the number of inhabitants, which numbered 380 in 1880, has been steadily dropping and now stands at around 100. These days the secluded nature of the valley and the of natural beauty draws visitors to Trenta.

▶ The best place to start your visit to the Valley is at the Trenta Lodge Information Centre (*www.tnp.si, open daily 10am–6pm 27th Apr to 31st Oct, 10am–2pm 26th Dec 26th Apr, tel. 053/889330*) in the centre of Trenta. The ground floor houses the information centre which provides free information for visitors to Triglav National Park as well as selling literature and souvenirs and can arrange guided tours within the Park. The Lodge also has self-contained apartments available for rent. The Trenta Museum (*guided tours are free for groups of 10 or more if arranged in advance, otherwise entry fees are €4 adults; €3 children, students and pensioners; €10 families; free for children under 5*) occupies the upper floors where natural exhibits about Triglav National Park include a relief of the Park, presentations of the geology, geomorphology and hydrology and exhibitions of the indigenous flora and fauna. A highlight is the multi-media presentation entitled 'Secrets of the Soča'. Alongside the Information Centre there is also a small shop (look for the '*Trgovina*'

The Soča Trail

sign, it looks like it's in someone's front room!) and an eco-restaurant.

Part of the Soča Trail crossing the Soča

▶ The Soča Trail (Soška pot) is a nature trail which runs alongside the Soča river from its source to Bovec. The entire trail measures 20km in length and is split into four sections. If time is limited, a visit to the upper-part of the trail contains many of the most interesting natural and cultural sights. The trail is well-marked throughout with Triglav National Park information boards providing

The Koča pri izviru Soče

▶ The source of the Soča River (Izvir Soče, 886m) where the water mountain slopes gushes out of the karst springs and joins the riverbed in a waterfall, can be reached by a 15min walk from the hut Koča pri Izviru Soče where food and refreshments are available (open 1st May – 31st October). The last few metres require some scrambling using handrails and ropes. An alternative way of reaching the hut is from bend 49 of the Vršič pass, crossing a small bridge where a sign shows 1km to the hut, which can be reached on foot or by car.

information about the important sights along the walk. It can be walked in either direction though the favoured route is from its start at the source of the Soča River thereafter continuing mostly downhill. As the trail is not circular, if you wish to walk a large section of the trail, the use of buses, travelling from Kranjska Gora to Bovec and onwards to Nova Gorica, is recommended for the return journey. The Information Centre in Trenta have up-to-date bus timetables (note: these buses only run during the summer months).

Butterflies at the Juliana Alpine Botanical Garden

Dr. Julius Kugy (1858–1944)

Dr. Julius Kugy was one of the greatest admirers of the Julian Alps and the Trenta Valley. He was a lawyer by profession, a humanist and an adventurer who, with the help of local mountain guides, was the first to climb many of the peaks of the Julian Alps, many by previously unknown routes. He wrote extensively of the beauty of the Alps and recorded his affection for the people of the mountains. In his memory the Slovene Mountainering Association erected a monument to him (Kugyev spominik) located in a prominent position beside the road at bend 48 of the Vršič pass. The monument is the work of the Slovene sculptor, illustrator and poet Jakob Savinšek (1922-1961).

▶ Along the upper-part of the trail is the Juliana Alpine Botanic Garden (*Alpinum Juliana, tel. 012/410940, open daily 8.30am–6.30pm 1ˢᵗ May–30ᵗʰ Sept, entry fees €3 adults, €2 children*) which was founded in 1926 by the botanist Albert Bois de Chesne (1871-1953) when he bought a piece of land in Trenta to fulfil his botanical dream and started to bring and plant specimens from the mountains working with Dr Julius Kugy (see p. 129). The garden contains over 600 different species of alpine and karst plants including many unique to Slovenia. The gardens are at their most beautiful in late spring, early May and the beginning of June but are also equally beautiful throughout summer until the autumn.

The Trenta Valley is a starting point for the ascent to Triglav

▶ The Trenta Valley is also one of the starting points for the ascent to Triglav. This approach from the western side is quieter than the other routes due to Trenta being harder to reach than the other start points and because it's a long climb of over 2,200m. The route starts at an altitude of just over 600m from the Zadnjica Valley before making the long monotonous zigzagging ascent (approx 4h) towards the Dolič saddle, where during the summer months the mountain hut Koca na Doliču (2151m) provides overnight accommodation and refreshments before continuing to the summit.

2 Bovec

1,700

Trg Golobarskih Žrtev 8, www.bovec.si 053/896444, open daily 8.30am–8.30pm

Kluže Festival (July and August)

The small town of Bovec is situated in the far northwestern corner of Slovenia in the wide flat Bovška Kotlina basin. The combination of the steep surrounding mountains of the Kanin range and the famous emerald green Soča River make for a stunning location. What's more Bovec has, in recent years, earned a reputation for being the "adventure capital" of the Soča Valley region. Bovec and its surroundings have a huge amount to offer outdoor enthusiasts during both the winter and summer months.

A view over Bovec

▶ Bovec doesn't have its own railway station, the nearest one is in **Most na Soči** 42km away and can seem a little cut-off as a result. During summer, however, buses run regularly from Bled to Kranjska Gora and onwards to Bovec and Nova Gorica. By car Bovec can be approached from the north either from Kranjska Gora (over the Vršič pass, passable only during summer, closed during winter) or from Tarvisio in Italy (over the Predel Pass usually open during winter). Approaching from the south, the road from Nova Gorica via Tolmin leads to Bovec (75km).

▶ During World War I Bovec suffered heavily and was almost completely destroyed. Rebuilding took place only for the town to then be hit by the severe Friuli earthquake in 1976, the epicentre of which was in Italy but which caused considerable damage to the town and its surroundings. Whilst fortunately no lives were lost in Slovenia, around 13,000 people found themselves without roofs over their heads. Weaker earthquakes shook the town in 1998 and in 2004.

Tolmin Gorge near Bovec

The Bovec area has a long, rich tradition of cheese-making

▶ Other than tourism, agriculture has traditionally provided people here with a living, in particular sheep and goat breeding. The Bovec area is especially well-known for the local **sheep cheese** (*ovčji sir*) which has a long and rich tradition and is well worth a taste either from a local restaurant or, better still, from one of the producers. The tourist information have a map and a leaflet, "Along the Bovska ovca sheep trail" with information about the cheese making process and listing all the dairies in the area.

▶ The **Kanin Ski Centre** (*www. boveckanin.si*) is the highest ski centre in Slovenia with slopes ranging from 1,600-2,300m. Even though the climate in Bovec is relatively mild as a result of the influence of the Adriatic sea and the warm winds which blow up through the valley, the ski season here can be long, often starting in December and lasting until May. The 2009/2010 winter season saw a new exciting development for Kanin when they joined together with the ski resort of Sella Nevea on the Italian side of the mountain, enabling skiing on both sides with just one ski pass, making this Slovenia's only transnational ski resort. The Kanin centre lifts also operate in the summer. It ascends to 2,200m which

Enjoying the Kanin mountains in summer

provides an ideal starting point for numerous hiking paths into the high mountains. The Kanin centre lifts can be easily reached on foot from the centre of Bovec (approx 15 minutes) following the road towards Tolmin and taking the turning directly opposite the petrol station.

The Kanin Ski Centre

▶ There are numerous walking options both in and around Bovec ranging from low-level valley walks to hiking the peaks towering above Bovec. The 1:25,000 Bovec Tourist Map has all the routes marked together with suggested itineraries. Valley walks are marked both on the map and on wooden posts with B1, B2 etc.

Hiking around Bovec can be a breathtaking experience

▶ A particularly pleasant low level walk is the one numbered B2 which offers lots of sights without too much exertion (7km). The walk starts from the far end of the car park of the Kanin ski gondala lift. The walk also passes the

leading to the unusual **source of the river Glijuna**, a spring gushing up from the rocks as though from nowhere. The route also passes the small but powerful **Virje waterfall** which can be heard long before it can be seen.

The potent Virje waterfall

newly opened 9 hole **Bovec Golf Course** (*www.golfbovec.si, 040/382229*). Shortly after it passes a man-made reservoir before

▶ For high level hiking, some of the more popular options include the ascents to **Rombon** (2208m) or **Visoki Kanin** (2587m) both of which offer magnificent views across the western Julian Alps and are easiest reached by taking the Kanin gondola to the top 'D' station from where the paths are well marked (5 and 3 hours respectively). During summer months and at weekends only, the mountain cabin **Planinski Dom Petra Skalarja** (2260m) is open and situated 45 minutes walk from the 'D' station (NB, the cabin is open only when the gondola is in operation).

▶ The **Bovec Sports Airfield**, situated directly opposite the town, offers paragliding, parachuting and panoramic flights with the chance to soar high above the valleys and mountains. The

Simply sublime views of the Julian Alps

combination of the valley and the mountains provide great thermal and wind conditions.

▶ The **Mountain Bike Park Kanin** (*www.mtbparkkanin.com*) is divided into three sections, two of which are suitable for all abilities, the third for advanced riders. The trail is 4.5km downhill and starts from the Kanin ski gondola 'B' station. The park has bikes for rent and can also arrange guided bike tours.

Mountain biking through the spectacular landscape around Bovec

Planinski Dom Petra Skalarja

▶ Lovers of water-based activities will be spoilt for choice with the **Soča river** which provides opportunities for canyoning, rafting, kayaking and hydrospeed. There are numerous picturesque gorges, waterfalls and bridges and of course countless places to stop and enjoy being by the river. Trips of various length are offered ranging from short gentle trips in the shallow rapids suitable for children to riding the full-on adrenaline-pumping rapids. As well as being a real haven for lovers of kayaking and rafting the Soča is also a fisherman's paradise. The best fishing is to be had from June through to September when the Soča

trout, endemic to Slovenia and the largest of the European trout species, is at its most prevalent. The Soča River is famous for its stunning emerald colour, which is rare because it lasts throughout the length of the river and is so clear and bright in places it seems like something out of a fairy tale. This became almost literally the case in 2008 when some scenes of the film "The Chronicles of Narnia" were shot around the river and the Bovec area.

The Boka Waterfall

▶ Whilst Bovec has a number of hotels, guesthouses and apartments, **camping** is particularly popular here and in the surrounding areas and there are a number of campsites occupying prime positions next to the Soča river.

▶ Travelling from Bovec towards Tolmin, between the villages of Žaga and Srpenica, the **Boka waterfall** (*Slap Boka*) is one of the most impressive and powerful waterfalls in Slovenia. The waters that gather high in the Kanin mountains converge and form

Canoeing along the Soča

a mighty force falling directly downwards over two stages totalling 144m. The waterfall is at its most impressive in late spring when up to a hundred cubic metres per second of water falls as a result of the layers of mountain snow melting. The waterfall can be seen from the road but for a close-up view, park at the Boka bridge (*Most Boka*) and follow the marked path for approximately 40 minutes to the view point at the foot of the waterfall.

▶ The **Kluže Fortress** (*Trdnava Kluže, open daily July & Aug 9am-8pm, June & Sept Sun– Fri 10am-5pm, Sat 10am-6pm, May & Oct only weekends 10am-5pm, entry fees €3 adults, €2 students and pensioners, €1 children*), 4km from Bovec in the direction of the Predel Pass, sits above the deep gorge of the Koritnica River. Originally the wooden fortress was built in the second half of the 15th century to prevent raids on the valley by the Ottomans. In the 17th century, Georg Phillipp von Gera, the then ruler of Bovec, built a stone fortress in its place and also discovered a nearby spring which would enable the fortress to withstand lengthy sieges. In 1797 an Austrian contingent of soldiers defended the fortress against the advancing French army under the command of Napoleon. As the defenders stood little chance of overpowering the adversary, they resorted to trickery by removing the bridge over the Koritnica Rover and many of the French soliders plunged to their deaths. The following day, however, the defenders were forced to surrender to their assailants who, in their rage, demolished the fortress. Today the fortress operates as a museum exhibiting local history and also hosts the Kluže

The Kluže Fortress

Festival (July and August) which comprises a number of open-air theatrical and musical events.

▶ The upper part of the fortress, named **Fort Hermann**, lies on the opposite side of the road and is accessible only on foot. There are two ways to reach it. Either by parking at the Kluže Fortress and taking the 30min military path which leads first through a tunnel (for which a torch is recommended). Alternatively the fort can be reached on foot directly from Bovec by a marked path (B4) starting from Trg Golobarskih Žrtev, opposite the post office. Despite its heavy defences, Fort Hermann was almost entirely destroyed by an Italian artillery barrage in 1915.

Visitors enjoy an open-air performance during the Kluže Festival

A view of Kobarid

3 Kobarid

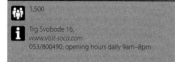

1,500

Trg Svobode 16,
www.visit-soca.com
053/800490; opening hours daily 9am–8pm

Kobarid, 21km south of Bovec, lies at the meeting point of two valleys - Breginjski Kot and the Soča valley. Set in stunning scenery and dwarfed by the surrounding mountains of Stol (1673m), Matajur (1642m) and Krn (2244m) Kobarid makes an ideal location for outdoor pursuits, but it is also popular with history buffs due to its turbulent past and a wealth of nearby historical sites.

▶ The town was the site of the World War I Battle of the Isonzo Front, also known as the Battle of Caporetto, named after the Italian name for Kobarid. The battle was made famous by Ernest Hemingway in his novel "A Farewell to Arms". The battle is well documented in the Kobarid Museum (see p. 136).

Unlike Bovec, Kobarid has a more Mediterranean rather than Alpine feel and appearance. Its mediterranean climate, sleepy atmosphere and Italian-style houses complete with terracotta roofs reinforce this.

The landscape around Kobarid is a Mecca for outdoors types

The delicious Kobariški Štruklji dessert

▶ The town and the vicinity have built some reputation for the quality and variety of its food offerings. The specialty is the famous local dessert, *kobariški štruklji* made from dough stuffed with walnuts, raisins and other secret ingredients. Everyone who prepares it has their own signature recipe and signs it with a fingerprint indented into the pastry.

Learn about the WWI Soča Front at the Kobarid Museum

▶ The **Kobarid Museum** (*Gregorčičeva ulica 10; www.kobariski-muzej.si; open daily April-Sept 9am-6pm, Sat, Sun & Hols 9am-7pm, Oct-Mar 10am-5pm, Sat, Sun & Hols 9am-6pm; entrance fees €5 adults, €4 pensioners and students, €2.5 children*) has won several European awards for excellence. The museum is devoted to presenting the rich history of Kobarid and in particular the events which took place on the Soča Front from May 1915 to November 1917. A good place to start your visit is in the **Krn Room** on the ground floor where a scale model of Mount Krn and its neighbouring peaks gives a perspective of the battlefields and their environs and also presents the initial assaults along the Soča River after Italy's entry into the war on May 24, 1915. The first and second floors house exhibitions telling the story of the twenty-nine months of fighting. The **Black Room** shows graphic photographs of soldiers praying before being sent into battle and of dead and dying soldiers. The **White Room**, describes the harsh conditions and suffering encountered by the soldiers waging war in this treacherous mountainous region. The

third floor documents the final campaign of the Soča Front and the twelfth Soča battle on October 24th 1917, the **Battle of Kobarid**. Another scale model and large maps illustrate the scale of the task the soliders faced and their extraordinary efforts to transport the necessary supplies across the mountains to the Soča valley.

▶ Many visitors to the museum choose to continue their immersion into the history of the Kobarid area by walking all, or part of, the **Kobarid Historical Trail**. The 5km trail starts from the north corner of the central square where a minor road leads between two pillars, one with a star on the top, the other with a cross. Here an information board marks the start of the

Walking the Kobarid Historical Trail

walk which, in terms of cultural and natural sights, must be one of Slovenia's most fascinating walks. A leaflet with a map and descriptions of the sights along the way is available at the tourist centre.

▶ The walk starts up the winding road where the Stations of the Cross line the roadside before reaching the octagonal **Italian Charnel House**. The house was opened in 1938 by Benito Mussolini and comprises three octagons, each smaller than the one before it, stacked and topped by the Church of St. Anton. Here, the large ossuary houses the remains of more than 7,000 Italian soldiers killed on the Soča front.

▶ The road now continues to the rocky elevation **Tonocov Grad** which due to its naturally secure position was used as a settlement from the Copper Age until the Middle Ages. The

The Church of St Anton

The late Roman ruins of Tonocov Grad

surrounding villages is not possible by public transport) can be reached by crossing Napoleon's Bridge and turning left. Drežnica is well worth a visit for the imposing **Church of the Sacred Heart** Construction of the church began in 1911 and despite the raging war and earthquakes that have struck the region, the church has remained intact ever since. The interior of the church is rich with paintings and images. On the lateral wall

settlement's heyday was in the late Roman and Antiquity periods when over twenty houses and several churches were built on the hill. The remains of these constitute one of the most important late Antiquity archeological localities in the eastern Alps.

▶ The walk also visits the spectacular **Kojzak waterfall** (*Slap Kozjak*). While not the highest, widest or most powerful of Slovenia's many waterfalls, Kozjak is certainly one of the most beautiful due its wonderful natural setting. Here at Veliki Kozjak the 15 metre column of water has carved an underground cavern where the luminous blue and green waters offer an unforgettable scene and photo opportunity.

Stunning views of the Julian Alps

there are two reliefs with two pairs of saints; the left one shows the Slavic apostles St. Cyril and St. Methodus, the right one shows the announcers of faith St. Mohor and St. Fortunatus. The Sacred Heart, surrounded by angels and pilgrims, is depicted on the wall behind the altar.

▶ Cattle breeding and cheese production takes place above Drežnica on Alpine dairy farms such as **Planina Zaprikraj** (1208m). The Planina can be reached by following the road to Drežniške Ravne (3km from Drežnica). The road continues a further 1km, but it is best to leave your car at the small parking area by the water

The enchanting Kozjak Waterfall

▶ For a longer walk, the **hike to Stol** (4 hrs), begins at a path to the left of the start of the Historical Trail and ascends through the forest. This long high ridge running west from Kobarid continues into Italy and offers stunning views across the upper Soča Valley, the Julian Alps and on into Italy and is also popular with mountain bikers.

▶ The village of **Drežnica**, 6kms from Kobarid (*note - access to Drežnica and its*

Zaprikraj is famous for its cattle breeds and cheese making

The Alpine meadows of Zaprikraj

The Tolmin Gorge, part of the Walk of Peace

trough where the tarmac ends and continue on foot as the road is very rough. The path takes about an hour to reach the Planina where, during the summer months, cheese can be purchased.

▶ A further 15min level walk from Planina Zaprikraj brings you to the **Zaprikraj First World War Outdoor Museum** (1259m). The museum represents the first line of defence in the Krn range which blocked the passage along the valley between Mount Krasji vrh and Vršič where the heaviest battles were fought in the autumn of 1915. Well-preserved trenches, caves and fortified positions, remains of cabins, gun and mortar positions and a restored memorial to Lieutenant Vito Neri who died in 1916 can be seen here.

▶ This is just one of the six Outdoor Museums that are located within the Soča Valley in the areas surrounding Kobarid, Bovec and Tolmin. The Outdoor Museums together with the most important monuments and memorials of the Isonzo Front have been connected to form **The Walk of Peace**. The route begins at Log Pod Mangartom and ends on Mengore Hill and

travels through the six outdoor museums, military cemeteries, chapels, forts, the Soča gorges and idyllic alps within Triglav National Park. Further details on the museums and the walk is available through the Walks of Peace in the Soča Region Foundation (*Gregoričičeva 8; www.potmiru.si; tel. 053/890167*) who also organise guided tours, with local historians,

The Zaprikraj First World War Outdoor Museum

by prior arrangement (€25 per hour for groups up to 30).

Biking the Walk of Peace trail

4 Nova Gorica

13,200

Bevkov trg 4,
www.novagorica-turizem.com
053/304600, Summer opening
hours Mon–Fri 8am–8pm, Sat &
Sun 9am–1pm, winter (15th Nov–
–15th Apr) 8am–6pm

A view of Nova Gorica's communist-era high-rises

The town of Nova Gorica (New Gorica) is a socialist new town on the Italian border. It was founded after WWII when Gorica, the capital of the former Slovene province of Goriška, was awarded to Italy in the post-war settlement. Today Nova Gorica and its Italian neighbour Gorizia blend almost seamlessly into one another but each has its own distinct character.

Being a relatively young town, Nova Gorica doesn't hold a wealth of interesting historical or cultural sights and these days it is famous for its casinos which are very popular with visiting Italians. The town's

Revolutionary sculptures on Nova Gorica Town Hall

location however, standing at the junction of the Soča Valley, the Vipava Valley and the Karst area, make it a good location for a base from which to enjoy the surrounding landscapes of wine-growing regions and the pleasant Mediterranean climate.

▶ The town is centres on the main road, Kidričeva ulica, which runs north to south. To the east of Kidričeva ulica on Trg Edvarda Kardelja is the **Town Hall** (*Mestna hiša*) which was built in 1950, and is a typical example of post-war architecture. Its facade is enriched with the sculptures of partisans and revolutionary motifs created by the sculptor

Boris Kalin. At the end of Kidričeva ulica, in the direction of the town of Solkan, stands the **Church of Christ the Saviour** (*Cerkev Kristusa Odrešenika*) which was built in 1982. Its modern exterior hides the beauty and grandness of its interior including a wooden statue of Christ and the Stations of the Cross, works of art done by the Slovene artist and sculptor Stane Jarem (born in 1931). Bevkov square (*Bevkov trg*), to the west of Kidričeva ulica, is the town's main shopping and cultural centre.

▶ Nova Gorica's **railway station** on Kolodvorska ulica, 1.5km west of the centre, is the town's oldest building. When it was built in 1906 it was the largest and most beautiful station in the region. Largely gutted during WWI it was rebuilt by the Italians after the war. After 1945 it remained on the very border between Italy and Yugoslavia, a small part of the Iron Curtain, swathed in barbed wire. Today, however, since the removal of the borders between the two countries and in honour of Slovenia joining the EU, the area in front of the station has officially been declared a common square shared by both countries, graced with a huge circular mosaic. Within

The train station is Nova Gorica's oldest building

Kromberk Castle, home of the Goriška Museum

the station is **The Museum collection: Border-line in the Goriška region 1945 – 2004** (*open Mon-Fri 1pm-5pm, Sat 9am-5pm, Sun 10am-5pm, entrance free*) displays photographs of this period of the region's history.

▶ **Kromberk Castle** stands on a hill approximately 1km from the centre of Nova Gorica. It was built before the end of the 16th century and was severely damaged in both World Wars, but was renovated both times. Since 1954 it has also been home to the **Goriška Museum** (*Goriški muzej, www.goriskimuzej.si, 053/359811, open Mon-Fri 8am-7pm, 8am-3pm winter, Sun&Hols 1pm-7pm, 1pm-5pm winter, Saturdays closed, entrance fees €2 adults, €1 children*) whose permanent exhibits include the Gallery of Ancient Art, the Gallery of 20th century Primorska artists and an exhibition of 19th century paintings.

▶ 2km south of Nova Gorica, the **Kostanjevica Monastery** (*Franciskanski samostan, www.samostan-kostanjevica.si, 053/307750, open Mon-Sat 9am-12pm and 3pm-5pm, Sun & Hols 3pm-5pm. Entrance fee €2.50*) was founded by the Capuchin Franciscans in the early 17th century. The monastery's rich and valuable library (**Škrabčeva knjižnica**, *open by appointment only*) contains over 10,000 books including 30 incunabula, the oldest dating from 1476. The highlight of a visit to the monastery is

The interior of the Church of the Annunciation of Mary

its garden which contains one of the biggest and most complete collections of Bourbon roses in the world.

▶ The nearby **Church of the Annunciation of Mary** has a rich history. It is home to priceless treasures from the past such as the tombs of the last members of the French Bourbon royal family, including King Charles X, who were exiled from France during the revolution of 1830. After seeking refuge in Scotland, then Prague, they finally came to Gorica where they were received as guests of Count Coronini.

▶ **Goriška Brda** is a hilly wine region that extends from the Soča River in the southeast to the Idrija River in the northwest and across the Italian border. The region is famous known for for its vineyards and cherry orchards.

▶ The centre of the Goriška Brda region and the main town is **Dobrovo** which is also home to the regions tourist

Kostanjevica Monastery

Traditional wine-growing in the Goriška Brda region

Dobrovo Castle is home to a famous wine cellar

information centre (*Grajska cesta 10, www.brda.si, 053/959594, opening hours*

Dobrovo nestled in the Goriška Brda

▶ The **Goriška Brda Wine Road** leads from the village of Plave to Vrhovlje near Kojsko. A drive along the road offers wonderful view over the hills, vineyards and orchards of the Brda region. The route passes through several small attractive villages with a distinctly Mediterranean character, such as Števerjan, **Kojsko** and **Vipolže** where you can stop at one of the many tourist farms which offer wine tasting and typical Slovene food.

Mon-Fri 8am-4pm, Sat&Sun summer only 10am-6pm). Standing above the town is the fortified two-storey 17th century Renaissance **Dobrovo Castle** *(Tel: 053/959586, open Tue-Fri 8am-4pm, Sat, Sun&Hols 10am-6pm, winter 12pm-4pm, Mondays closed, entrance fees €2 adults, €1 children).* The castle is home to the **Brda Wine Cellar** (*Vinoteka Brda, www. vinotekabrda.si, tel: 053/959210, open Tue–Sun 11.30am–9pm*) which was created to bring together over 200 different wines and over 40 local producers for on-site tastings and visits to the vineyards.

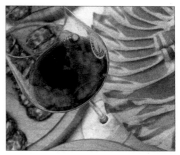

The Goriška Brda region is famous for good food and good wines

Šmartno, a particularly pretty village on the Goriška Brda Wine Road

5 Idrija

6,000

Vodnikova ulica 3,
www.idrija-turizem.si
053 743916, opening hours
May-Oct Mon-Fri 9am-6pm, Sat,
Sun & Hols 10am-4pm, Oct-May
Mon-Fri 9am-4pm, Sat 10am-4pm,
Sun & Hols - Closed

Events: Idrija Lace Festival (June)

A view of Idrija

1 Gewerkenegg Castle

2 Antony's shaft

3 Church of the Holy Trinity

4 Idria war museum

5 Lace making school

6 Town Hall

HOTELS:

1 Hostel Idrija

RESTAURANTS:

1 Gostilna Kos

2 Kavarna Gabron

The town of Idrija, famous for its mercury mines, is located in a basin at the confluence of the Idrijca and Nikova rivers and is surrounded on all sides by the steep Idrija and Cerkno hills. The town's development and growth were founded on the discovery of mercury in 1490 and the Idrija Mine went on to become the second largest mercury mine in the world, accounding for more than 13 percent of total world production. The mine has, however, been closed due to declining mercury prices and concern for the local environement.

▶ A good place to find out more about mercury is at the **Idrija Municipal Museum** (*www.muzej-idrija-cerkno.si, Prelovceva 9, tel: 053 726600, opening hours daily 9am-6pm, entrance fees €3 adults, €1.70 children*) which is housed within the impressive **Gewerkenegg Castle** *(Grad Gewerkenegg)*. The name Gewerkenegg means "mine castle" in German. The castle, which was completed in 1533, was originally constructed for the needs of the mercury mine and was used as a warehouse for storing wheat, mercury and cinnabar

Back to nature in the hills around Idrija

Gewerkenegg Castle, home to the Idrija Municipal Museum

The stunning Renaissance interior of Gewerkenegg Castle

and served for many centuries as the headquarters of the mine administration. The Renaissance style complex comprises three cylindrical corner defence towers and an entrance tower which was renovated in the Baroque style in the mid-18th century.

The entrance to Anthony's Shaft

The clock tower bears the image of Mercury, the god of trade. In 1997 the Museum won the coveted title of Best Technical Museum in Europe. Today as well as the museum, the castle houses a music school, lace shops and a restaurant. As one would expect many of museum's exhibitions are based on mercury and all things pertaining to it. However there are also numerous other fascinating exhibitions including Rocks and Fossils of the Idrija and Cerkno Regions, a Mineral and Petrographic collection, The History of the Idrija Region, The Period of the Italian and German Occupation, Rural

Frescoes and A History Written in Thread – Idrija Lace.

▶ Another place you can get an insight into what life must have been like for the mine workers is the Idrija Mercury Mine named **Anthony's Shaft** (*Antonijev rov*). Its entrance point is in the Šelštev building (*Kosovelova 3, www.rzs-idrija.si, tel: 053 771142, tour schedule Mon–Fri 10am & 3pm, Sat, Sun & Hols 10am, 3pm & 4pm, entrance fees €6 adults, €4 children, € 4.50 pensioners*), which was previously one of the main entrances to the town. Upon arrival visitors are shown a short film (in several languages) about the history of the mine. Then its time to don the provided overcoats and helmets and set off on a 1½ hour guided tour of the underground world of the mine. Reconstructions show how the miners dug, loaded and transported

Anthony's Shaft

the ore in carts and offers a glimpse into how hard life must have been in the narrow deep shafts. At the end of Anthony's Main Road, the underground **Chapel of the Holy Trinity** was dug out in the mid 18th century. From the chapel the miners then descended more than a thousand steps down into the depths of the mine. The chapel is simply decorated with a relief of the Holy Trinity and statues of Saint Barbara and Saint Achacius, the patron saints of miners. From the chapel the tour continues through the shafts, descending to the lowest point around 100m, before returning to the light of day.

Exhibits at the Idrija War Museum

▶ To the north of the town's central Mestni trg, through a passageway leading to Trg Svetega Ahacija is the Magazin building. Formerly a granary and warehouse it now houses a cinema and the **Idrija War Museum** (*Vojni Muzej Idrija, open daily except Mon 10am-12pm & 1pm–5pm, entrance fee €3 adults, €2.50 children & students*). The private museum houses five collections covering the First and Second World Wars, the Italian occupation, The National Liberation War, the military forces in times of socialist Yugoslavia and the War of Independence of Slovenia.

▶ The **Church of the Holy Trinity,** to the north of Mestni trg, is Idrija's oldest church. Initially a wooden chapel was erected here shortly after the discovery of mercury in 1490. In 16th century a Gothic stone presbytery and wooden nave had been added. Further embellishments followed in 1703 including lateral golden altars and the central image on the main altar of the Coronation of the Virgin painted by the Austrian painter Carl von Reslfeld (1658-1735). During the first half of the 19th century, the church fell into disrepair due to neglect. Fortunately, the Archbishop of Ljubljana, an Idrijan, secured its preservation and today it is fully restored back to its authentic form. The presbytery's stained-glass windows were designed by the Slovene artist Lojze Čemažar (b.1950).

▶ Idrija is known both nationally and internationally for its lace. The oldest document testifying to the existence of lace-making in Idrija dates from 1696. The lace-making skills were brought to Slovenia when Czech and German miners came to Slovenia to work in the mine. Making and selling lace products provided additional income to the miners' families.

The **Idrija Lace-making School** (*Čipkarska šola Idrija, Prelovceva 2, www. cipkarska.sola.si, tel: 053 734570*) provides courses and workshops for adults and children. Every June the School prepares a new lace exhibition (*open from the first day of the Lace Festival until the end of August, opening hours daily 10am-1pm & 3pm-6pm. Outside of summer, the exhibition is open Mon-Fri 10am-1pm. Entrance fees €2.5 adults, free for children under the age of 15*) to showcase the work of students. The school offers guided tours of the exhibitions, lace-making demonstrations and a selection of handmade products for purchase.

Idrijski žlikrofi are the food speciality of the town. Whilst the origin of the recipe remains unknown their importance was recognised when in 2010 they became one of a few Slovene dishes which have received European protected status. Žlikrofi are made of dough filled with potato, chives, marjoram and pork crackling and formed into their specific crescent-like shape. Traditionally they are served with a sauce of lamb and vegetables but to-day they are served in many different guises. Whilst visiting Idrija they are a must try.

Idrija lace

Traditional lace-making paraphernalia

6 Vipava Valley

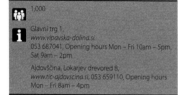

1,000

Glavni trg 1,
www.vipavska-dolina.si,
053 687041, Opening hours Mon – Fri 10am – 5pm,
Sat 9am – 2pm

Ajdovščina, Lokarjev drevored 8,
www.tic-ajdovscina.si, 053 659110, Opening hours
Mon – Fri 8am – 4pm

The wide, fertile Vipava Valley south of Nova Gorica is famous for its vineyards and world-class wines. The valley's location together with its mild climate, an idyllic mix of Mediterranean and Continental, make for perfect conditions for wine production. It is said that spring lasts two months longer here than in other parts of Slovenia, hence the vineyards are even more productive. Although the valley has a generally mild climate, it is often subject to the North Eastern Bora (*Burja*) wind, which can be a mixed blessing (see p. 127).

▶ The entire valley is shadowed by the mighty **Nanos Plateau**, the highest point of which is Suhi Vrh (1313m) with magnificent views of nearby Mount Snežnik, the Karst area, the Gulf of Trieste and the Trnovski Gozd plateau. The Nanos plateau formerly offered shelter to the members of the TIGR organization, the first rebels against fascism in Europe, and later to the Partisans (see p. 146). A monument dedicated to the victims of the battle stands outside the mountain cabin, Vojkova Koča. There are several marked paths to the peak including those starting from villages Podnanos and Razdrto. On reaching these villages simply look for easily visible red and white circular way-markers. Due to the limestone formation of the mountain, it is full of interesting features such as sinkholes, caves, cracks and springs. Whilst not particularly high, the steep paths (marked *Strma pot*) can be quite challenging, however, steel ropes and handholds are provided to assist and there

The vineyards of the Valley with the Nanos Plateau in the background

DON'T MISS! The tradition of Osmica, derived from the Slovene for eight (*osem*), dates back to the middle of the 18th century when Empress Maria Teresa issued a decree allowing wine producers to sell their produce and allow visitors to visit their farms and vineyards to taste the wines and home-made food. Nowadays, Osmicas take place twice a year in spring and in autumn. During this time local farms and vineyards, some of which are tourist farms and the like whilst others are merely family run farms, open their doors for eight days and the festivities are often accompanied by singing and dancing. Osmica's are marked with signs simply displaying the number 8 and should you be fortunate to be in the area at this time, it's a great way of enjoying some authentic Slovene hospitality.

are also longer gentler routes making Nanos largely accessible to all.

▶ The Vipava wine region has thousands of hectares of vineyards along the Vipava Wine Road, with 30 wine-growing villages marked by brown tourist signs. Everything is relatively close-by and accessible; a car is the most practical form of transport though this of course might get in the way of your wine tasting experience. Alternatively walk or cycle along the marked Upper Vipava Valley path. The tourist offices in Vipava and Ajdovščina have a brochure and map entitled 'The Vipava Wine Road' and can also arrange wine-tasting visits to vineyards. Tourists are also welcome to visit the vineyards independently but are advised to call ahead.

Up to 25 varieties of wine are produced by the winegrowers in the valley. The most well known amongst them being the Merlot and Cabernet Sauvignon reds and the Sauvignon Blanc and Chardonnay whites while many domestic varieties are also

The Vipava Valley is famous for its wide range of excellent wines

produced. Previously the region produced mainly white wines but today it is also increasingly famous for its excellent red wines. If you want to sample authentic and original Vipava wines, try the local Zelen and Pinela varieties.

▶ The largest settlement and economic and cultural centre of the valley is **Ajdovščina** (pop. 6,400). The town has had a long and turbulent history and has many remains from as far back as Roman times. It is the only town in the country with an almost

TIGR – the beginnings of anti-fascism in Europe
The TIGR organization (the acronym stands for Trst, Istra, Gorica and Reka and is reminiscent of tiger, which is also Slovene for tiger), was one of the first anti-Facist organizations in Europe. The organization began its secret meetings in 1927 on the Nanos plateau and was active until 1941. Its members were Slovene and Croat nationalists with links to Yugoslav and British intelligence services. The organization fought against the provisions of the Rapallo Treaty (1920) that turned their homelands over to Italy, as well as against the Fascist Italianization that was instituted. TIGR carried out violent attacks and acts of sabotage against Italianized institutions, including local schools, and destroyed Italian army equipment and warehouses. In 1941 nine members of the organization were accused of terrorism and espionage and five of them were executed, whilst other prominent members were either sent to concentration camps, killed or exiled, effectively leading to the end of the organization.

intact Roman fortress, the settlement of Castrum, which can be reached via a number of small squares leading from the town's main square. The fortress, with fourteen defensive towers, was built around 270 AD and it is possible to stroll around the entire fortress on the path leading around it.

▶ The Parish church of St John the Baptist in Ajdovščina is the home of one of the oldest and most renowned paintings of the Stations of the Cross in Slovenia which depict the final hours, also know as the 'Passion' of Christ. The author of these masterpieces was the popular local church painter, Anton Cebej (1722-1774), who also painted the ceiling frescoes and altar paintings in the mid-18th century.

A view of the village of Vrhpolje on the Vipava Wine Road

The interior of the church of St John the Baptist in Ajdovščina

▶ The Pilon Gallery (*Prešernova ulica 3, www.venopilon.com, 053/689177, open Tue-Fri 8am–4pm, entrance free*) was founded in 1973 by Dominique Pilon, son of the Slovene expressionist painter and photographer Veno Pilon (1896-1970) who was born in Ajdovščina. Following his father's death, Dominique donated his father's works to the town. Its collection comprises a great deal of Pilon senior's paintings and photographs. It comprises two buildings, one of which is Pilon's home and one which was previously his father's bakery. The facades and interiors of both buildings have been well preserved in their original form.

▶ The second biggest town in the valley is the pleasant, peaceful town of Vipava. This picturesque town boasts 25 bridges and is a source of several springs of the Vipava River. A particularly pleasant part of the town is Podskala which can be reached via the small alley next to the tourist office in the main square, sign-posted as leading to the Source of the Vipava. This pleasant shady area is home to the Podskala Restaurant and a couple of bars, reached by one of the many bridges and are an ideal place to relax and admire the view.

▶ The ruins of the Old Vipava Castle *(Stari grad)* stand on a steep hill overlooking the town. Built in the 12th century, in 1565 it was claimed by the Lanthieri Counts who abandoned it sometime during the 17th century, after which it fell into disrepair. Today, although the castle lies in ruins, it is still a popular

The soothing flow of the Vipava River

The abandoned ruins of Old Vipava Castle

Tabor Castle sits serenely on the Vipava River

In 1762 the Lanthieris renovated the mansion in a baroque style and it remains so today. The mansion was last inhabited up until 1910 by Count Carlo Federico Lanthieri. His death signalled the end of this branch of the Vipava Counts and the mansion was subsequently used by army as recently as 1991. In 2009, a significant number of previously hidden frescoes on the ceiling and walls were uncovered. These frescoes are thought to be from the 17th century and to be the work of the same artist who painted the resplendent frescoes at nearby Zemono Manor (*see below*).

spot for a walk from Vipava (app. 30min) as its elevated position offers beautiful views across the Vipava Valley.

▶ **Tabor Castle** *(Grad Tabor)*, otherwise known as Lower Castle *(Spodnji Grad)* was built in the 14th century in order to provide protection for the adjacent stone bridge across the Vipava River. The small castle had many owners and, as with many of the notable buildings in Vipava, it too also owned from 1624 until the end of World War I by the Lanthieri family (note the relief of the Lanthieri family arms dated 1653 on the portal). Today a part of the main building, the defensive tower and part of the protective wall are preserved.

▶ Alongside Tabor Castle, the stucco covered **Lanthieri Mansion** (also known as the New Castle – *Novi grad*), also built by the Lanthieri family in the mid-17th century, is a prime example of period Venetian architecture. The estate was visited in 1728 by the young Carlo Goldoni, the future virtuoso of Venetian baroque drama, who remembers it in his memoirs as a place of excellent wines and excessive drinking.

▶ Following the building of the mansion, the Lanthieris then went on to build and layout the castle park, **Vipava Park**. The well-kept park, which today functions as the

The Lanthieri Mansion, once home to the Vipava Counts

town park, stands in the foreground of the mansion. It was modelled on a traditional English park and contains a stone fountain and numerous sculptures.

▶ Amongst the castles and manors in the valley, **Zemono Manor** *(Dvorec Zemono)* is by far the most impressive. It was built on a hill 2km northwest of Vipava in the 17th century also by the Lanthieri counts. The renaissance style manor, built in the shape of a cross, is the only such example of secular architecture in Slovenia. The manor, which was used as a summer residence and hunter's lodge, has never been permanently inhabited. The entire building is surrounded by arcaded entrance halls whilst its interior is richly painted with secular Baroque frescoes. Today the mansion's

The 17th century Zemono Manor, photographed by Marijan Močivnik

The elegant interior of the "Restaurant pri Lozjetu" in the Zemono Manor

cellar is home to an up-market restaurant and wine cellar "Restaurant pri Lojzetu", which markets itself as the place 'slow food' was invented in Slovenia and is also a popular wedding venue. From the manor there are splendid views towards the valley making Zemono worth a visit, even if you don't intend on dining in the restaurant itself.

7 Cerkno

👥 2,000

ℹ️ Močnikova ulica 2 (entrance from Glavni trg), *www.cerkno.si/turizem* 053/734645, open Mon-Fri 8am-4pm, Sat 8am-noon

🧍 Cerkno Carnival (February)

Cerkno lies in a secluded, hilly landscape

Cerkno lies in a basin in the Cerknica River Valley, on the border between the Primorska and Gorenjska regions and is the administrative, economic and cultural centre of the Cerkljanska region. Thanks to its secluded, hilly location, the area has developed its own unique characteristics including its dialect and customs. Though the **Cerkno Hills** and the **Cerkno Ski Centre** have long been attracting visitors, Cerkno itself is relatively new to the tourist map. Since the opening of the Cerkno Hotel which provides visitors with a base for hiking and cycling in the summer and skiing in winter, the town and its surroundings have becoming increasingly popular. Unfortunately due to its location, unless you have your own transport, Cerkno isn't the easiest place to reach. By car it is easiest to reach via Škofja Loka. The nearest train station is in Most na Soči, 29km away, but buses run from Idrija, Ljubljana and Škofja Loka.

▶ The centre of Cerkno is the small **Glavni Trg** square, where all the town's services, including the tourist information centre,

are. Should the tourist office be closed, an information board at the bus station has many marked circular walking routes whilst a number of red signs show walking times and directions for hiking routes.

The *Lafarji* figures in Cerkno Museum

▶ The **Cerkno Museum** (*Bevkova ulica 12, www.muzej-idrija-cerkno.si, tel: 053 723181, open Tue-Fri 9am–3pm Sat, Sun & Hols 10am–1pm & 2pm–6pm, closed Mondays, entry fees €2.10 adults, €1.30 children*) is

Cerkno's small town centre

The Franja Partisan Hospital

pri Cerknem (*7km from Cerkno*) is one of Slovenia's most important and remarkable historic monuments. The hospital, which was named after its chief physician Dr. Franja Bojc Bidovec, operated as secret World War II hospital run by Partisans to treat wounded soldiers from December 1943 until the end of the War. Its remote location, deep in the forest and hidden in a ravine by the Pasica Stream, meant that the occupying forces were unable to locate it. Another advantage of its location was the abundance of fresh water from the stream which it used to power a hydroelectric generator. The hospital complex, which comprised 13 buildings, housed an impressive array of facilities including an operating theatre, x-ray apparatus and a convalescence area. Unfortunately, the hospital suffered severe damage and was almost totally destroyed during flash floods in 2007 which turned the Pasica stream into a raging torrent. The renovated hospital reopened in May 2010, however of the 800 original preserved items, only 225 were

found on the main through road, a minute's walk from the main square. The museum houses two permanent exhibitions; *The Cerkno Region through the Centuries* and *PUST is to Blame!* The latter tells the story of the *Cerkljanski Laufarija* (the Cerkno Runners), the most recognisable carnival figures in Slovenia and for which Cerkno is famous. The name *Laufarji* refers to the entire group of characters, taken from the German word *laufen* (to run) whose distinguishing features are the wooden masks and clothing made from natural materials such as ivy, straw and moss. The museum exhibits the costumes for all the 25 figures of the Laufarija family.

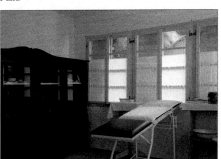

Exhibits at the Partisan Hospital

▶ The **Franja Partisan Hospital** (*Partizanska Bolnica Franja, open 1st Apr-30th Oct daily 9am–6pm, www. muzej-idrija-cerkno.si, entrance fees €3 adults, €1.70 children*) in Dolenji Novaki

found and restored. The hospital can be reached from the centre of Cerkno either by car or on foot (*2½ hours walk*). In both cases the road leads towards the village of Dolenji Novaki where, just after passing the settlement of Log, signs direct you to the hospital and car park.

▶ The **Cerkno Ski Centre**, 10kms from Cerkno (*www. ski-cerkno.com*), is situated at an altitude of 900-1287m on the Črni Vrh mountain. It has 18km of ski runs (4km easy, 8km medium, 6km advance), 5kms of cross-country skiing and a new Snow Fun Park which opened in 2010, ideal for adrenaline seekers. The Centre, one of the most modern in Slovenia, has six chair lifts and two t-bar lifts and is also

The Cerkno Ski Centre has become increasingly popular

The lush green of the Cerkno Hills

very child-friendly. At the top of the main lift station, an alpine style restaurant offers typical Slovene dishes together with panoramic views across the Julian Alps. A ski bus service runs from Cerkno to the Ski Centre.

The Dom na Pozrenu mountain cabin

▶ The **Cerkno Hills** are also ideal for walking and there are numerous options for walks of various lengths and difficulties. One of the most popular hikes in the area is to **Porezen** (1,630m), the region's highest peak. The mountain cabin **Dom na Poreznu** (1,590m) is open end of June to mid-September during fine weather. Here, from 1918–1941 Italians fortified the top of the mountains and underground passages and remains of the fortifications can still be seen. There are several options for the ascent to Porezen. Those without transport can reach the peak directly from the centre of Cerkno where a sign shows 3hrs 30mins one-way. A shorter

alternative starts from the village of Poče from where the ascent takes approximately 2 hours.

▶ The **Divje Babe Archaeological Park** *(open 1ˢᵗ Apr–30ᵗʰ Sept daily 9am–5pm, tour fees €4 adults, €2 children, children under 4 free)*, located near Cerkno in the direction of the village Reka, was established in 2005 on the site of the oldest known archaeological find in Slovenia. The most notable find is a flute fashioned from the femur from a young cave bear. The flute, thought to be at least 45,000 years old and associated with the time of the Neanderthals, is claimed to be the world's oldest known musical instrument and is now on display in the National Museum of Slovenia in Ljubljana (see p. 61). Visits to the park are only possible with a guide and must be arranged in advance through the Cerkno Tourist Information Centre.

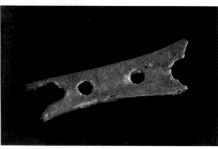

The oldest known musical instrument in the world

The Škocjan Caves grandiose entrance hall

8 Škocjan Caves

The entrance to the Škocjan Caves

The Škocjan Caves, (*Škocjanske Jame*) are a spelioligist's dream and offer an entirely different experience to that of the Postojna caves 33km away. Škocjan is considered by some to be the more 'authentic' experience and there is no denying that its vast underground gorge together with its huge chambers are truly magnificent. The importance of the caves has been acknowledged both in the international scientific world and by UNESCO which, in 1986, placed the caves on its list of natural and cultural world heritage sites.

The nearest town to the caves is Divača, 4km away and is the marked exit if arriving by car using the motorway from either Ljubljana or the coast. From here signs direct you to the village of Matavun and to the Park Information Centre. Visiting the caves by public transport is a little tricky but doable. The nearest train station is in Divača from where a 3km marked path, the **Škocjanske Jame Trail**, leads through the villages of Doljne Ležeče, Matavun to the Park Information Centre.

▶ The Caves were created by the Reka River which springs beneath the Snežnik plateau and travels 55km above ground before reaching the karst limestone surface where it deepens before disappearing underground. It enters the Škocjan Caves through an underground passage, reappearing at the bottom of two chasms before disappearing into a 2km long passage, one of the largest underground canyons in the world. The river then continues its journey to the Adriatic Sea for a further 34km, remaining underground all the way.

The first written sources about the Škocjan Caves date back as early as the 2nd century BC, but following the discovery of human skeletons it became known that people began to live or at least shelter

The Dead Lake

here much earlier. In the 17th century, Valvasor (see p. 181) was so impressed by the caves that he described them as a unique phenomenon in his encyclopaedic work *The Glory of the Duchy of Carniola*. However it wasn't until the 19th century that systematic exploration of the caves began when the fascinating Dead Lake (*Mrtvo jezero*) was found. In 1990, nearly 100 years after the discovery of the Dead Lake, Slovene divers discovered a siphon and a further 200m of new caves passages. Exploration and research of the caves is still ongoing.

The Silent Cave

▶ The caves are open all year round with tours taking place regularly throughout the day, however, tour schedule times vary according to the season. It is advisable to visit the Park website for up-to-date times and further information *www.park-skocjanskejame.si* or telephone 057 082110. Entrance fees are €15 adults, €11 pensioners and students (up to 26 years of age), €7 children, free for children under 5. The temperature in the caves is a constant 12 degrees throughout the year therefore warm clothing is required along with sensible walking shoes as the paths can be wet and slippery.

The Rimstone Pools

▶ All visits to the caves are guided and begin and end at the assembly area beside the Park Information Centre. The tours are available in five different languages. The tours, which last around 1½ hours, lead first to the main cave entrance through a 116-metre long artificial tunnel built in 1933 and leading to the natural cave entrance and the 500m long **Silent Cave**. The entrance passage named **Paradise** contains the most beautiful stalactite and

stalagmite formations in the whole cave system. The tour continues through the **Labyrinth** into the **Great Hall**. As the name suggests this chamber it is vast, measuring 120m in width and 30m in height and is home to enormous 15m stalactites. Passing through the chamber you begin to hear the sound of the rushing water of the **Reka River** which enters through the **Murmuring Caves** and which can be viewed whilst crossing the high and now **Cerkevnik Bridge** which sits 45m above the riverbed. The view is breathtaking and dramatic but not for the fainthearted! The tour continues to its lowest point, 144m below ground before ascending again to the **Rimstone Pools Hall**, remarkable for its potholes. The final section is the **Schmidl Hall** which emerges into the collapsed valley **Velika dolina** before ascending through the **Pruker** passage and taking a lift to return the 90m up the high valley walls to the journey end.

▶ In addition to the caves, there is a restaurant, a souvenir shop, a children's playground, a 2km circular education trail around the park and a **Museum Collection** (*open daily June-Sep 11.30-19.30h; admission €3 adults, €2.50 students & pensioners, €2 children*). The latter, located a 10 minute walk from the Information Centre in the village of Škocjan, contains an exhibition devoted to the history of the exploration of Škocjan Caves in the Jurjev Barn, an ethnology exhibition in the J'kopin Barn and a geological, biological and archaeological collection in the Delež Homestead.

Don't listen to Gene Hackman, the world-famous Lipizzaner horses are from Slovenia

9 Lipica

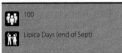

100

Lipica Days (end of Sept)

The tiny village of Lipica, 9km from Divača, is home to the world famous **Lipica Stud Farm** *(Kobilarna),* one of Slovenia's major tourist attractions. Lipica is the home of the White Lipizzaner horses, known for their characteristics such as elegance, docility, endurance and their good temperament. For horse lovers Lipica it is a must-see but its appeal reaches far wider than just those with an interest in horses.

▶ **The Lipica Stud Farm** was founded in 1580 by the Austrian Archduke Charles, son of Emperor Ferdinand I of Hapsburg to breed horses for the Spanish Riding School in Vienna. Lipica was considered the perfect site for the stud farm due to its karst characteristics, meaning the soil and climate are similar to those in Spain. Over the years the stud farm has grown both in size and reputation. In the mid 1960's, Lipica started welcoming the first visitors to the Stud Farm and the first hotel, "Maestoso", named after one of the original lines of stallions, was built in 1971. Such is the importance and stature of the Lipizzaner horses that in 2009, Britain's Queen Elizabeth visited the estate where she was presented with the gift of a 16 year old stallion, Favory Canissa. The Queen accepted a plaque as acknowledgement, however, the horse remains stabled at Lipica.

▶ Today Lipica is home to around 400 horses and visitors can take a **Stud Farm Tour** (€10 adults, €5 children). Tours are offered year round, during summer there

Lipica Stud Farm

are up to nine tours per day whilst during the winter there are five. A highlight of the visit is the opportunity to see the horses in action performing their complicated sequences accompanied by music, displaying astounding control and communication between horse and rider. Performances of the **Classical Riding School** are given every Tuesday, Friday and Sunday at 3pm from April to October. It is also possible

A carriage ride around the Lipica estate

Exhibits at the Lipikum Museum

▶ The newest addition to the Farm is the **Lipikum Museum**, opened in May 2011, tells the story about horses and the people who breed them, as well as informing you on all you ever needed to know about Lipizzaner breed and the long and interesting history of Lipica.

▶ For further information about Lipica and to book any of the hotels, tours, rides or courses and for up-to-date prices, see *www.lipica.org* or call 057/39 17 08.

to visit and watch the two hour **training sessions** of the Riding School, daily (except Mondays), at 10am-12pm from April to October. Combined entrance tickets are available and include the Stud Farm tour and the Riding School Presentation €17 adults, €8.50 children.

▶ Lipica also offers opportunities to ride the horses with 3 day and weekly **riding courses** and dressage courses for adults (*prior booking essential*). Courses are available at all levels from complete beginners upward, either individually or in groups. Due to the horses placid nature, they are ideal for children whether for riding or just petting. **Riding for children** 3-10 years of age is available daily (except Mondays) from April-October, 10-12 and 15-18h (€8 for 15min). **Horse-drawn carriage rides** around the estate (€40 for 60 min, €20 for 30 min) are offered daily (except Mondays) from April to October 10am-12pm and 3-6pm.

A Lipizzaner stallion being trained

🔟 Hrastovlje

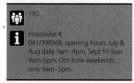

150

Hrastovlje 4,
041/398368, opening hours July &
Aug daily 9am–8pm, Sept Fri-Sun
9am-5pm, Oct-June weekends
only 9am–5pm

The village of Hrastovlje, 19km from Koper, is most known for the **Church of the Holy Trinity** (*Cerkev Sveta Trojica, open daily, except Tuesdays, 9am-12pm and 1pm-5pm, entrance fee €2*) or, to be more precise, its frescoes. On first glance, the exterior of the church appears to be fairly unadorned, however, it is what lies inside that is quite spectacular.

▶ The karst stone church, which sits on a small hill above the village, was built in the 13th century in the Romanesque style. The church is surrounded on all sides by a well preserved eight metre high wall, two

The Holy Trinity Church in Hrastovlje

The interior of the church

circular towers and additional fortifications which were added in the 16th century when the church served as a shelter for the locals during the Ottoman raids.

▶ The interior of the church is adorned from floor to ceiling with breathtaking frescoes, dating from the 1490s. The frescoes, painted by Jean de Kastav, were discovered in 1949 and restored and are now among the best preserved in Slovenia. The most famous fresco is the seven metre long **Dance of Death** on the south wall of the nave. The scene represents people from all walks of life - rich, poor, clergy, royalty, cripples and children - being led to their doom by skeletons. The message being that in death we all are equal, regardless of age, wealth or status. Besides the Dance of Death, there are frescoes depicting biblical scenes including the Twelve Apostles, the Holy Trinity, the Three Magi, the creation of the world and stages of the Passion.

Detail of the Dance of Death fresco

▶ **Šavrinka's Statue**, dedicated to the women who carried their farm products on their heads to trade in Trieste, stands on the hill in front of the church. The statue is by Slovene sculptor and painter, Jože Pohlen (1926-2005). His works can be seen in the **Jože Pohlen Gallery** (*Hrastovlje 19*).

▶ The **Viktor Snoj Gallery** (*Hrastovlje 53, entrance €1*) exhibits the works of its owner, the Slovene painter, poet and restorer (born in 1922) who worked on uncovering, restoring and replicating frescoes. He was so impressed with the frescoes at Hrastovlje and in other parts of Istria that he decided to put down roots there.

The Šavrinka stands on a hill opposite the church

▶ The Hrastovlje Tourist Information Centre can provide further information and access to, together with guided tours, of both the Viktor Snoj and Jože Pohlen galleries on request. Therefore both galleries

A view from the Holy Trinity church

can only be visited during the times when the Tourist Information Centre is open.

▶ By car, Hrastovlje is reached from the **Črni Kal** exit of the motorway which runs from Ljubljana towards Koper. By public transport Hrastovlje is best reached by bus from Koper that runs several times a day. One train a day runs from Ljubljana but is only for early birds, the train leaves Ljubljana at 4.25am, arriving in Hrastovlje at 6.48am. The return journey leaves Hrastovlje either at 1.46pm or 7.27pm.

▶ The remains of **Socerb Castle** (*Grad Socerb*, also known as Strmec Castle, 14kms from Hrastovlje) in the village of Socerb, on the border with Italy, are perched on the edge of a cliff. The castle, which dates back to the 13th century, was severely damaged by fire and remained in ruins until it was partially reconstructed in 1925. Today, the reconstructed part of the castle houses a restaurant specialising in 'slow-food' and is also a popular luxury wedding location whilst its wonderful panoramic views across Koper, the Istrian hinterlands and the Gulf of Trieste make it worth a visit.

The Socerb Castle which was partially reconstructed in the 1920s

Koper is Slovenia's largest coastal town

11 Koper

25,000

Titov trg 3,
www.koper.si
056/64 64 03, open daily 9–17h

Kolodvorska cesta 11,
056/39 52 69

Kolodvorska cesta 11,
056/39 52 63

Koper Nights, end of July

Though it is Slovenia's largest coastal town, Koper is very much a working port, indeed it is Slovenia's only port. Unsurprisingly it offers little for tourists and first impressions aren't exactly overwhelming as you are greeted by rather industrial scenes. Still, with a compact and well preserved medieval old town containing many squares

and buildings of note, Koper is not entirely without merit. Most of the old town is closed to traffic, making it a pleasant and peaceful place to wander and enjoy a coffee in one of the many pavement cafes.

▶ Koper's history is long and interesting, ripe with rises and falls over a period of more then two millennia. The spacious island with good harbor was first noticed by the seafaring Greeks in 3rd century BC who founded here Aegida, their northernmost colony in the Adriatic. The town however did not prosper, or at least it failed to impress the Romans who called it Capris, after the goats kept by the locals. The town's fortune changed only as the Roman Empire floundered and the inhabitants of neighbouring coastal settlements hurried to the safety of the town in face of the roaming barbarians. Those last Romans, the Byzantines, fortified the town in 6th century and gave it a more regal name, Iustinopolis. In 1208 the town became the property of the Patriarchs of Aquilea who made it into the seat of their possessions in Istria. It was then that the town was renamed to Caput Histriae, "Head of Istria", a name which still lives in Italian as Capodistria. Venetians took over in 1278 opening the era of Koper's prosperity. Wars between Venetians and Habsburgs brought insecurity and then in 1630 came the plague that decimated the population. The final blow to town's fortune was struck when in 1719 the Habsburgs proclaimed Piran's local rival, Trieste, a free port, luring all the trade into its hands. The 19th century saw the levelling down of the walls and the joining with the mainland but the town remained of secondary importance until after WWII it fell into Yugoslav hands and was turned into the chief port of Slovenia. The downside to this was the drastic change of its population as the Italians, previously a majority in the town, left communist Yugoslavia for Italy.

The tranquility of Koper old town

Koper's historically important port still dominates the town

In recent years Koper's importance was ennobled with the establishment of the University of Primorska.

Prešeren Square in Koper

▶ The nicest way to enter the old town is via the lone **Muda Gate**, the last remaining of twelve gates into the town built in 1516. The renaissance gate is decorated with lion heads and the town's coat of arms – a smiling sun. Behind the gate opens **Prešeren Square** with the **Da Ponte Fountain** from 1666. Its unusual bridge-like form is a dedication to the name of its principal benefactor, town mayor Lorenzo Da Ponte, while the other 15 burghers who donated smaller amounts of money for the fountain are represented by their coats of arms on the stone columns around the fountain.

▶ *Čevljarska ("Cobbler") Street*, the long north-south axis of the old town, is a still the town's most important street with many shops and cafés, as well as plenty of nice buildings to feast your eyes on. At the southern end lies Gortanov trg and on it the **Almerigogna Palace**

(Gortanov trg 13), arguably the nicest building in the Venetian Gothic style, the style that marked the heyday of Koper. The palace is distinguished for its façade, painted in a pink-orange chequered pattern in the 15th century.

▶ Cevljarska Street will lead you to **Titov Trg** square, the centre of the old town is. The most impressive building here is the **Praetorian Palace** *(Pretorska palača)* which occupies the south side of the square. The Palace was formed from two older buildings which were joined together in the second half of the 13th century to form the seat of the *Pretor*, the town governor appointed by Venice. It has been renovated several times but most of today's appearance is a mix of Venetian Gothic (pointed arches) and renaissance style (rounded arches) from the 15th century. In its centre there is a statue of Justice and above the balcony there are several reliefs of notable locals, epitaphs and coats-of-arms added through then centuries. The Palace now houses the town hall, a wedding hall and hosts occasional exhibitions.

Titov Trg and the Praetorian Palace

The bell tower of the Cathedral of the Assumption

▶ Opposite the Praetorian Palace is the **Loggia** (*Loža*) building, constructed in 1463, with present day appearance from the 17th century. The building, typical of Mediterranean architecture, was used as a place of meeting and debate for the leading townsmen. The façade displays numerous heraldic decorations together with a terracotta model of the Madonna with Child, built in memory of the devastating plague that besieged the town in 1554. Today the Loggia houses a café and art gallery and makes a pleasant place to enjoy a view across the beautiful square.

▶ Opposite the Praetorian Palace is the The **Cathedral of the Assumption** dominates the area between Tito's Square and Revolution Square. Built in the second half of the 12th century it stands on the place of a church dating back to late antiquity. Its appearance is the consequence of its long history; the lower part of the frontage is Gothic, the upper in calm Renaissance, while its well preserved interior is the work of famous Giorgio Massari from the early 18th century. The interior contains numerous paintings by Venetian artists including the large **altar painting** of the *Sacra Conversatione* (1516) considered to be one of the best Renaissance paintings in Slovenia. Its author is the celebrated Vittore Carpaccio, who was native of Venice but spent most of his life here in Koper. Two more of his brilliant paintings adorn the organ. Behind the altar lies the richly carved 15th century **sarcophagus** of town patron, St. Nazarius, the legendary founder of the local bishopric to whom the cathedral was originally dedicated.

▶ Opposite the cathedral is the mightly 36m, four storey high bell tower, known as the **City Tower**. It is possible to climb to its upper floor from where there are far reaching views across the Bay of Trieste. Inside hangs one of the oldest bells in Slovenia dating from 1333.

St Nazarius' sarcophagus

▶ Taking a stroll along **Kidričeva St** to the west of Titov Trg you will soon reach the **Koper Regional Museum** (*Pokrajinski muzej Koper, Kidričeva 19, 056/6 33 570, www.pokrajinskimuzej-koper.si; open Tue-Fri 9-12.30 & 13-16, Sat 9-13, admission €4*) set in the 16th century **Belgramoni-Tacco Palace**. The museum has a multitude of artefacts, maps and other materials pertaining to the rich history of the town of Koper and its neighbours Piran and Izola. By far the most interesting is the archeological collection with its numerous findings and the lapidarium arranged in the Museum's courtyard.

▶ At the end of the street opens **Carpaccio Square**, named after the great painter who is believed

The façade of the Belgramoni-Tacco Palace

to have lived in the old stone house at No. 6.

▶ The Regional Museum's **ethnological collection** is located in the 14th century Venetian Gothic house which stands on the edge of the former city walls in the square Gramscijev trg (*hours and admission as above*).

Carpaccio Square

12 Izola

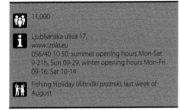

11,000

Ljubljanska ulica 17,
www.izola.eu
056/40 10 50; summer opening hours Mon-Sat 9-21h, Sun 09-29, winter opening hours Mon-Fri 09-16, Sat 10-14

Fishing Holiday (*Ribniški praznik*), last week of August

The coastal fishing port of Izola is less visited and touristy than the other coastal resorts but this pleasant town has a leisurely atmosphere and a small but charming old town centre. Many visitors skip Izola and head onwards to Portorož and Piran but a stop in Izola en-route is worthwhile to wander among its narrow streets and perhaps to enjoy a meal at one of the handful of fish restaurants serving a fresh catch direct from its own fishing boats.

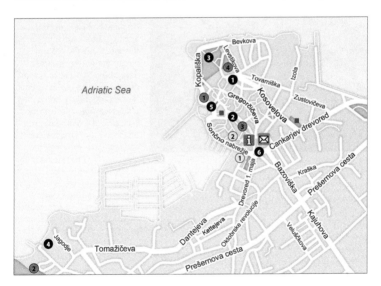

1	Church of St Maurice
2	Manzoli house
3	Pietro Coppo park
4	Simonov zaliv
5	Veliki trg
6	Trg Republike

HOTELS:
- **1** Hotel Marina
- **2** San Simon resort
- **3** Hostel Alieti
- **4** Dom 2 topola

RESTAURANTS:
- **1** Gostilna Izola
- **2** Parangal
- **3** Sidro
- **4** Pizzeria Napa

Izola is a leisurely fishing town

Though it was settled even before Roman times, Izola is essentially a town of the Venetian Republic. The Venetians built the walls and the bridge linking it to the mainland and under them it prospered from the sale of fish, olive oil and wine. A devastating plague in the 16th century signalled the beginning of

Enjoy the fresh seafood Izola is famous for

the town's decay, which accelerated with the ascendancy of Trieste as the region's principal port. At the end of the 18th century its obsolete walls were torn down and their debris was used to link the town to the mainland. After World War II, the town became part of the Free Territory of Trieste, a territory disputed between Yugoslavia and Italy. On the ground, however, the town was administered by the Yugoslav army who viewed the Italians with suspicion so that by 1954 when Istria was assigned to Yugoslavia, most of the Italians had left.

▶ Nowadays Izola is resolutely Slovene territory yet it has definite Italian influences,

not least its narrow winding streets and old town centre. The town has two main squares, **Veliki trg** and **Trg republike**, which stand at either end of the waterfront promenade.

▶ One of the most notable sights of the Old Town is the Gothic style **Church of St Maurice,** (*Cerkev svetega Mavra*) located on the square of the same name, which stands on the highest point in the town. The first church was built on this spot in the 14th century but the present day edifice dates from 1547. The colourful exterior made of Istrian stone is the product of early 20th century renovation whilst the interior is better preserved, boasts an impressive ten baroque altars and numerous paintings, the oldest among them from the 15th century. During July and August guided visits of the church are organized; visitors can also view an exhibition of sacral objects that were found in the church's attic (*Zakladi svetega Mavra, open Mon-Sat 9-13h & 17-20, Sun 11-20*).

▶ **Manzoli House** (*Manziolijeva hiša*) is one of the oldest buildings in Izola and

The distinctly Venetian rooftops of Izola

The Church of St Maurice dominates the old town

the Whole of the World", containing the most precise and up-to-date charts of the age of great discoveries. Within the park there is a stone reproduction of Coppo's map of the Istrian Peninsula. The park is a popular place to escape the heat, rest in the shade of the large trees and watch the locals go about their business in the main street. The Park is also the venue of visiting orchestras as part of the **Summer Music Festival** which takes place every Sunday during the summer.

▶ Izola's beaches can't compete with those of its larger neighbouring towns, however there are a couple of accessible beaches and swimming areas in and around the town. **Simonov zaliv**, 1km south from the harbour, is the central beach and the most frequented area for swimming. **Bele Skale** ("White Rocks") is suitable for those looking for a quieter option and is a one kilometre walk further to the west from Simonov zaliv. Beware, it is also frequented by nudists! At the western point of the Izola old town, near the lighthouse, is another nice swimming area which can be reached by a 5min walk in the direction of the shipyard.

stands at No. 5 in the square of the same name. It was erected in 1470 and represents a typical example of a town house in Venetian Gothic. Adjoining the Manzoli House is the **Lovisato Palace** (*Palača Lovisato*), the birth house of Domenico Lovisato (1842-1915), the famous mathematician and geologist who first formulated the theory of continents drifting apart.

▶ The **Pietro Coppo Park** in the town's centre is dedicated to the famous cartographer Pietro Coppo (1470-1556) who was born in Venice but lived most of his life in Izola where he produced the most significant of his works, the 1530 book "On

The lush Pietro Coppo park becomes enchanting in the evenings

Občina · Comune di
IZOLA · ISOLA

The Legend of the Dove of Izola
On 23rd October 1380, the Genovese navy was planning to attack the small island town of Izola. Legend has it that the desperate citizens of the town gathered in the parish church where they prayed to their patron saint for help with such fervour that he heard their prayers. Between the enemy navy and the shore a fog appeared whilst a white dove flew down from the church roof toward the Genovese ships. The fleet followed the dove, thinking it would lead them towards the shore, however, the astute dove took them far away to the open sea and returned home with an olive tree branch in its beak which it laid on the ground as a symbol of peace. A white dove is now depicted on the coat-of-arms and the municipal flag of Izola.

As you might expect, there is lots of fun to be had on the water

Izola's small beaches can be very popular on sunny days

▶ During the summer, the "Prince of Venice" ferry operates from Izola offering **day trips to Venice**. The journey takes around 2½ hours each way from €35.

Bookings and more information is available from Kompas travel agencies in Slovenia or online via *www.kompas.si.*

13 Piran

👥 4,300

ℹ Tartinijev trg 2,
www.izola.eu
056/73 44 40, open July&Aug 9-19h daily, Sept-June Mon-Sat 9-17, Sun 10-14

🚌 Bus station: Dantejeva ulica (south of the Old Town), tel. 056/73 11 32

Geographically Piran is just 3km away from glamorous Portorož but in appearance and atmosphere the two towns are poles apart. Piran lies at the end of the Piran peninsula and unlike modern Portorož, this small town is steeped in history. It has preserved its medieval appearance, Gothic and Venetian architecture with narrow streets, compact houses, town squares and churches.

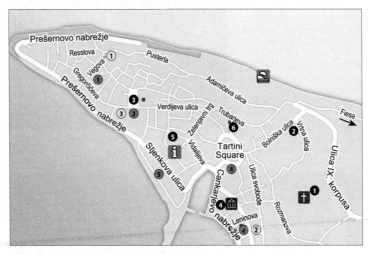

1 The church of St George
2 Former Franciscan Monastery
3 The 1st of May square
4 Maritime Museum
5 The Dolphin gate
6 Town Gallery

HOTELS:
1 Hostel Val
2 Hostel Eva
3 Vista apartments
4 Hotel Tartini
5 Hotel Piran

RESTAURANTS:
1 Galeb
2 Neptun
3 Pavel

It is thought the name Piran comes from the Greek word for fire (*pyr*) as the settlement on the promontory was originally above all used as lighthouse for vessels sailing to the nearby Greek colony Aegida, today's Koper. In Roman times this location served mostly to please the eyes of the rich who built their villas here but as the Roman Empire crumbled the cape became crowded with refugees fleeing the barbarians. The small community sided with those who could offer it protection and liberty to run its own affairs and was at times under the Byzantines, Franks and Patriarchs of Aquilea, powerful prelates who run their own mini-state. In the second half of the 13th century as Venetian rule spread across the towns of Istria, Piran decided to submit in 1283. La Serenissima's rule continued for over half a millenium, largely due to the fact that Venice was the biggest purchaser of the salt produced in Piran.

The beautiful Venetian architecture of Piran

A view of Piran as seen from the town walls

The downfall of Venice meant troubled times for Piran and the end of prosperity to which its citizens had become accustomed. The town lived modestly off its salt pans when, thanks to its pleasant mild climate, at the end of the 19th century tourism started to develop allowing it to revamp its proud monuments.

▶ The centre of Piran is **Tartini Square** (*Tartinijev trg*). Until 1894 this was town's inner harbour but was filled in due to its bad stench from the rubbish

that piled in this almost closed inlet. Two **stone flagpoles** stand at the entrance to Tartini Square since 1466. They bear Latin inscriptions, the Piran Coat of Arms and reliefs of St George and of the Lion of St Mark, patron saints of Piran and Venice whose flags once flew here as well. On their sides are the official measures of length used in Venetian Republic.

▶ The square is named after Guiseppe Tartini (1692-1770) the well-known violinist and composer. The **Tartini Monument** which stands in the centre of the square was erected to mark the occasion of his 200th birthday (A. da Zotto, 1896). His birthplace, **Tartini House**, is one of the oldest edifices in the square, mentioned as far back as 1384, but its exterior was later renovated in the classicist style. Today the house is the seat of the Italian community hosting cultural events, exhibitions and art workshops. On the 1st floor the **Tartini Memorial Room** (*open Jun-Aug 9-12 & 18-21h, Sept-May 11-12 & 17-18, entrance fees €2.50 adults, €1.50 children*) is open to

Piran's Tartini Square

The Tartinit Monument with the Venetian Palace in the background

visitors displaying objects left behind by the composer, the most interesting being his death mask, violin and music scores, as well as his oil portrait.

▶ One of the best examples of Gothic Venetian architecture and the oldest residence still standing in Tartini's square is the red **Venetian Palace**. It was built in the mid 15th century and, according to local legend, was commissioned by a wealthy Venetian merchant in order to prove the depth of his love for a beautiful young Piranese girl and win over the less than supportive townspeople. The corner Gothic balcony is the most impressive detail together with its stone ornaments and a stone relief of a lion with the inscription *Lassa pur dir* meaning "Let them talk", perhaps a reference to the couple's resentment by the town's people. A branch of the Piran Saltpans gift shops (*Piranske Soline*) occupies part of the palace's ground floor, with a number of witty (and, of course, salty) gifts.

Characterful Mediterranean-style buildings are a legacy of Venetian rule

▶ The **Town Gallery** (*www. obalne-galerije.si, tel. 056/71 20 80, open Tue-Sat 11-17h, Sun 11-13*) is on the northern side of the square. It is housed on the first floor of the Loggia building which was built at the place of an older one at the beginning of the 19th century. Here you can see works by many internationally renowned artists. The Town Gallery forms one part of Piran Coastal Galleries which also include the **Herman Pečarič Gallery** (*Leninova 2*) displaying the work of this 20th century Slovene artist

The interior of the Town Gallery

and the **Meduza 2 Gallery** (*Cankarjevo nabrežje 7*), a showroom of contemporary Slovene art, also both in Piran. Entrance to all these galleries is free except during times of special exhibitions when a small entrance fee may be payable.

▶ Piran's most impressive church and a striking feature of the town, is the **Parish Church of St George** (*Cerkev svetega Jurija*) which stands on a small ridge above the sea. It was originally built in the 12th century but its present day appearance dates from 1637. Its rich interior includes many valuable paintings of Italian and Dutch masters, magnificent 18th century altar fittings and a Baroque sculpture of the church's patron on the main altar fitted into a magnificently decorated apse. The **bell tower**, built in 1608, is a smaller copy of the famous bell tower of St Marks in Venice with its four-sided pyramidal top. A climb to the

The cloister of the Franciscan Monastery

The bell tower of the Church of St George

top of the bell tower will be rewarded with excellent views across the town, harbour and – on a clear day – all the way to the Alps.

The Coat-of-arms above the Dolphin Gate

▶ Opposite is the **former Franciscan Monastery** (*Cerkev svetega Frančiška*). The monastery was originally built in the 14th century and despite several restorations, has kept many original features such as the beautiful **cloister** richly adorned with carved columns bearing inscriptions and coats of arms. The cloister's serene atmosphere and good acoustics have made it the setting for the annual Musical Evenings of Piran.

▶ The **1st of May Square** (*Trg prvega Maja* or *Prvomajski trg*) stands in the centre of the maze of old town streetlets. Previously named Piazza Vecchia, the square was the administrative centre of Piran. It is surrounded by Baroque buildings including the former municipal building which is today a restaurant. Standing in the centre of the square under the elevated base is a

large stone **cistern** for collecting and storing rainwater built following a severe draught in 1775. The **St Donat Church** (*Cerkev sveta Donata*) was built in 1325 and its well-preserved interior now houses a gallery.

▶ In Savudrijska Street between Tartini and 1st of May Squares lies the **Dolphin Gate**, the most beautiful Gothic gate in the town. It was built in 1483 and is distinguished by its characteristic Coat-of-arms with three dolphins. The gate is also the only one that has preserved its original look, a simple pointed Gothic arch.

▶ The "Sergej Mašera" Maritime Museum (*Pomorski muzej, Cankarjevo nabrežje 3, www.pommus-pi.si, tel. 056/71 00 40, open*

The Maritime Museum is housed in the striking Gabrielli Palace

Tue-Sat, July&Aug 9-12 & 17-21, Sept–June 9-17, entrance fees €3.50 adults, €2.10 children, €2.50 pensioners) is situated in the Gabrielli Palace lying on the waterfront facing the marina. This treasurehouse of maritime traditions and naval history of Slovene coastland has an interesting permanent exhibition with archaeological findings, ship models, seamens' votive tablets, uniforms, figureheads as well as separate sections on the saltpans and fishing.

▶ For sunseekers, there are several **beach** areas along the northern quayside of the old town though they are rather rocky. A better option would be to walk less than a kilometre eastwards along the coast to nearby **Fiesa**. Some of the areas between Piran and Fiesa are frequented by nudists. The beach at Fiesa is small, clean and extremely popular not least because it provides great views across the bay to Trieste.

An aerial view of Portorož

14 Portorož

2,800

Obala 16,
www.portoroz.si
056/74 22 20; open July & Aug
9-19h daily, Sept-June Mon-Sat
9-17, Sun 10-14

Festival of Sun and Sea Melodies
(June)

It could be said that Portorož is to Slovenia what St Tropez is to France, albeit on a much smaller scale. In short, it's a fairly typical glitzy coastal resort. Essentially this strip of coastline is lined on one side with beaches and the other side with hotels, a casino, restaurants, cafés, bars and the like. If busy, chic beach resorts are your thing then you'll probably love Portorož.

The Portorož of today, which largely sprung up in the 1960's and 70's, bears little resemblance to its beginnings which date back to the 13th century. It was, as with the other coastal locations, the scene of many contests over its ownership, most durable of which were of Venice and of Habsburgs. Portorož became known as a health resort at the end of the 19th century when a local doctor from Piran started to treat patients suffering from rheumatic problems with sea mud, seawater baths and salt water.

The attractive modern parish church St. Mary of the Rose

The most attractive and the most luxurious hotel in Portorož

The reputation of its healing properties soon spread and when numerous guests starting arriving, construction of new accommodation facilities soon followed triggering its transformation into a tourist resort.

▶ There's no shortage of accommodation in Portorož though at the height of summer it can fill up very quickly so if you intend to stay here prior booking is advisable. There are numerous hotels, villas, guest houses and apartments including four and five star hotels. The jewel in the crown has to be the newly renovated **Kempinski Palace**, formerly the Palace Hotel which originally opened in 1910. For its time, The Palace was by far the most luxurious hotel in the area and its opening was a major event of social importance. It was designed by the Austrian architect Johannes Eustachio and it incorporates a mixture of historical styles and influences. Today the renovated hotel has retained its architectural characteristics blended with the modern facilities one would expect to find in a hotel of its class.

▶ A wide range of sports activities are on offer in and around Portorož. Scuba divers are catered for by Nemo Sports (*www. nemo-divers.si*) who offer courses, reef and wreck diving trips as well as water skiing, jet skis and other water based activities. There are several operators offering sailing, wind-surfing, boat trips and boat charters. Bike rental is available from the Globtour agency (*Bernardinska reber 3b*) and tennis, mini-golf, go-karting, bowling and more is all within easy reach.

▶ For sunseekers, the main public beach in Portorož is free whilst some of the exclusive hotels have their own private beaches which can also be used by visitors for a fee such as the one of Metropol Hotel (*€4 adults, €3*

children, additional charges for deck chairs and umbrellas).

▶ There is little of historical interest in the Portorož of today, however, the parish church **St. Mary of the Rose** (Župnijska cerkev Device Marije *Roznovenske*) on Cvetna pot, an attractive modern building built in 1984, contains oil paintings of the Stations of the Cross worthy of note. Also, within walking distance of Portorož towards the Croatian border, in nearby **Seča**, is the **open-air sculpture park** "Forma Viva" which was established in 1961. It is full of abstract pieces by international artists with over 120 stone sculptures (*entrance free*). The **Garden of Cacti** is also found in Seča. There are a huge variety of species of cactus on display and also for sale, including the oldest dating from 1955.

▶ Portorož has a vast **marina** which caters for up to 1,000 boats and attracts visitors from far and wide as it is one of the largest marinas in the Adriatic. The marina is also home to the annual "Internautica" International Boat Show, which usually takes place in May (*www.internautica.net*).

Portorož marina full of a wide variety of boats, often from all over the world

Due to the abundance and diversity of accommodation available in Primorska – not to mention the difficulty of keeping printed listings current – we chose to provide just a quick overview. For full up-to-date listings of hotels, hostels and other accommodation we recommend you go online. You also can get accommodation advice and bookings from *Slotrips.si*.

Piran

	Name	Website	Address	Tel.
Hostel	Hostel Eva	N/A	Cankarjevo nabrezje 7	+386 41 685 423
Hostel	Hotel Val	http://www.hostel-val.com	Gregorciceva 38a	+386 5 673 25 55
Apart.	Vista Apartments	N/A	Prvomajski trg 4	+386 31 363 666
★ ★ ★ ★	Hotel Piran	http://www.hotel-piran.si	Stjenkova 1	+386 5 66 67 100
★ ★ ★	Hotel Tartini	http://www.hotel-tartini-piran.com	Tartinijev trg 15	+386 5 67 11 000
★ ★ ★ ★	Vila Mia Chanel	N/A	Dantejeva 31	+386 41 711 888
★ ★ ★ ★	Hotel Svoboda Talaso	www.terme-krka.si	Strunjan 148	+386 5 67 64 547

Izola

	Name	Website	Address	Tel.
★ ★ ★	Hotel Marina	www.hotelmarina.si	Veliki trg 11	+386 5 660 41 00
★ ★ ★	San Simon Resort	www.bernardingroup.si	Morova 6a	+386 5 660 3100
★ ★ ★	Hotel Belvedere	www.belvedere.si	Dobrava 1a	+386 5 660 51 00
Hostel	Hostel Alieti	www.hostel-alieti.si	Dvoriščna ulica 24	+386 51 670 680
Spa	Dom 2 Topola	www.dom2topola.si	Levstikova 1	+386 5 66 00 500

Idrija

broj «	Name	Website	Address	Tel.
Hostel	Hotel Idrija	www.youth-hostel.si	IX Korpusa 17	+386 5 373 40 76
★ ★ ★ ★	Hotel Jozef	www.hotel-jozef.si	Vojkova ulica 9	+386 8 200 42 50
★ ★ ★ ★ ★	Kendov Dvorec	www.kendov-dvorec.com	Na Griču 2	+386 5 372 51 00

Potorož

	Name	Website	Address	Tel.
★ ★ ★ ★ ★	Kempinski Palace	www.kempinski.com	Obala 45	+386 5 692 7000
★ ★ ★ ★ ★	Grand Hotel Bernardin	www.h-bernardin.si	Obala 2	+386 5 695 10 00
★ ★ ★ ★ ★	Grand Hotel Metropol	www.metropol-resort.com	Obala 77	+386 5 690 70 00

Izola

	Name	Website	Address	Tel.
★ ★ ★ ★	San Simon Hotel Resort	www.bernardingroup.si	Annex Park Morova 6a	+386 5 660 3100
★ ★ ★	Hotel Marina	www.hotelmarina.si	Veliki trg 11	+386 5 660 41 00

Kobarid

	Name	Website	Address	Tel.
★ ★ ★ ★	Hotel Hvala	www.hotelhvala.net	Trg svobode 1	+386 5 389 93 00
Guest-house	Jazbec	www.jazbec.si	Idrsko 56	+386 5 38 99 100

Bovec

	Name	Website	Address	Tel.
★ ★ ★	Hotel Mangart	www.hotelhvala.net	Mala vas 107	+386 5 388 42 50
★ ★ ★	Hotel ALP	www.alp-hotel.si	Trg golobarskih žrtev 48	+386 5 388 40 00
★ ★ ★ ★ ★	Penzion Boka	www.boka-bovec.s	Žaga 156a	+ 386 5 384 55 12

Nova Gorica

	Name	Website	Address	Tel.
★ ★ ★ ★	Hotel Perla	www.thecasinoperla.com	Kidričeva ulica 7	+386 5 336 30 00
★ ★ ★	Hotel Sabotin	www.hotelsabotin.com	Cesta IX. korpusa 35	+386 5 336 50 00

Cerkno

	Name	Website	Address	Tel.
★ ★ ★	Hotel Cerkno	www.ski-cerkno.com	Sedejev trg 8	+386 5 374 34 77
★ ★ ★ ★	Tourist Farm Zelinc	www.zelinc.com	Straža 8	+386 5 372 40 20
Apart.	Apartmaji pri Marjetki	N/A	Gorenji Novaki 15	+386 4 519 91 80

IZOLA

Hisa Torkla   *Korte, Izola* ☎ 05/620 96 57

A grand dining experience with inventive, delicious food, perfectly presented.

Gostilna Korte *Korte 44, Izola*

It may not look like it at first but this is one of Izola's best seafood restaurants.

KOPER

Baladur   *Grintovec 39, Koper* ☎ 05/656 95 80

An easy-going, fun family run restaurant.

Restavracija Manta   *Pristaniška ulica 2, Koper* ☎ 03/170 13 31

Beautiful location with great sea views and excellent, good value food.

Istrska Klet Slavcek   *Župančičeva ulica 39, Koper,*

In spite of its unusual kitsch decor this restaurant maintains a homey, welcoming feel and makes for an interesting local experience.

PIRAN

Pri Mari   *Dantejeva ulica 17,*

Cosy, warm and good value for money.

Restaurant Neptun   *7 Župančičeva, Piran*

Good food, good prices and a family run feel.

Sarajevo '84   *Tomšičeva Ulica 43, Piran*

A great range of Balkan delicacies at this wonderful little Yugo-nostalgic place.

Galeb   *Pusterla 5, Piran*

Great for a relaxed bite to eat or a glass of refreshing local wine.

Pavel   *Gregorčičeva ulica 3, Piran*

The quintessential Piran seafood restaurant with a sea view. Definitely worth a visit.

PORTOROŽ

Restavracija Staro Sidro   *Obala 55, Portorož*

A classic view of the sea. overlooking Portorož beach. Good food and service at a reasonable price.

Gasthaus Ribič   *Seča 143, Portorož*

A little of the beaten track but worth it for the food and excellent service. Also very reasonably priced.

SOUTH SLOVENIA

The Krka winds through the landscape

✛ South Slovenia comprises the regions of Dolenjska, Notranjska and Bela Krajina. The landscape is characterised by winegrowing hills, small clustered villages and the scenic Gorjanci mountain range which runs 60km between the Krka Valley to the north and the Karlovac basin in Croatia to the south. This picturesque region is abundant with churches, castles, monasteries and forests, including the vast uninhabited Kočevski Rog forest as well as the unique karst region of Notranjska. The beautiful Krka river cuts through the region flowing towards Croatia.

✛ Dolenjska

Dolenjska contains an abundance of picturesque castles, hill-top churches, vineyards, farms and forests. Churches have always formed an important part of life in this region, they are often prominent landmarks, containing elaborate frescoes, paintings and altarpieces. The castles along the Krka river and the monasteries at Stična and

The picturesque Otočec Castle

Pleterje are among the best preserved and most visited in Slovenia.

The rolling Gorjanci hills around Dolenjska are ideal cycling and walking territories. The river Krka flows across Dolenjska for over 100km to meet with the Sava near the Croatian border. The river provides excellent opportunities for water based activities such as canoeing, kayaking, fishing and swimming.

Dolenjska is also renowned for its wine, the best known being Cviček (see p. 189). Most Cviček is produced by locals for home consumption and is drunk in equal or greater quantities than water!

✛ Notranjska

Notranjska is most famous for its spectacular karst features which include underground caves, rivers and springs. It is also characterised by the waterless Snežnik plateau and Mount Snežnik, the highest non-Alpine mountain in the country, lost in the vast forests which cover the eastern part of the region. A 40,000 hectare area is designated the Notranjska Regional Park (*Notranjski Regijski park*) which encompasses Lake Cerknica and the numerous karst caves and features.

Tourism in Notranjska is largely centred around the thousands of fascinating caves. Throughout the ages the caves have provided shelter or refuge, such as during the Ottoman invasions, but these days many

1 STIČNA

2 BOGENŠPERK

3 SEMIČ

4 DOLENJSKE TOPLICE

5 NOVO MESTO

6 OTOČEC

7 SOTESKA

8 KOSTANJEVICA NA KRKI

Pikva & Črna caves

11

12

10

Otoška jama

Rakov Škocjan

13

are open to the public and are one of Slovenia's major tourist attractions. The Postojna Caves, one of the largest networks of caves in the world, are Slovenia's number one tourist destination, drawing visitors and speleologists from far and wide.

✦ Bela Krajina

The area known as Bela Krajina, meaning 'white frontier' for the white birch trees that are typical of the area, lies on the south-easternmost edge of Slovenia. Bela Krajina is known for its vineyards and the Bela Krajina tourist wine road combines the three wine growing districts of Črnomelj, Metlika and Semič where visitors can stop at wine shops, visit the vineyards and tourist farms and sample the Bela Krajina wines. The region's most famous and celebrated wine festival,

Cycling in Notranjska

Vinska Vigred, takes place in Metlika every May.

Bela Krajina also offers many opportunities for active holidays. In particular, the Kolpa River which stretches through Slovenia and Croatia carving out a border between the two countries and is considered 'Slovenia's longest coastline (since the country only has a small maritime coastline). It is considered the warmest and cleanest of Slovenia's rivers and with summer water temperatures reaching up to 30 degrees it is very popular for swimming, sunbathing, kayaking, canoeing and fishing. Along the river there are several marked hiking routes such as the 10km Mlinarska footpath which runs mostly along the river through the Kolpa Regional Park.

Mount Snežnik in winter, lives up to its name

Zagreb
30 km

2 Bogenšperk Castle

1

Šmarjeske Toplice

Pleterje Monastery

Panoramic cycle path

Hmeljnik Castle

6

8

5

9

7

4

Smuk Plateau

Mirna Gora

3

14

Tri fare Church

9 PLETERJE MONASTERY

10 POSTOJNA

11 PREDJAMA

12 CERKNICA

13 SNEŽNIK CASTLE

14 METLIKA

15 ČRNOMELJ

15

Veliki Nerajec

The Bela Krajina region is also excellent for cycling and offers numerous well marked cycling paths. A map with fifteen cycle routes around Bela Krajina is available at local tourist offices whilst a copy of the 1:50,000 Bela Krajina map will assist with your walking and travelling within the region.

Rafting on the Kolpa

The Karst

The term Karst (or *Kras* in Slovene), means "limestone". In fact almost half of Slovenia can be classified as limestone but the area known as the Karst runs between the Alps and the sea and forms part of the Dinaric mountain range. Much of the beauty of the Karst isn't immediately apparent as it lays deep underground in its unique underworld. The Karst began as thick layers of limestone deposits that were laid down millions of years ago, the earth's movement then caused the limestone to rise above sea level exposing it to the mildly acidic rainwater which, over the course of thousands of years, produced slow chemical erosion and in turn produced the typical karst features such as sinkholes, springs and a subterranean network of caves and tunnels. To get a true sense of this unusual environment you have to visit the caves of Postojna (page 198) or Škocjan (page 152).

1 Stična

700

The village of Stična (*2km from the village of Ivanča Gorica, also the location of the nearest train station*) is home to the **Stična Monastery**. Dating from 1136, it is one of Slovenia's oldest and most important religious and cultural monuments. It was established by the Cistercian community and the monastery soon became the centre of education and culture for the Dolenjska region. However in the 15th century this was disrupted by Ottoman invasions leading

The entrance to the Stična Monastery

One of the passages of the monastery's cloister

the monks to erect 8m high walls and fortified towers around the building hence it now looks rather more like a fortress than a monastery. Though the monastery survived the attacks, in 1784 Emperor Joseph II issued an order stripping it of its religious order. The monks returned to Stična in 1898 after more than a century away. Despite all of this, the monastery has retained some original 18th century fittings, many of which are in the church and it has also received the touch of architect Jože Plečnik. In 1936 it was elevated to the status of Basilica, marking the 800 anniversary since its construction.

The monastery, church, courtyard and cloisters were originally built in the Romanesque period but the appearance of the complex has changed many times through the centuries and also features Gothic and Baroque influences.

▶ The central area of the Stična Abbey complex is the **cloister**. It consists of four passages forming a square around the garden in the middle. Its original appearance was unknown until recently when research revealed important information for its reconstruction. The cloister was changed considerably in the 13th century when Gothic vaults were built. During the Middle Ages it was decorated with frescoes depicting prophets and stories from the Old Testament which can still be seen on the porch arches; the most important murals were painted by the distinguished Gothic painter Johannes von Laibach.

▶ The **church** was built in the 12th century, a pillared basilica with three naves and semicircular apses to the east. Two of the apses are still visible in the eastern courtyard, whereas the remains of the apse of the main nave are preserved under the paving of the presbytery. An original Romanesque wall is exposed in the right chapel next to the presbytery. In the 17th century, under the guidance of

The church of the Stična Abbey complex

Abbot Jakob Reinprecht (1603–1626), the Romanesque church was rebuilt in the Baroque style. A further Baroque renovation of the church took place during the time of Abbot Viljem Kovačič (1734–1764). Most of the church's interior furnishings; altars, pulpit, benches and organ, date from the late Baroque period or from the second half of the 18th century. The only Romanesque traces preserved in the interior are the ground plan and the two rows of arcades with six pairs of semicircular arches.

The Slovene Museum of Christianity

Textiles on display as part of the museum's collection

▶ Today it is again a working monastery, the only active Cistercian monastery in Slovenia and thus can be visited only by prior arrangement (*017 877 100*). Situated within the monastery's old prelature, a Renaissance building next to the church, the **Slovene Museum of Christianity** (*www.mks-sticna.si, 017 878576, open for guided tours only Tues – Sat 8:30 am, 10 am, 2 pm and 4 pm; Sundays, 2 pm and 4 pm, entrance fee €4.50 adults, €2 children, €7 families*) showcases the history of Christianity in Slovenia and the development of the Cistercian order.

2 Bogenšperk

Bogenšperk Castle (*www. bogensperk.si, 018 987664, closed Dec-Feb; July and August open Tues–Sat 10am–5pm, Sun & Hols 10am–6pm, closed on Mondays; March and November open Sat & Sun 10am-5pm only. Remaining months open Tues–Sat 10am–5pm, Sun & Hols 10am-6pm, Mondays closed. Entrance fees €3.50 adults, €2.50 children, €2.70 pensioners*) stands on a hill near Šmartno pri Litiji on the road from Litija to Ivančna Gorica, close to the geographical centre of Slovenia. The beautiful Renaissance castle, one of the best preserved in Slovenia, is known for its architecture and for being the home of **Janez Vajkard Valvasor** (1641 – 1693, *see box on page 181*). The castle is worth visiting if you have a car but unfortunately rather off-the-beaten-track as far as public transport is concerned with the only alternatives being to travel by taxi or on foot from the nearest bus and train stations in Litija (*23km from Ivančna Gorica*). Bogenšperk is a further 7km south towards Šmartno pri Litiji.

Bogenšperk Castle from the air

▶ The castle in its present form was built in 1511 by the Wagen family after an earthquake destroyed the previous fortress. Valvasor owned the castle from 1672 to 1692 and spent these two decades of his life here devoted to his scholarly exploits. He partially remodelled the castle by deepening the well and by building an underground cellar and the Chapel of the Holy Virgin. Unfortunately due to debts Valvasor incurred in order to get his work published, he was forced to sell the castle in 1692 and died a year later. The castle then changed

The Castle was home to Janez Vajkard Valvasor (see opposite)

owners several times but since 1998 the Community of Litija has been the owner of the castle.

▶ The three-storey castle today houses a **museum** dedicated to Valvasor, offering an insight into his life and work. His former study is beautifully preserved together with a reconstructed printing press, a graphics collection and his former library which is now used as a (hugely popular) wedding venue.

The Castle houses a museum dedicated to one of the most celebrated Slovenes in history, Janez Valvasor

▶ In other rooms there are several further collections. The **Geodetic Collection** exhibits the development of surveying, geodesy and cartography in Slovenia and around the world from antiquity to the present time. The **Geological Collection** displays rocks, fossils and minerals collected in the region. The **Hunting Collection** shows trophies from hunting associations, the main attraction being the 360kg trophy of a brown bear which was hunted in 1978 near Kocevje. The **Superstition Collection** depicts superstitions in Slovenia, particularly belief in witchcraft dating from the second half of the 17th century. **The National Costume** collection was designed by workers from the Slovenian Ethnographic Museum (see p. 63). The collection offers a unique insight into clothing styles in Slovenia in the second half of the 17th century. The author of the exhibition took her ideas mostly from the illustrations and descriptions in Valvasor's book. Costumes from different regions of Slovenia are in immaculate detail as well as showing the process of cloth-making.

A copper printing press in the museum's collection

Some of the other collections housed in the Castle

The lavishly decorated interior of Bogenšperk Castle

JANEZ VAJKARD VALVASOR (1641-1693)

Janez Vajkard Valvasor was certainly a man of many talents and to many he was one of the greatest Slovenians to have ever lived. He showed, among other accomplishments, a flair for history, geography, ethnography, topography and cartography. Much of what we now about Slovenian history and culture before the 17th century can be attributed to his writings. His single most important work remains the monumental *Glory of the Duchy of Carniola*, published in 1689 totalling 3532 pages and including 528 illustrations and 24 appendices, which provides a vivid description of Slovene lands of the time.

Valvasor was born in Ljubljana in 1641. Aged 17 he graduated from the Jesuit school in his hometown in 1658 but chose not to continue his studies, embarking instead on a journey across Europe to broaden his horizons. He travelled for fourteen years, even visiting North Africa. During this period, he fought in the Austrian-Turkish war, and later served in a French-Swiss infantry regiment. It was not a conventional tour undertaken by young men of the time but from it Valvasor gained valuable experience and knowledge.

In 1672 Valvasor acquired Bogenšperk Castle near Litija and set about carrying out his ambitious publishing plans for which he established his own writing, drawing and printing workshop. During the course of his research and travelling, he also compiled a library containing a valuable graphics collection, various scientific and musical instruments, minerals, coins and antique objects.

Unfortunately, he did not reap the rewards of his lifetime of research. Having spent a fortune on writing and publishing his books, he was forced to sell the castle, his vast library and his collection of prints to pay off his debts; a year later he died.

Since his death, Slovenia has recognized his great contributions in many ways including his depiction on the 20 tolar banknote (the country's currency prior to the adoption of the Euro), the annual Valvasor awards for innovation and a statue of him which stands in Valvasor Square in front of the Natural History Museum in Ljubljana (see p. 61). Also, his great work The Glory of the Dutchy of Carolina, originally written in German, is now in the process of being fully translated into Slovene.

3 Semič

👥 2,000

ℹ️ Stefanov Trg 7,
tic.semic@ric-belakrajina.si
073/56 52 00, open Mon-Wed
8-15h, Thu & Fri 8–16, Sat 9-12

The small pleasant town of
Semič (11km from Metlika) is a
good base from which to enjoy
many of the activities on offer
in the Bela Krajina region. If
coming from Dolenjske Toplice
the journey downhill into the
town opens up breathtaking
views across the town and the whole of the
region. The centre of Semič has a handful
of shops and bars plus one small hotel
(Hotel "Smuk"). A visit to the tourist office
in the main town square will equip you
with the required maps and information

Semič is a quiet little town – perfect for exploring the
surrounding countryside

The hunting lodge and church atop Smuk Plateau

for the numerous walking and cycling
opportunities starting from Semič.

▶ The **Smuk Plateau** rises above Semič
and is a popular location for walking,
cycling or hunting. A well-marked footpath
starts from the information board in the
town square, Štefanov Trg.
The path leads first rather
steeply up the roads, amongst
the vineyards and then gently
ascends through the forest (for
approximately 45min). The
ruins of **Smuk Manor**, which
was abandoned at the end of
the 19th century, rise up to the
west of the Baroque **Church
of St Lawrence**. The church
was once used by the Lords
of Smuk Castle, whose family
coat-of-arms can still be seen
in the pulpit. The circular
Semiška Gora path also starts

and ends on Štefanov Trg. The path travels
past various cultural, historical and natural
sites and through part of the **Bela Krajina
wine road.**

▶ **Mirna Gora** is one of the highest peaks
in Bela Krajina (1047m) and a popular
hiking destination. There are
a number of paths to the top
ranging in length and duration.
A good starting point for the
walk to the top is from the
village of Vrčice (5km from
Semič towards Dolenjske
Toplice) turning where the road
sign shows 5km to Planina
and 8km to Mirna Gora. From
here it is approximately two
hours walk to the mountain
cabin *Planinski dom Mirna
Gora* which sits near the top at
1000m whilst the actual top is
a further 10 minutes walk. The
road is also suitable for mountain-biking to
the peak.

▶ **The Bela Krajina Wine Road** begins in
Semič and runs through the wine growing
areas of the region where you can stop
at vineyards and tourist farms, meet the
owners and sample their produce. A feature

The Mirna Gora mountain refuge *Planinski dom Mirna Gora*

of the road includes a stop at the **Wine Information Centre of Bela Krajina** in Črnomelj *(Trg Svobode 3, 063/056530)* where along with tasting the wines, they can teach you about the characteristics of each wine, production techniques and growing conditions and can arrange visits to local wine producers. The wine road runs via the village of **Rožanec** (5km from Črnomelj on the road towards Semič and Dolenjske Toplice) where the "Mitrej" is found. This is an ancient relief carved into a rock most likely originating from the 2nd century. It portrays the image of the god Mithras sacrificing a sacred

Tourists are welcome at vineyards on the Bela Krajina Wine Route

bull. The monument is highly prized by archaeologists and has been preserved in its natural environment.

4 Dolenjske Toplice

 3,200

Sokolski trg 4, *www.kkc-dolenjske.si.* 073 845188, Open May-Aug Mon-Fri 9am-6pm, Sat 9am-3pm, Sun & Hols 9am-12pm (off-season hours vary)

The village of Dolenjske Toplice *(13km from Novo Mesto)* is one of only a handful of 'real' spa towns in Slovenia and is dominated by the Thermal Spa first built in the 17th century. Dolenjske Toplice can be reached by regular bus from Novo Mesto (approximately 20 minutes) and the nearest train station is also in Novo Mesto.

The spa town of Dolenjske Toplice

▶ **The Bathers House**, complete with its three pools was built in the 18th century by Prince Ivan Vajkard, of the Ausperg family. He also built hotel Vital, one of two hotels still standing today and which was,

at that time, the most prominent building in the entire region. The Princes of Ausperg completely renovated the hotel and resort several times, the last being in 1899 when the hotel Kristal was built.

▶ The village grew up around the thermal springs and nowadays **Zdraviliski Trg** (Health Square) is the village's central square as well as being the centre of the health resort and where almost everything is located. The square attractively blends the modern state-of-the-art facilities of the health resort with the surrounding 19th century village. The resort itself comprises the two 4* hotels (Vital and Kristal), a camp site, indoor and outdoor pools and the new Balnea Wellness Centre (*www.terma-krka.si, 073 919400*).

Legend has it that Hotel Vital is built on the spot where the healing waters were discovered (see box on p. 184)

A view onto Zdraviliski Trg and Hotel Kristal

The exceedingly modern Hotel Balnea

▶ The healing power of the warm water in the pools has been known and used for centuries. The water contains minerals and its temperature (36–38˚C) is equal to that of the human body making it most appropriate for treating ailments such as inflammatory and degenerative rheumatism, gynecological illnesses and osteoporosis. However many people also visit the pools simply for fun, relaxation, enjoyment and a sense of wellbeing. The pools are open to paying visitors as well as hotel guests.

▶ There are a number of marked walks and bike rides starting from the village centre, details of which are available from the tourist office, which is housed in the **Cultural & Congress Centre** (*Kulturno Kongresni Center*).

▶ One such walk is the 4.5km **Cvinger path**. Cvinger is a forested hill (262m) west of the village. The path leads to the village of **Meniška**, the largest settlement in the area. The name, meaning 'Monk's village' reveals that the village used to be part of the **Stična Abbey** (see p. 178). For an interesting diversion, a marked path turns off from Meniška to follow the **Cvinger Archeological Path**, exhibiting iron-age smelting furnaces.

One of the elegant pools of Hotel Vital

Enjoying the fresh air

The Legend of the Water and the Dog
Legend has it that once upon a time in Dolenjske Toplice lived a sexton, who loved his dog very much. One day the dog was running through the village as a cart came through. The dog started to leap up at it, fell under the wheels and the last wheel ran him over. The dog, squealing with pain, dragged itself from the road. When the sexton noticed that his dog was missing he started to search the whole village but couldn't find his dog. Later that evening, when he was crossing the Sušica brook, which flows through the village, he heard a noise on the riverbank. Moving closer to the noise he found his dog lying in a pool, trying to relieve the pain caused by the accident. As he bent down to stroke it, he unintentionally touched the water and was surprised to find the pool was warm – its temperature was equal to the human body. Thus, according to legend, the first creature to become aware of the effects of the thermal water in Dolenjske Toplice was a dog.

5 Novo mesto

22,800

Glavni Trg 6,
www.novomesto.si
073 939263, Open Apr-Oct Mon-Fri
9am-7pm, Sat 9am-4pm, Sun 9am-
12pm, Nov-Mar Mon-Fri 9am-6pm,
Sat 9am-2pm

Cviček Fair (May)

A view of Novo Mesto from the Krka River

The name Novo Mesto means 'New Town', rather ironic nowadays as the town was established in 1365. The town, situated on a bend of the Krka River, was entirely surrounded by a defensive wall with two gates forming the main communication route from the Gorenja (Ljubljanska) gate via the Main Square to the Dolenja (Karlovška) gate. Prosperity initially came to the town through trade, much of which was with neighbouring Croatia, although further development was hindered by natural disasters and Ottoman raids. The town's historic centre was heavily damaged during bombing raids in World War II and the human casualty toll was high. In the second half of the 20th century Novo Mesto expanded beyond its defensive walls and industrialization and urbanization

accelerated thanks to the town's favourable transport routes and terrain and it soon became the administrative, cultural, religious and business centre of Dolenjska.

Today Novo Mesto is the largest town in southern Slovenia and the capital of the Dolenjska region. The town comprises two distinct areas, the new town and the old town, and is certainly a town of two halves. The new town is, as the name implies, a modern business centre, home to international pharmaceutical company "Krka", and "Revoz", a local subsidiary of Renault, and one of Slovenia's biggest employers and exporters. For a town where much of the focus is on cars, there are certainly a lot of them and this

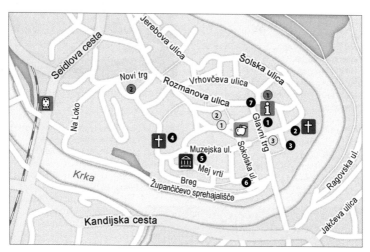

1 Mestna hiša
2 Church of St. Leonard
3 Franciscan Monastery
4 Chapter Church of St. Nicholas
5 Dolenjska Museum
6 Jakac House
7 Marble fountain

HOTELS:
1 Hostel Situla
2 Hotel Krka

RESTAURANTS:
1 Pizzeria Štingelj
2 Restaurant Tilak
3 Kavarna Tratnik

A view of the old town from the air

is undoubtedly one of its drawbacks. However a pleasant surprise lies in store in the pedestrianised old town which has preserved its medieval appearance and is a riverside oasis of calm and green.

▶ The old town contains almost all the town's sights of importance and interest. Most of the sights are found on or near the **Main Square** (*Glavni Trg*) which is arguably the biggest and one of the most beautiful in Slovenia. It is lined with shops and arcaded buildings, many of which are former rich merchants' houses that were built in the second half of the 16th century. Although the facades have been altered, the late Gothic features are still in evidence including vaulted arcades and stone pillars. The **marble fountain**, dating from 1955, which sits in the upper part of the Main Square sits atop a stone column in the centre of a stone basin. Upon it are carved verses taken from "On the Square" a poem by the renowned Slovene impressionist and Neo-Romantic poet Dragotin Kette (1876–1899), who lived and studied in Novo Mesto.

▶ The **Town Hall** (*Mestna Hiša, Glavni Trg 6*) on the eastern side of the square dates from 1905. Its ground floor has an archway opening up to the Main Square. Neo-Renaissance as well as Neo-Gothic elements were used to shape the main façade and

The spires of Novo Mesto's churches at dusk

even though many consequent layers of stucco have been applied, the original murals have remained intact in some parts of the building. The coat of arms of the town's founder, Austrian Archduke Rudolf IV, is on the exterior.

▶ Behind the town hall on Jenkova Ulica, is the **Church of St Leonard** (*Sveti Lenart*), built by Franciscan monks who came to Novo Mesto from Bosnia to flee the Ottoman invasion. The Bishop of Ferrara gave the Chapel of St. Leonard to the Franciscan order in 1469 and the Franciscans were allowed to tear

The fountain on the Main Square cheerily lit at night

down the chapel and replace it with a new church. During the following decades the church was restored and added to several times but the structure remained practically unchanged until 1866, when the main façade was rebuilt in Gothic Revival style. The 18th century interior decoration and furnishings were designed mainly by the Franciscan monks themselves. The colourful Gothic stained glass windows and wooden pulpit were added in the early 20th century. The altars were painted by the Baroque painter Janez Metzinger (1699-1759) and several of his paintings can also be found in the church.

▶ Next to the church in Frančiškanska Ulica is the

Francisan Monastery (*Frančiškanski Samostan*) which the monks built on a piece of land they bought adjoining the church. The monastery library has a collection of over 12,000 rare books and manuscripts, including many precious incunabula over 600 years old. The library is not usually open to the public but group visits are possible by prior arrangement.

▶ The oldest building in the town is the **Chapter Church of St. Nicholas** (*Cerkev Sveta Nikolaja*) which is in a dominant position perched above the old town on Kapiteljska Street. Its present day appearance dates from 1429 when an older Gothic building, dating from the second half of the 14th century was altered and extended. A particular feature of the church is its broken symmetry, a result of it having been rebuilt many times in different styles. The upper portion of the 55m tall octagonal bell tower was rebuilt in 1860 in a Gothic Revival style. The Gothic exterior is made of crushed limestone with no stucco. Inside, the main altar features a picture of the patron of the church, St. Nicholas with Ss Hermagoras and Fortunatus by Tintoretto set in a neo-Gothic frame. It is one of the most valuable altar paintings in the country. On the side altars there are paintings by the Slovene Baroque painter Valentin Metzinger (1699-1759). The crypt, which is a rather rare element in Gothic churches, has three naves with crossed vaults placed on four pairs of octagonal columns. Near the church, a small reminder of the city walls, which were eventually demolished in 1786, are still visible today at Šance on

The Town Hall on the Main Square

Kapitelj Hill behind Hotel Krka. A 100 meter footpath runs along the walls and leads downhill to the Loka Sports Centre.

▶ The **Dolenjska Museum** (*Muzejska ulica 7, www.dolmuzej.com, 073 731130, open summer Tue-Fri 8am-5pm, Sat 10am-5pm, Sun 9am-1pm, winter Tue-Fri 8am-4pm, Sat 9am-1pm, Sun 9am-12pm, entrance fee €5 adults, €3 children & pensioners*) was created to showcase the history of the town and the Dolenjska region. It has been in operation since 1953, expanding from its one original building to today's five buildings which house five permanent exhibitions.

The Church of St. Leonard was built by Franciscan monks fleeing Ottoman invasions

The Franciscan Monastery is positioned prominently in the town

▶ The entire first floor of the **Križateije building**, which has been the seat of the museum since 1951, now houses the largest and most important of the museum's exhibits, the **Archaeology** collection. Novo Mesto is known for the rarity of its archaeological heritage and numerous unique artefacts, particularly those from the early Iron Age period. This impressive collection includes grave findings uncovered in the Kandija suburb of Novo Mesto featuring a wealth of metal, glass and amber material from women's graves and metal weapons, bronze helmets and armour from men's graves

The spire of the Church of St. Nicholas rises above the rooftops of Novo Mesto

A glass-bead necklace displayed as part of the Museum's Ethnographical collection

from the period of the Halstatt Culture. The importance of Novo Mesto in the early Iron Age is illustrated by eight decorated bronze situlas, which rank among the very finest artistic works of their time, and an exhibition entitled 'An Archaeologic Picture of Dolenjska' displaying numerous artefacts covering a period spanning from the Palaeolithic to the Early Middle Ages.

▶ The **Ethnology** collection is housed in the building known as **Ropasova Hiša**. Its exhibits cover a wide spectrum of folk art including paintings on glass, wooden folk sculptures, painted furniture and a collection of farming implements which depict and symbolise the annual cycle of peasant life and farm work throughout the year. Further rooms contain displays of horse-breeding and crafts including the preserved candle workshop showing the traditional methods of candle-making and original furnishings from the Novo Mesto gingerbread workshop.

▶ The **Recent History** exhibition remains almost unchanged from the socialist era. It represents the time from the beginnings of the worker's movement up to the liberation of Novo Mesto in 1945 with emphasis on events during the Second World War. It contains thousands of photographs, documents of both Partisans and occupation forces.

▶ Novo Mesto was home to the artist **Božidar Jakac** (1899-1989), one of Slovenia's most famous painters and artists. **Jakac House** (*Jakčev Dom, Sokolska Ulica 1, open Tue-Sat 9am-5pm, last Sun of each month 9am-1pm, entrance fee €1.50 adults, €1 children*) is located in the area known

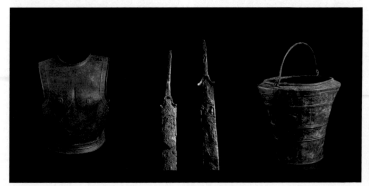
Bronze exhibits of the Dolenjska Museum Archaeology collection

A tourist boat sails along the Krka River past Breg

as **Breg** (meaning 'riverbank') which is found by turning right shortly before the far end of Glavni Trg. Breg is one of the most picturesque sites in the town due to its location. Here a dense row of simple but picture pretty houses were built around 1786, on the remains of and using materials from, the demolished city walls. Božidar Jakac was born in Breg which was generally inhabited by the less wealthy town folk which can be seen from the modest design and layout of the houses. The Gallery houses a permanent collection of over 800 pieces of his work together with the **Young Božidar Jakac** collection, showcasing the earlier period of his life from 1910-1923. There are two further permanent exhibitions; an art exhibition of the Dolenjska Museum containing works covering the period from the 17th to 20th century and an art education exhibition with works representing every different artistic genre and technique.

Cviček wine

Cviček is nowadays amongst the most popular wines in Slovenia. This wasn't always the case, however, as it was previously regarded by some as barely being worthy of the label 'wine'. In the Middle Ages the region where Cviček is made was a famous wine-growing region but as the old viticultural system declined, so did the quality of wine produced, becoming gradually more sour, hence people started referring to it as Cviček (an old Slovenian word denoting very sour wine) and the name stuck. These days, however, it is a very different wine, drunk widely throughout the country. Although it is red in appearance, it is actually a blend of red and white grapes more akin to a rosé. Cviček is produced in the south-eastern of Slovenia in the Dolenjska region where the climatic conditions are favourable for the required blend of grapes; Modra Frankinja (Blue Franconian) which gives it its full flavour, Žametna Črnina makes it drinkable and adds to its acidity and Kraljevina, a white grape which regulates its acidity. Occasionally Laški Rizling (Italian Riesling) is also added. It is light in both colour and alcohol content, typically just 7.5-8.5%. Cviček does not improve with age and is best drunk young.

Cviček is largely grown by locals who have their own private vineyards and small outbuildings (zidanice) where the wine is taken to mature. Travelling through the Dolenjska region, one cannot fail to notice the abundance zidanice dotted throughout the countryside where Cviček is a staple part of life culminating in the annual Cviček festival which takes place in Novo Mesto every May.

6 Otočec

700

Rock Otočec (June)

Otočec (6km from Novo Mesto) is home to Otočec Castle, Slovenia's only castle on an island. The castle and gardens stand on a tiny island in the middle of the Krka River, and are among Slovenia's most picturesque sights. The castle has rectangular fortress walls, including four circular-shaped towers and a rebuilt

The Otočec Rock Festival, increasingly popular but in definite contrast to the surroundings

These days the Castle is a luxurious world-class hotel

central defence tower above the entrance to the inner courtyard.

Otočec Castle was first mentioned in 1252 and throughout its history has undergone numerous transformations and had many owners. From the Counts of Višnja Gora, who established the Stična monastery (see p. 178), it was next owned by the Counts of Andechs and the Babenbergs. In 1246 the Czech King Premysl Otokar II of Bohemia, who was involved in several years of conflict to gain control over the region, gave the castle as a gift to the bishop of Freising. In the early 16th century its owners were the Villander family, who gave the castle its Renaissance look, until the castle was bought by Baron Ivan Lenkovič, the Commander-in-Chief of the military border region in 1560. In 1942 the castle was burnt down by the Partisans but was restored in 1961 and redeveloped into a hotel. Ownership finally passed to Krka, the well-known pharmaceutical company and its subsidiary Terme Krka, who also manage a number of other spa hotels in Slovenia.

▶ Today the 5★ **Otočec Castle Hotel** (*www.terme-krka.si*) is one of the most famous and luxurious hotels in the country.

Otočec Castle surrounded by lush greenery and the sparkling waters of the Krka

Its setting makes for a unique and romantic stay and its 16 rooms are exceptionally luxurious. It is especially popular for weddings and offers a number of themed ceremonies including one in which the 'Count of Otočec', dressed in a traditional period costume, welcomes guests to the civil ceremony which takes place either in the Knight's Salon or at the wedding arch. The Castle's restaurants and gardens are open to non-residents.

Otočec in winter is a sight full of mystery and old world charm

▶ In addition to the Castle Hotel, Otočec offers a choice of alternative accommodation with something to suit all budgets. The 4★ Sport Hotel or the 2★ Bungalows are less than 300 metres away and the Otočec Camp is also situated on the riverbank.

Fine dining to be had in the elegant restaurant

▶ For sports lovers, the Otočec area offers a wealth of choices. The **Otočec Sport Centre** offers indoor and outdoor tennis courts and a multipurpose court. The Centre also features the **Otočec Tennis Academy** as well as saunas, a fitness studio, table tennis and a bistro. Bikes can be rented from the Sport Centre to explore the surrounding areas. Fishing along the Krka River is another popular activity and fishing permits can be obtained from the Sport Hotel. Rowing boats are available to rent from the camp and the new **Otočec Golf Course** is also set along the banks of the river surrounded by forest.

▶ There are many walking options in the area including the 17km **Cviček Trail** which is a pleasant circular path through the heart of Cviček land (see box on p. 189), with magnificent views of the Krka river valley and the Gorjanci hills. The marked walking trail starts from the centre of Otočec, near the fire station before the underpass. Follow the road for Paha and Herinja through the underpass which continues along the Lešnica valley. The path is not demanding with only one ascent to Nova Gora (581m) which is the highest point of the hike. The path also passes **Hmeljnik Castle,** built in the 12th century as one of the first castles in the area and also an early example of Romanesque architecture in Slovenia. Its double walls and a staircase tower are Gothic and Renaissance additions, while it was renovated into a modern stately home in the 19th century. In 1942, the castle was also burned down by the Partisans, however from the late 1950's, the ruins were slowly rebuilt. The path then continues to **Trška Gora** a hill largely covered with vineyards some of which are the property of the nearby Stična monastery. There are extensive views across Novo Mesto, the Krka river and the Gorjanci hills from the top of the hill and from here the path then descends among the vineyards before returning to the start point.

▶ A more strenuous 3½ hour walk but with rewarding views leads to **Gospodična** (822m) and **Trdinov Vrh** (1178m) via the villages of Tolsti Vrh and Suhadol. Views towards the

The new Otočec Golf Course set in tranquil natural surroundings

Kamnik Savinja Alps from the summit Trdinov Vrh are simply magnificent but you may wish to stop earlier at the mountain cabin **Planinci dom pri Gospodični**. For those with a car, you can shorten the walk by driving from Otočec in a south-easterly direction to Gabrje and start your walk from there.

The spa at Šmajerske Toplice

▶ The village of Šmarjeske Toplice (5km from Otočec) is home to a spa resort of the same name, run by the Terme Krka group (*www.terme-krka.si; tel: 073 843*

The spooky ruins of Hmeljnik Castle

400). The centre is based around health and wellbeing as well as being a therapy centre for cardiovascular diseases and sports injuries. Accommodation at the resort is offered in three 4★ hotels or in the nearby apartments. Facilities include two indoor and three outdoor pools, the Vitarium Spa & Clinic and three rehabilitation centres. The highlight is the 'wooden pool' which is built above the thermal water spring which is at 32°C. Its special feature is the fact that water flows through the pool coming in from one side and going out from the other meaning it has a constant influx of fresh thermal water, maintaining the water temperature and healing properties.

7 Soteska

The tiny village of Soteska (13km west from Novo Mesto) grew up around the fortified Soteska Manor which, together with its adjoining buildings, is the focal point of the village. The magnificent Soteska Manor, which stands on the left bank of the Krka River, replaced the Old Soteska Castle which formerly stood on the opposing river bank, was described by Valvasor (see p. 181) as one of the finest architectural achievements of its time. The nearby park with its Devil's Tower and the parish Church of St. Erasmus complete this heritage sight.

Soteska Manor, gutted during WWII

▶ **Soteska Manor** was built by Duke Jurij Žiga Gallenberg in the 17th century. The Gallenberg family, who gained the title Lords of Soteska, owned the Manor until 1733 during which time they enlarged and beautified it to the extent it became known as one of the most remarkable in the region. In 1943 the Manor was burned down by the Partisans who had also previously removed and hidden all its precious contents and

artworks. The Manor was later used as a source of building material, a kind of quarry, by the local population. Inside the rectangular shaped Manor, the arcaded courtyard was flanked by four single storey tracts supporting four corner towers and it was known for its richly painted rooms. Plans were put in place to renovate the Manor which sadly never came to fruition and today only the Manor's ruins remain.

▶ The **Old (*Stara*) Soteska Castle** was first mentioned in 1311. The isolated position of the castle led to its abandonment in the

16th century and it was later destroyed by the Partisans. From the surviving ruins the foundations are indicative of typical Romanesque construction techniques which were known for their precision and were very sophisticated for their time. A late Gothic moat, dungeons cut deep into the rock and the keep with its double curtain wall and towers are still visible today. The ruins have been protected as a cultural monument, however, access to them is not recommended as the area has not been made safe.

An illustration of the Old Soteska Castle

▶ The Renaissance-style park, was originally laid out at the same time as the old castle, however, at the end of the

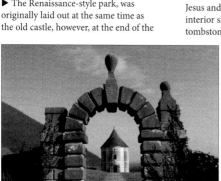

The Devil's Tower (*Hudičev Turn*)

17th century, a new Baroque park was designed beside the river and the manor. The centre of the park is the clover shaped **Devil's Tower** (*Hudičev Turn*), so named by villagers who were rather suspicious of the hedonistic lifestyles of the aristocracy during the Rococo period. The interior is richly painted and decorated in the illusionist style with a scene depicting the kidnapping of the young Ganymede by Zeus, On the first floor, other partially visible paintings are imaginative works (showing rather a lot of naked flesh!) dating from the 17th century.

▶ The **Church of St. Erasmus** (*Sveti Erazem*) which is also closely connected with the manor was built circa 1664 by the Lords of Soteska on the site of an earlier church. Inside, a painting of the patron saint hangs amid the scenery painted

on the altar walls and two beautiful Baroque altars in the side chapels remain intact. The left altar is dedicated to the Crucifixion of Jesus and the right one to St. Thecla. On the interior side of the chancel arch there is the tombstone of the former owner Ivan Adam Gallenberg and his family's coat-of-arms is on the other side. The ceiling of the presbytery, though now largely destroyed, was painted by the Austrian artist Franc Kurz Goldenstein (1807-1878) in 1856 who also painted the only known portrait of the great Slovene poet France Prešeren (see p. 97).

▶ A further outbuilding houses an open-storage exhibition depot of the Technical Museum of Slovenia and encompasses a collection of vehicles including a wagon and carriage collection which are constantly complemented and rotated.

▶ There is an official car park with information panels besides the road and opposite the manor's ruins. From here it is possible to walk to the old castle ruins

The church of St Erazmus

The Krka River at Soteska

on the right bank of the river and also to the church. For scheduled visits, which include a tour of the ruins of Soteska Manor, the Technical Museum Exhibition Depot and the Devil's Tower, you must make prior arrangements via the Dolenjske Toplice tourist office (*www.dolenjske-toplice.si*, *073/84 51 88*).

8 Kostanjevica na Krki

The small picturesque town of Kostanjevica na Krki (22km from Novo Mesto) is built on an islet on a bend in the Krka River at the foot of the Gorjanci hills. At just 500m long and 200m wide Kostanjevica, named after the abundance of chestnut trees (*kostanji*) surrounding it, is the smallest town in Slovenia. It is also known as the Venice of Dolenjska due to frequent flooding. You won't need a map to explore the town; it consists of just two parallel streets with a church standing at either end.

The picturesque location of Kostanjevica na Krki

The town has remained the same since medieval times though sadly much of it is now long overdue for conservation and many of the buildings need more than just a lick of paint. Combined with the nearby Kostanjevica Castle and the Kostanjevica Cave it makes for a fascinating place to visit.

▶ The parish **Church of St. Jacob** (*Sveti Jakob*) is the oldest building in the town

The Church of St. Jacob, the oldest building in the town

and stands at the northern tip of the islet. Originally built in the 11th century, the current 13th century church was renovated in the Baroque style. Two stone portals still remain from its original Romanesque appearance and on the south outside wall is a fresco of St. Christopher dating from the mid 14th century.

▶ At the other end of the town, the small gothic **Church of St. Nicholas** dates from the 16th century and has frescoes painted by the local artist Jože Gorjup (1907-1932), born at No. 8 Talcev Ulica. More of his work can also be seen in the **Gorjup Gallery** (*viewing by arrangement with the Božidar Jakac Gallery*), located within Kostanjevica Elementary School. The gallery's international art collection of the 20th century is large and is changed and supplemented with new works every few years.

"Polja", a landscape by Vladimir Lamut

The Church of St. Nicholas

▶ The **Lamut Fine Art Salon** (*Oržanova 5, 074 988152, open Tues-Sun 9am-6m, entrance free*) is devoted to the Slovene graphic artist and painter Vladimir Lamut (1915-1962), renowned for his oil landscape paintings who created much of his work in the town.

Kostanjevica Castle, once a monastery now houses an art gallery

▶ The nearby Cistercian monastery, also known as **Kostanjevica Castle** (*Kostanjeviški Grad, Grajska Cesta 45, 1.5km southwest of the town*), is reached through an avenue of linden trees leading to the colourful building. Above the main entrance is a fresco painted in 1737 by the Slovene painter Franc Jelovšek. The cloister, with a two-storey arcade, is one of the largest in central Europe. The monastery was established by the Carinthian Duke, Bernard Spanheim in 1234 and it has been rebuilt, altered and expanded several times. In 1786 Hapsburg Emperor Joseph II dissolved the monastery and the altars and other church fittings were taken away or sold as the monastery buildings slowly deteriorated. In 1942 it was torched by the Partisans and in 1956 the bell-tower collapsed. Since 1958 it has been gradually and consistently renovated and

a large part of it now houses the excellent **Božidar Jakac Gallery** (*www.galerija-bj. si, 074 988140, open Tues-Sun 9am-6pm summer, 9am – 4pm winter, entrance fee €3 adults, €1.50 children, €5 families*). The Gallery exhibits over 3500 paintings and sculptures, mostly by 20th century artists, with permanent collections by Božidar Jakac, Tone Kralj, Zoran Didek and Janez Boljka and featuring the **Pleterje Collection of Old Masters**, 17th and 18th century oil paintings, belonging to the nearby monastery. **The Lapidary** contains original examples of monastery's architectural art, decorative panels and a reconstructed model of the monastery church. The gallery also hosts special exhibitions by Slovene and foreign artists in the former monastery church, created specifically for this location. Further oak sculptures are located in the gardens around the monastery, in the town and in nearby areas. This international sculpture symposium, which began in 1961, is known as '**Forma Viva**' and holds over 100 exhibits with contributions from artists worldwide.

▶ **Kostanjevica Cave** (*Kostanjeviška Jama, www.kostanjeviska-jama.com, 041 297001,*

An outdoor exhibition of the Božidar Jakac Gallery

*open daily 10am-6pm Jul & Aug, open
weekends only from Apr-Oct, entrance €6
adults, €4 children)* is just 1km southeast
of the town. No-one knew about it until
1937 when its entrance suddenly burst open
because of flooding water. It was developed
and opened to the public in 1971 when
electric lights and paths were installed.

The so-called Crisis Hall of Kostanjevica Cave

Whilst it doesn't compare in size or stature
with the caves at Postojna (see p. 198)
or Škocjan (see p. 152), it is nevertheless
interesting and easily accessible for a guided
tour. The cave is also the natural habitat of
horseshoe bats as well as other fascinating
cave animals and plants.

▶ Details of a number of scenic walks
and bike rides that start from the town
including the 8km **Resslova Forest Path**
or the 15km **Panoramic Cycle Path** are
listed at *www.kostanjevica.si* – sadly still
only available in Slovene. The tourist office
in Kostanjevica closed a few years ago
however tourist information is available
from the Božidar Jakac Gallery.

The countryside around Kostanjevica na Krki is
perfect for long walks

9 Pleterje monastery

The tiny village of Drča,
situated in a valley at the foot
of Gorjanci hills, is home to
the **Pleterje Monastery** (*www.
kartuzija-pleterje.si*) the only
active Carthusian Monastery
in Slovenia. Due to the monk's
strict orders, the monastery
is not open to visitors with
the exception of the adjoining
gothic **Holy Trinity Church**
and the monastery shop. The
monastery's attractive and

The Pleterje Monastery complex from the air

peaceful location and surroundings are,
however, well worth a visit. Drča is located
3km south of Šentjernej and 6km west of
Kostanjevica. It is easiest reached by car,
however buses do run from Novo Mesto to
Kostanjevica na Krki, alight at Šentjernej
and from here the final 3km must be made
on foot.

The monastery has had an interesting
and protracted history. The Carthusians
came to Slovenia in 1160 and to Pleterje
in 1403. The monastery was founded

by Herman II, a Count of Celje, a great
supporter of the order, who was eventually
buried here. It suffered several attacks by
the Ottomans who eventually burned it
down in 1471. It was rebuilt with fortified
ramparts, towers and a solid walls until it
came to resemble a fortress. In 1593, due
to the material and spiritual decay of the
monastery, Archduke Ferdinand II handed
Pleterje over to the Jesuits of Ljubljana who
retained it until 1772. After the suppression
of the Jesuit Order, the monastery passed

into the ownership of the state until 1839 when it was privately owned. In 1899 it was regained by the Carthusian Order and rebuilding of the complex took place according to the plans of the Order in France whose principles dictate that all monasteries are built alike with a well-considered layout; a grouping of hermitages (or cells) linked to one another by a cloister which ends at the communal grounds. The church, refectory, and the

The Pleterje Monastery

The portal of the Gothic church with a fresco of Mary and the Holy Trinity

Chapter are separated by an entrance door to the workshops and the lodging of the monk in charge of the day to day running of the house.

Despite the monastery itself being inaccessible to the public, the Carthusian

Charterhouses are known worldwide and regularly attract a large number of curious visitors and admirers from far and wide. You might spot some of the white robed monks working in the grounds; these are the lay monks (brothers) whose role is to provide for the needs of the monastery enabling the cloister monks (fathers) to devote their time to the silence of the cell. The cloister monks, all of whom are or will be priests, are totally dedicated to contemplation. They operate in silence and maintain a strict separation from the world. They live in their 'cells' along the cloister only leaving for the appointed hours of liturgy, choir or the monthly recreation walks. The cells are actually two-storey small houses with their own enclosed garden. Food, which is abundant, well prepared and strictly vegetarian, is received through a small window by the entrance twice a day except on the one day a week when the monks have 'abstinence' meaning they take only bread and water.

▶ The Gothic **Holy Trinity Church** outside the cloisters is open to visitors (*8.30am-6.30pm daily except Sundays*).

The monks make their own wine, spirits and honey products

Pleterje is still a working monastery and encounters with the monks are likely

Of note are the fresco depicting Mary and the Trinity above the main portal, the ribbed vaulted ceiling and a low wall along the aisle used to separate the clerics from the other faithful that came to the church. In the sacristy of the church an audiovisual presentation about the monastery and the life of the monks is available (usually for groups of at least five).

The impressive Gothic arches of the monastery church

The monastery **shop** (*open Mon-Sat 7.30am-5.30pm*) sells products such as wine, fruit juice, herbal teas, fruit brandies and bee products all made from the produce of the 30 hectares of agricultural land. Some of the wines can even be ordered online (*see website above*). **Fruit brandies** made and aged in Pleterje's cellar in wooden casks are another speciality. The pear brandy contains a whole pear in each bottle that will leave you wondering how they got the whole pear inside the bottle; the secret being that the bottle is placed over the pear whilst it is still on the tree and it grows and ripens inside the bottle before the brandy is added.

▶ The **Pleterje Path** (*Pleterska Pot*) is a 4km long circular walk which starts at the entrance to the church. It first leads up through the forest where boards provide more information about the forest flora and fauna then the path continues amongst rolling hills and vineyards and offers wonderful views over the monastery, its gardens and orchards. Towards the end of the path you reach the **Pleterje Open Air Museum** (*073 377 680; open daily Apr–Nov 9am–5pm, Dec–Mar open 10am– 4pm daily except Mon & Tue; entrance fee adults €2.50, children and pensioners €1.90, families €7*), a collection of buildings which represent typical 19th century Slovene farmhouses and outbuildings built from wood and with thatched roofs.

One of the traditional houses of the Pleterje Open Air Museum

10 Postojna

8,800

Ljubljanska Cesta 4, *www.postojna.si* 057/280 788, Open Mon-Sat 10am-6pm, Sun 10am-2pm

Titova Cesta 2, 05/721 01 80

Kolodvorska Cesta 25, 05/296 23 47

Christmas Fair

The Postojna Park area, at the entrance to the caves

The town of Postojna, the centre of the Notranjska region, lies at the north end of the Pivka River valley and is famous as being the destination of the **Postojna Cave** (*Postojnska Jama*). Postojna was first mentioned in 1226 and at first the town developed along the foot of the Sovič hill. Later, after the construction of the railway and the discovery of the inner parts of the Postojna Cave, the town acquired city status and it spread further to the edges of the basin.

▶ Covering an area over 20km, **Postojna Cave** is not only Slovenia's number one tourist attraction but is also one of the largest and most visited caves in Europe. The cave, actually a system of several connected caves, is undoubtedly hugely impressive but they is also hugely popular and timing your visit wisely is recommended to avoid queuing amongst the hoards of tour groups. It is for this reason that some people prefer to visit the Škocjan caves (see p. 152). If however you have children in tow, Postojna is by far the best choice and offers plenty of child-friendly diversions.

An electric train whisks visitors around the caves

The gigantic system of caves in Postojna has been carved by the underground course of the Pivka River. The passages open to tourists are on the dry level, while the

The so-called "Spaghetti Hall"

river has long ago retreated underground. The length of all the corridors and halls surpasses 17km but it is not its sheer size but also the beauty of stalagmites and stalactites, pillars and curtains that has made the cave famous.

▶ Postojna Cave has had a long and interesting history. Since prehistoric times parts of its entrance served as a refuge and it has been visited since the Middle Ages although in those days visitors didn't venture too far. Near the entrance to the cave in the **Passage of Old Signatures** you can see travellers' signatures with the oldest dating from 1213. Meanwhile in the Vivarium (*see below*) the **Gallery of New Signatures** contains signatures where in the 19th century, following discovery of the inner sections of the cave, visitors were permitted to sign their names on the walls. Today, the signing of names is no longer permitted as it could damage the precious cave environment. The first descriptions of the caves was published by J. W. Valvasor in his work, *The Glory of the Duchy of Carniola* in 1689 (see p. 181). Valvasor considered Postojna Cave to be the largest and longest but at the same time the grimmest of all

the caves he had seen. Exploration of the caves inner sections was not made until 1818 when it was visited by Emperor Franz I Habsburg in whose steps followed the first organised groups. Following new discoveries and the arrival of the Vienna-Trieste railway Postojna became one of the most visited show caves in the world.

▶ On arrival at Postojna Cave you are confronted with the rather dated looking Hotel "Jama" (since the complex was sold in 2010, plans are afoot to renovate and revive the hotel and surroundings), a tourist complex selling all manner of cave-related souvenirs, and several fast food restaurants. You can quickly whisk past these distractions and head to the caves themselves.

The White Hall of Postojnska Jama

After purchasing your tickets, almost 6km of the caves await you. Note that the temperature inside the caves is a constant 8-10°C and the floor is wet, so warm clothing and sensible footwear is advisable. The tour lasts approximately 1½ hours. The first 4km are covered on an electric train which travels from the cave entrance through the many caverns to the Great Mountain Hall. From here, large signs direct visitors to the waiting area for their chosen language (a choice of Slovene, English, German and Italian) for the remainder of the tour and where you await your guide. The guide escorts you through the remaining rooms pausing occasionally to explain their formation and answer questions. The sheer diversity of shapes and colours of stalactite and stalagmite formations as well as expansive cave areas are quite phenomenal.

The Pikva River sinks underground to carve out the Postojna cave system

A wide variety of entrance tickets to the caves and other attractions in the area is available including package details for the Vivarium, Predjama Castle and the Park of Military History. Entrance prices and tour times can be found at *www.postojna-cave. com*.

▶ There are many smaller but equally interesting caves near Postojna. The most popular are **Pivka and Črna Caves** (*tel. 05/700 01 00; guided tours at 9 and 15h daily in July and Aug, only weekends in Jun and Sept, the rest of the year only by appointment*) which are linked by a man-made tunnel. Both are part of the Postojna cave system and have been carved out by River Pivka. The entrance is through the Pivka Jama camping grounds some 3km to the north of Postojna and this is also where you will purchase your tickets. A steep descend down 300 wooden steps takes you to the Pivka Cave continuing on the walkway above it's the course of the river and its two lakes. Črna Cave is dry and takes its name from the soot of torches lit by visitors. Not all of it is black and it has some very nice cave ornaments shining with tiny crystals.

The Olm or "Human Fish" is the only species of its kind in Europe

▶ The **Proteus Vivarium** is an exhibition housed in a cave setting where you can learn about the form and history of the cave, its underworld life, as well as view the vivarium which contains live specimens of cave fauna. Amongst the animals on display are cave crickets, bats, beetles and fish with special attention being paid to the **"human fish"** (*proteus anguinus*), the most famous and fascinating cave animal in the world. At 25-30cm long it is also the largest of all the cave-dwelling animals. The human fish has adapted to living in the eternal darkness of the cave environment and despite having atrophied eyes, has a highly developed sense of smell, touch, taste and an especially sensitive inner ear.

There are many smaller but equally interesting caves

The breathtaking Planinska Jama

▶ **Otoška Jama** lies next to Postojna on the road towards Predjama (see below). Though it is small in comparison with the

others (only 672m) the visit is a wholly different experience since you embark on a 45min guided where the only light is that of your torches. The cave is open only by prior appointment with the Postojna tourist info centre.

▶ The impressive cave, **Planinska Jama**, near the village of Planina has only 100m of its halls open, but is still worth a visit as the largest water cave in the country offering great shots for photographers. You can arrange a boat tour through the Postojna Cave tourist office.

⑪ Predjama

The tiny village of Predjama (pop. 85) is situated 11km northwest of Postojna at the edge of the Pivka Basin. A walk up its green valley will bring you to **Predjama Castle**, one of the most memorable sights in Slovenia. This impressive piece of medieval fortification is perched on a 123m cliff nestled impressively into the surrounding karst rocks. Most visitors to Postojna make the short onward trip along the picturesque road to Predjama and indeed combined entrance tickets are available (*see below*).

The medieval Predjama Castle is built into the rock face

The oldest surviving records of Predjama Castle's existence date from the second half of the 13th century. Its most famous inhabitant was **Erasmus von Luegg**, a knight who inhabited it in the second half

Erasmus von Luegg as depicted in a painting that can be seen in the Castle

of the 15th century. After a quarrel in which he killed a kinsmen of his lord, Frederic III of Habsburg, Erasmus became a baron outlaw, attacking merchants on the roads and amassing wealth in his impregnable castle. In 1484 the Emperor sent troops to punish him but the siege of Predjama castle dragged out to over a year. During this time Erasmus entered and left the castle via a secret passage defying the Austrian army's fruitless attacks and even mocked the Habsburg soldiers by throwing them freshly-picked cherries as evidence that he was able to come and go as he pleased. The story goes that in the end Erasmus was betrayed by one of his servants who signalled to the imperial troops when his master went to the toilet, the only weak spot in the castle wall, so that one well aimed cannonball sealed Erasmus' fate. Erasmus is believed to be buried in the square at Predjama, next to the 15th century **Church of Mary of the Seven Sorrows** which contains many restored frescoes and is a beautiful example of Late Gothic architecture.

After Erasmus' death the original castle was destroyed only to be rebuilt in 1570 in its present day form. At the beginning of the

17th century, a secret exit that was in a small sinkhole close to the edge of the Predjama cliff was walled up when it was discovered that thieves had been entering the castle and carrying away a large number of valuables. After World War II, cavers began exploring this passage which is today known as **Erazem's Passage** and is now open to visitors (*see below*).

The Castle looks even more splendid at night

The castle is a true warren of passages, rooms, chambers and walkways with low ceilings (mind your head!) which lead up, down and around the four-storey building. Many of the rooms contain reconstructions showing their original functions. Other rooms are designated museum rooms with portraits and oil paintings including one of Erasmus

Many of the Castles rooms contain period reconstructions

himself. On the third floor a lookout terrace provides fine views over the valley below.

The castle is open daily between 10am-4pm but with longer opening hours in the summer months (see *www.postojnska-jama. eu*). There is a free parking area near the castle and a small kiosk selling entrance tickets and guides. The entrance fee for the castle only is €8 adults, €5.50 children but there are a number of combined tickets available (*Predjama Castle and Cave - €13 adults, €8 children, Postojna Caves and Predjama Castle €21 adults, €16 children*). If coming by public transport the nearest place the buses will take you is **Bukovje** village wherefrom it's a leisurely 2km walk to the castle.

▶ Beneath the castle the **Predjama Cave** is really a network of caves and passages around 140 metres deep. To date over 13 kilometres of the caves have been explored, making it the second largest cave system in Slovenia. This karst underworld was created by the Lokva stream which hollowed out the limestone strata of the Nanos and Hrušica plateaus. The underground stream surfaces in Vipava, over 13kms away and then flows to the Adriatic.

Casual visitors are able to explore around 1km of the trail but must be of a reasonable fitness as a little climbing is required and the trail is unlit so torches and appropriate clothing and footwear are necessary. There are three routes into the caves, the best known of these is via the Stable, where traces of Late Stone Age and Copper Age habitation have been discovered, along with finds dating from Roman times. A particularly interesting feature is the Passage of Names, with signatures of visitors from the 16th century onwards. Due to its position and temperature conditions, the cave has gained some interesting inhabitants, a colony of bats, and for this reason entrance

The caves beneath the Castle are the second longest in Slovenia

The stalactites and stalagmites of Predjama Cave

to the cave is not possible in winter, when the bats are hibernating. Experienced speleologists are able to further explore the numerous passages in this mysterious underworld.

Cave visits last around 45 minutes and take place at 11am, 1pm, 3pm and 5pm from May to September. Entrance is €7 for adults and €4 for children. Longer one to six hour tours can be organised by prior arrangement.

🔢 Cerknica

👪	3,500
ℹ️	Cesta 4. Maja 51, *www.cerknica.si* 017/09 36 36, open 8.30–15.30 daily
🎭	Cerknica Carnival (Sunday before Shrove Tuesday)

Cerknica's famous disappearing-reappearing lake

The town of Cerknica is famous for the disappearing-reappearing **Cerknica Lake** (*Cerkniško Jezero*), a rare natural phenomenon. For the majority of the year the Cerknica karst is a typical dry field with the Stržen stream flowing through it. However, in springtime and autumn or with any abundant rainfall it mysteriously transforms into the largest lake in Slovenia, 10km long and 5km wide. When full, the lake even has an island with a tiny village on it – Otok, on its south side.

It is hard to believe, but the lake can fill up within a day and disappear again almost as quickly. The phenomenon has puzzled people as far back as Greek geographer Strabo and remained unexplained until Valvasor (see page 181) explained it in a paper sent he to the Royal Geographic Society in London. Underneath the field is a maze of caves with numerous siphons and sinkholes which are fed by the waters of underground streams, when the system fills faster than it can outflow (again underground) the water gushes out, creating the lake.

Today the lake dries up far more often than in the past and it has become very unpredictable. Part of the problem is due to the dense vegetation covering the lake. In the past herds of cattle grazed the pastures but now this tradition remains in only one part of the Cerknica karst. However Notranjska Regional Park plans to try to restore the lake, though this will take years to fulfil.

Cerknica Lake when fully reappeared

▶ If you're not lucky enough to be in Cerknica when the lake is full, there are still plenty of other things to see and do in the surrounding areas. The town itself is small with only one real main street, Cesta 4. Maja, and has a handful of shops and, on Saturdays during the summer, a small market. Head south of the city to the village of **Dolenje Jezero**, which stands on the shore of the lake, when it's there. There you will find the **Museum of Lake Cerknica "Jezerski hram"** (*tel. 01/709 405 3, http://jezerski-*

Cerknica Lake, now you see it, now you don't

Stunning views from Planinsko Polje

hram.si, admission adults €7, children €5 that has a multimedia presentation and a scale model of the phonomenon, as well as a small ethnological collection.

▶ The water from the lake creates **Unica River** in Planinsko Polje a few miles to the north. When full the river is very popular with fishermen. The tourist office in Cerknica can assist with fishing licences, maps and further information.

▶ If you wish to walk in the area, a fine choice is the path which leads from the centre of town to the top of the **Slivnica** peak (1114m) where the mountain cabin

Dom na Slivnici awaits you for a rest and refreshment or to pause and admire the view. The car park behind Bar "Kekec" in the centre of town is the starting point for the walk which is well marked. It should take a little over an hour to reach the cabin.

▶ On the south edge of the field, the **T'Dolenj farm** (*Kmetija T'Dolenj, tel. 041/36 34 21, kmetija.tdolenj@gmail. com*) offers guided tours of their Venetian sawmill and granary

The mountain cabin Dom na Slivnici in winter

built in 1746. They also produce and sell apple vinegar, liqueurs and spirits from their home-grown apples, pears and plums and can give a presentation of the distillation process.

▶ The picturesque karst valley of **Rakov Škocjan** is just minutes from Cerknica. This wonderful area was first discovered by tourists at the beginning of the 20th century and the area was designated

The Rak stream flows under a stone bridge

a regional park in 1949, among the first in Slovenia. The 2km long karst valley is created by the Rak ("Crab") stream that has carved out numerous caves and bridges in the limestone.

▶ The valley, which is well marked, can be entered from either end, either coming from Cerknica or when leaving

The karst features of Rakov Škocjan

Mali Naravni Most

the motorway towards Unec. There are parking areas at either end so you can either stop and look at one end and continue by car to the other end or walk through the valley (approximately 3h end to end). In the southern part of the valley stands the impressive remains of a tunnel known as the **Little Natural Bridge** (*Mali Naravni Most*) whilst standing at the other end is the **Big Natural Bridge** (*Veliki Naravni Most*). An educational footpath leads through the park with information boards (currently only in Slovene).

13 Snežnik Castle

Snežnik Castle (*Grad Snežnik, www.postojna-cave.si, only guided tours on the hour 10-18h May-Oct and 10-16 in Nov-Apr, €4 adults, €3 children, €8 families*), the best preserved castle in the Notranjska region, stands at the end of the tranquil Lož Valley (*Loška Dolina*), next to the village of **Kozarišče**.

The castle dates back to 1268 when it was first mentioned in manuscripts as Schneeberg Manor. It was first owned by the Aquileian Patriarchs and later had several different

Snežnik Castle

The pleasant grounds around the Castle are perfect for long walks

owners, the last of which was the German Schönburg family that used it as a summer residence and hunting post up until the end of World War II. The family's household items, period furniture, numerous hunting trophies and the castle's original fittings have been well preserved giving visitors a real glimpse into life in the past whilst a further room is full of fantasy Egyptian-style furniture.

The castle is built on a rock at the source of the Obrh and Brezno springs which have been dammed into a large pool. The oldest part of the castle is the three-storey tall core while the lower stone walls surrounding it date back to the renaissance. The outer towers and the arched stone bridge leading to the entrance

Mount Snežnik looking majestic on a summer's day

are 19th century additions. The picturesque surroundings have been arranged into a park with walking and riding paths but these are yet to be restored to their original appearance.

▶ Be sure not to miss the **Dormouse Collection** (*Polharska Zbirka, tel. 01/705 76 37, open Wed-Fri 10-13 & 15-17h, weekends 10-13 & 14-19*), housed in a former dairy adjacent to the castle. This small museum must be surely fairly unique and contains everything you could possible wish to know about the humble dormouse as well as – like it or not - catching and turning this plump rodent into delicious specialties.

▶ A stage of the E6 European Hiking Trail leads from Snežnik Castle to the **peak of Snežnik** (1796m), some 15km to the south, the highest non-Alpine mountain in Slovenia. If you don't want to walk all the way, a good starting point for shorter hike is Leskova Dolina on the main road towards Ilirska Bistrica. From there you have a bit over 3hrs of walking on a marked trail. Just below the top is the Draga Karolina mountain refuge (*tel. 051/61 53 56, open daily in August, May-July & Sep-Oct on weekends and holidays*).

The Draga Karolina mountain refuge

14 Metlika

👥 3,200

ℹ️ Trg Svobode 4,
www.metlika-turizem.si
073 635470, Open Mon-Fri 8am-5pm, 9am-1pm
(off-season hours vary)

🧗 Vinska Vigred wine festival (May)

Metlika (30km from Novo Mesto) is one of the two most important towns in Bela Krajina (the other being Črnomelj) and is certainly the more attractive of the two. The town is on the border with Croatia with only the **Kolpa River** and the border control post, separating the two countries.

A view over Metlika old town

Metlika has had a turbulent and interesting history since it was granted town rights in 1365. Beginning in 1408 it was subject to numerous attacks by the Ottomans who at one point actually occupied the town. The town was attacked and set alight seventeen times over the course of the next 170 years and also survived a major earthquake at the end of the 17th century. The townsfolk gradually re-grouped and rebuilt and, rather fittingly, it was here that in 1869 Slovenia's first fire brigade was established. During World War II the town was once

The Kolpa on the border with Croatia

Metlika Castle, an imposing fortress, seen through autumn leaves

again damaged by the Italians who burnt many of the buildings to the ground but the townspeople showed their fortitude and rebuilt the town once more.

Metlika has a compact town centre which, from the outskirts, doesn't look too promising, it too has fallen victim to the new large supermarkets that are springing up at a rapid pace throughout the country. However the attractive old town, built in the 18th century on a hill above the town retains much of its character.

▶ The **old town** consists of three main squares, Mestni Trg, Trg Svobode and Partizanski Trg which house all its main sights. **Metlika Castle** (*Metliški Grad, Trg Svobode 4*), formerly a fortress, played a key role in the defence against the ferocious Ottoman raids in the 15th and 16th centuries. Entrance is through the three-story tower that opens into a spacious

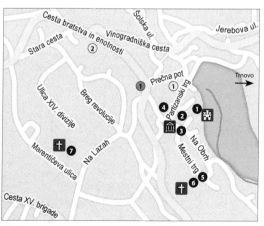

HOTELS:

1 Hotel Bela Krajina

RESTAURANTS:

1 Restaurant "Gastro"

2 "Kava Bar" Cafe

1 Metlika Castle

2 Slovenian Fire Fighting Museum

3 Trg Svobode

4 Partizanski Trg

5 Mestni Trg

6 Church of St. Nicholas

7 Church of Ss. Cyril & Methodius

arcaded inner courtyard. After the fires in 1705 and 1790, renovations followed and the castle survived World War II without sustaining any major damage. The Castle now houses the **Bela Krajina Museum** (*www.belokranjski-muzej.si, 073 063370, open Mon-Sat 9am-5pm, Sun & Holidays 10am-2pm, entrance fees €3 adults, €2 children, €2.50 pensioners*). Exhibits in three rooms show archaeological and cultural history together with ethnological collections from the region

An old-school fire pump at the Fire fighting Museum

The Church of St. Nicholas in the town square

from prehistoric times to the middle of the 20th century. On the ground floor there is a winegrowing exhibition and a winery where visitors can sample and buy the locally produced Bela Krajina wines.

▶ Next door to the castle is the **Slovenian Fire Fighting Museum** (*Slovenski Gasilski Muzej, Trg Svobode 5, 073 058697, open Mon-Sat 9am-1pm, Sun & holidays 9am-12pm, entrance free*) which was opened to mark the 100th anniversary of the first fire brigade in Slovenia. The museum's exhibitions are housed in two areas. The first presents the development of fire fighting until World War II and includes numerous photographs together with fire fighting equipment, uniforms, medals, tools and fire engine models. The hall area documents the founders of Slovene fire-fighting and contains an impressive hook ladder from 1889. The cellar houses old fire engines received as donations from the Technical Museum in Bistra.

▶ The town also boasts three churches. The most impressive is the **Church of St. Nicholas** (*Cerkev Sv. Nikolaja*) in Mestni Trg and the only of the three in the old town. Originally from 1334, it burnt down during the Ottoman invasion in 1578, was rebuilt, then burnt down again in 1705. Today's Baroque church was modelled on the church of the Virgin Mary in Ljubljana and has frescoes of the Day of the Judgment. The **Church of Ss. Cyril & Methodius** in Marentičeva Ulica was built in 1903 and is one of only two Greek Catholic churches in Slovenia. The local Greek Catholic priest is the only Slovenian iconographer and has exhibited numerous works around the world.

▶ A pleasant walk and just 2km south-east from Metlika, is the village of **Rosalnice** with its three famous pilgrimage churches '**Tri fare**'. The three gothic churches clustered together within high cemetery walls were built in 15th and 16th centuries. All three of them have been subject to significant remodelling throughout the

The Greek Catholic Church in Metlika

The 'Tri Fare' gothic churches in Rosalnice

the three, is dedicated to **Our Lady of Sorrows**. Its interior is especially impressive and contains a late Baroque altar and pulpit along with numerous statues and frescoes. The central church, dedicated to **Ecce Homo**, meaning 'Behold the Man', is the only of the three with a bell tower. Its most notable feature is the main altar which is flanked by images of saints and wall paintings dating from 1862. The third church is dedicated to **Our Lady of Lourdes**. On its exterior, graffiti dating back to 1565 has been uncovered as have the remains of a fresco of the Crucifixion dating from around 1500.

ages but still bear Baroque and Gothic hallmarks. The northern church, the largest and considered to be the oldest of

15 Črnomelj

5,700

Trg Svobode 3,
www.belakrajina.si
073/056530, open Mon-Fri 8am-11pm, 12pm-4pm, Sat 9am-12pm

Jurjevanje (June)

Črnomelj Castle dates back to the 12th century and houses the town museum

Črnomelj (*45km from Novo Mesto*), the largest town in Bela Krajina, lies at the confluence of the Dobličica and Lahinja rivers. It is generally considered to be the shabbier of the regions two major town's (the other being Metlika), but it is still worth visiting for its history and you can

form your own opinion. Unlike Metlika, medieval Črnomelj managed to escape the wrath of the Ottoman invasions. Despite

Črnomelj from the air

The Church of St. Peter on Trg Svobode

muzej.si, 073/056530; visits by arrangement, entrance fee €1 adults, €0.50 children). It exhibits the natural and cultural heritage of the town with emphasis on the 19th and 20th centuries as well as a display of a 20th century worker's kitchen featuring the 'cuisine of our grandparents' from the 1950's.

▶ There are two churches in the old town core. The single spire Baroque **Church of St. Peter** in the main square (*Trg Svobode*) is nothing remarkable except for the Roman tombstones which are built into the walls. More interesting however is the nearby gothic **Church of the Holy Spirit** (*Ulica Mirana Jarca*) which is located on ancient grounds where

their numerous and incessant attempts to take it, the town's good fortifications and well-placed hill-top lookouts to the west, meant it was never conquered and actually thrived during the 16th century. Over time, however, Črnomelj lost its significance and prosperity until, like Metlika, the building of the railway line in 1914, had a strong influence on the re-development of the town. During World War II, the town played a significant role hosting the first session of the Slovene Parliament.

▶ There are not a huge number of sights to see within the town itself but the town's position and proximity to the river Kolpa and the wine growing areas, have helped boost its popularity. **Črnomelj Castle** (*Črnomaljski Grad, Trg Svobode 3*), parts of which date from 1165, now houses offices, a restaurant and the **Town Museum Collection** (*www.belokranjski-*

The Gothic Church of the Holy Spirit is one of the focal points of the town

human traces from the Neolithic period have been found. It contains a mosaic and apse from the late antiquity (4th-5th c.). It was first mentioned in 1487 but has witnessed many ups and downs including being severely damaged during World War II. It was renovated and reopened in 2007 and is now once again the central focus of the old town.

▶ At the **Wine Information Centre of Bela Krajina** (*Trg Svobode 3, 063/056 530*) you can get acquainted with the local wines. Along with tasting the wines, they can teach about the characteristics of each wine, the technology of production and growing conditions and can arrange visits to wine growers and makers.

Find out about Črnomelj's wine cellars at the Wine Information Centre

The marshlands of the Lahinja Regional Park

▶ The **Lahinja Regional Park** *(9km south of Črnomelj)* comprises the source and the upper 7km of the river Lahinja, its many marshlands rich in flora and fauna and the fascinating villages of Veliki Nerajec and Pusti Gradac *(see below)*. The park also offers several marked theme trails for walking or cycling and you can also go boating on the river (boats available to hire at the tourist farm "Klepčeva Domačija") in the village of Pusti Gradac).

▶ The village of **Veliki Nerajec**, which won a European award for "Countryside Development and Village Renovation", is home to the **Park Information Centre** housed in a 200 year old ex-residential house which also contains an arts and crafts gallery. As well as giving out information about the park itself, the centre offers an insight into the traditional way of life of the people of Nerajec and by arrangement a local can show you around the village and let you sample the village speciality *ajdova potica* made from buckwheat flour, water, salt and cottage cheese. In the centre of the village is the Kholz Family Chapel (*Kapelica Sveta Družine*) made by Austrian sculptor Joseph Rifesser in 1906.

▶ The tiny village of **Pusti Gradac** is the sight of a rare uninhabited prehistoric settlement. Guided trips can be arranged (via the Park Information Centre) to view the archaeological sites of Okljuk and Draga as well as the site of a 16th century castle and a display of archaeological items. The Klepec mill and Venetian sawmill in the village are both still active and here you can also purchase flour. A great way to see more of the Regional Park is by walking or cycling on the marked path which leads from Pusti Gradac through the forest past Mala Lahinja to the nature reserve at Lahinjski Lugi and to the source of the river Lahinja (approximately three hours on foot).

The lush greenery bordering the Lahinja

Due to the abundance and diversity of accommodation available in South Slovenia – not to mention the difficulty of keeping printed listings current – we chose to provide just a quick overview. For full up-to-date listings of hotels, hostels and other accommodation we recommend you go online. You also can get accommodation advice and bookings from **Slotrips.si**.

Novo Mesto

	Name	Website	Address	Tel.
Hostel	**Hostel Situla**	www.situla.si	Dilančeva ulica 1	+386 7 394 20 00
★★★★	**Hotel Krka**	www.terme-krka.si/si/hotel_krka	Novi trg 1	+386 7 39 42 100
★★	**Hotel pri Belokranjcu**	www.hotel.pribelokranjcu.si/	Kandijska cesta 63	+386 7 302 84 44

Metlika

	Name	Website	Address	Tel.
★★★	**Hotel Bela Krajina**	www.hotel-belakrajina.si	Cesta bratstva in enotnosti 32	+386 7 305 81 23

Postojna

	Name	Website	Address	Tel.
Hostel	**Hostel Proteus**	www.youth-hostel.si	Tržaška cesta 36	+386 5 726 52 91
★★★	**Hotel Sport**	www.epiceco-hotels.com	Kolodvorska ulica 1	+386 5 720 22 44
★★★★	**Hotel Kras**	www.epiceco-hotels.com	Tržaška cesta 1	+386 5 700 23 00

Dolenjske Toplice

	Name	Website	Address	Tel.
★★★★	**Hotel Kristal**	www.terme-krka.si	Zdraviliški trg 7	+386 7 39 19 991
★★★★	**Hotel Vital**	www.terme-krka.si	Zdraviliški trg 1	+386 7 391 94 00

Otočec

	Name	Website	Address	Tel.
★★★★★	**Otočec Castle Hotel**	www.terme-krka.si	Otočec	+386 7 384 86 00
★★★★	**Hotel Šport**	www.terme-krka.si	Otočec	+386 7 38 48 600

Postojna

Restaurant Špajza   *Ulica 1 Maja, Postojna* ☎ 05/726 45 06

A warm, welcoming family run little restaurant. Resonably priced good food.

Pizzeria Minutka   *Ljubljanska cesta 14, Postojna*

A decent pizzeria and good value for money.

Jamski Dvorec   *Jamska cesta 30, Postojna* ☎ ☎ 05/700 01 61

A touristy restaurant just at the entrance to the caves. Decent food and excellent service.

Novo mesto

Don Bobi   *Kandijska cesta 14, Novo Mesto*

A classy restaurant perfect for a romantic dinner. Surprisingly reasonable prices.

Restaurant Grad at Otočec Castle   *Grajska cesta 2, Novo Mesto*

Extraordinarily good food in a truly unique setting. Well worth spending a little more for.

Gostilna in prenočišča Vovko   *Ratež 48, Novo Mesto*

A fulfilling dining experience. Welcoming and friendly service.

NORTHEAST SLOVENIA

Vineyards near Maribor

✛ Facing fierce competition from the natural wonders of the Alps, the Karst and the Adriatic, Northeast Slovenia doesn't often make it onto visitors' lists of things to do and see. This is a shame since the region boasts a rich Roman inheritance, Slovenia's oldest and grandest thermal spas, the eastern Alps, historical cities and plentiful vine-covered hills. For anyone who really wants to get to know Slovenia, a visit to its less travelled half is a must.

✛ Northeast Slovenia, as defined for the purposes of this guide, comprises three historical provinces. The largest of the three is Štajerska (historical Styria), starting from the Alpine valleys in the west and ending with the tame scenery of the Jeruzalem wine-country. In the northwest is Koroška, a small portion of Carinthia wrestled from Austria, amounting to just three valleys deep in the Alps. In the East is Prekmurje ("beyond the Mura river"), a region of plains and rolling hills as closely linked to its previous master Hungary as to the rest of Slovenia.

✛ People from the capital or Gorenjska often see this region as being all about agriculture and industry. It is true that Slovenia would have a hard time without the country's industrial centre, Maribor, without the hops of the Savinja Valley, beer from Laško or the wheat of the Prekmurje plains but this does not make it a less desirable destination. In terms of character,

A view of the Pohorje Massif near Maribor

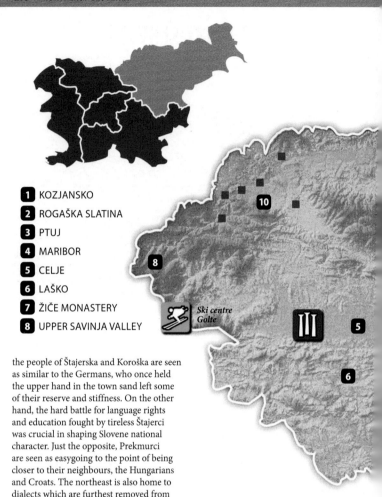

1 KOZJANSKO

2 ROGAŠKA SLATINA

3 PTUJ

4 MARIBOR

5 CELJE

6 LAŠKO

7 ŽIČE MONASTERY

8 UPPER SAVINJA VALLEY

Ski centre Golte

the people of Štajerska and Koroška are seen as similar to the Germans, who once held the upper hand in the town sand left some of their reserve and stiffness. On the other hand, the hard battle for language rights and education fought by tireless Štajerci was crucial in shaping Slovene national character. Just the opposite, Prekmurci are seen as easygoing to the point of being closer to their neighbours, the Hungarians and Croats. The northeast is also home to dialects which are furthest removed from

The captivating Alpine scenery of Logarska Dolina

literary Slovene. Competition with the capital, however, makes folks from Maribor keen on keeping this distinction alive, just as a desire for uniqueness keeps Prekmurci speaking what could easily be a separate language.

✦ If it is hard to characterise Northeast Slovenia in terms of geography and character, there is nothing easier than pointing tourists to what it has to offer. Start with what most people come to Slovenia for – winter sports – and you will discover the Pohorje Massif and the ski slopes near Maribor (p. 229). If you're into beautiful Alpine scenery head for the picture-perfect Logarska Dolina (p. 247) or the less travelled corners of mountains Peca and Uršlja Gora for all kinds of outdoor sports (p. 250). If this wears you out, indulge yourself with a stay in one the spa towns, from the grand old lady of Rogaška Slatina (p. 221), via

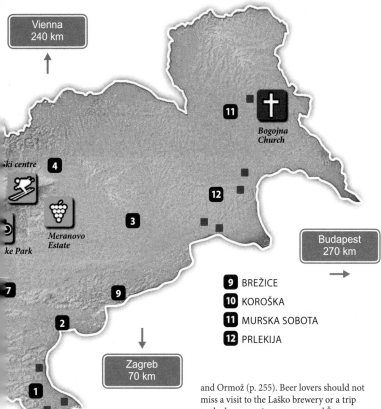

Vienna
240 km

ki centre **4**

3

Meranovo
Estate

ke Park

7

9

2

1

11

Bogojna
Church

12

Budapest
270 km

Zagreb
70 km

9 BREŽICE
10 KOROŠKA
11 MURSKA SOBOTA
12 PRLEKIJA

Dobrna to Moravske Toplice and their hot sulphur-laden black waters (p. 254). Wine lovers will be delighted by the sight of hill after hill of vineyards between Ljutomer and Ormož (p. 255). Beer lovers should not miss a visit to the Laško brewery or a trip to the hop-growing areas around Šempeter (p. 241). To round things off, visit Ptuj (p. 224), arguably Slovenia's prettiest town, with its castle, small streets and squares, as well as many reminders of it Roman past, or buzzing Maribor whose students keep reminding the rest of the country how hard they like to party (p. 229).

Mt Peca dominates the landscape of Koroška

1 Kozjansko

ℹ Podčetrtek – Škofja Gora 1 (main intersection);
www.turizem-podcetrtek.si
03/81 090 13; open Mon-Fri 8am-3pm, Sat 8am-1pm
Bistrica ob Sotli – Bistrica o/S 17;
03/800 1500; open

The rolling countryside of Kozjansko

Kozjansko is the name for a region along the Sotla river that forms the border with Croatia roughly between Podčetrtek in the north and Bistrica ob Sotli in the south. The region has long time ranked amongst the poorest in Slovenia but its relative isolation has in recent years been turned to its advantage by promoting it to visitors as a corner of unspoiled natural beauty. What puts Kozjansko on to the tourist map is above all the Regional Park, established in 1981 to protect its great natural diversity.

10am Fri & Sat; all day ticket adult/child Mon-Fri €10.50/8) with no less than eight pools and all the other amenities to suit even the fussiest guests. Its thermal waters, gushing from several springs, are of various temperatures but are all slightly radioactive (hence the spa's old name) and said to have curative powers for a number of ailments.

The modern buildings of Olimia Spa

▶ If you approach to Kozjansko from the north you will first encounter the **Olimia Spa**. Its older name Atomske Toplice ("Atomic Spa") was dropped with a recent face-lifts that has turned it in one of the most up-to-date and popular spas in Slovenia. The spa blends with the townlet of Podčetrtek as have their names so don't be confused if less precise maps don't distinguish between them.

▶ The Olimia Spa has two parts. On the north is the **"Aqualuna" water park** with 3000m² of pools and slides *(tel. 03/829 77 00; www.terme-olimia.com; open 1 May-31 Sep 9am-6pm every day; admission adult/child Mon-Fri €11.50/9, Sat, Sun & holidays €13.50/10.50)*. The larger part of the spa is one kilometre down the road. Here there are three hotels, bungalows and two restaurants arranged around the **spa centre** *(03/829 7805; open Sun-Thu 8am-10pm, Fri & Sat 8am-midnight, saunas only from 11am Sun-Thu and from*

▶ Round the next bend on the main road or a short walk through the woods behind the hotels brings one to **Podčetretek**. First mentioned in 1209 by its German name Landsberg that continued to be used until 1918, in the 15th century the place got the rights to hold markets on Thursday, which led to the forming of its unusual name (literally "Under Thursday"). The road to the right from Podčetrtek's modern centre takes you to the old centre past the small **Museum of Old Village Equipment** *(Trška cesta 46; tel. 03/810 92 56; open by appointment)*.

The Aqualuna water park

Podčetrtek

century. The **old pharmacy**, situated in one of the towers, was established in 1765 by Paulines who were known for their study of medicine. The wooden shelves and ceramic utensils in its round interior are modern day reproductions but the marvellous **wall paintings** are originals by Anton Lerchinger, created in 1780. He painted famous surgeons, medical herbs, the preparation of medicines etc. in a Rococo style. In this unique setting the welcoming monks will offer you tea, tinctures and

▶ Taking the road to Olimje from Podčetrtek's main roundabout will lead you to the **Church of St Mary on the Sand** (*Cerkev Marija na Pesku*) notable for its massive early Baroque belfry and its steep roof. Inside, there are interesting paintings from 1712 as well as altars and organ from the same period. Further down the road is the **"Haler" restaurant** (*tel. 812 12 00*) where they brew their own pilsner and dark beer and also offer guided tours of the brewery by prior arrangement.

The Church of St Mary on the Sand

creams made with herbs grown in the monastery garden.

▶ Back on the main north-south road, we pass through tiny scattered villages in a countryside ideal for biking. **Bistrica ob Stoli**, whose houses lie scenically grouped on a plump hill, lies 14km to the south of Podčetrtek. Contrary to its name, the stream passing by is not the Sotla but the Bistrica. The townlet's name features in all Slovenian schoolbooks as the place of two battles, the first in 1475 when raiding Turks defeated the local army and the second in 1573 when feudal lords cut down rebelling peasants, ending their insurrection. During the Nazi occupation of WWII Bistrica, as all the other settlements in the region, was

The Olimje Monastery

▶ The core the charming **Olimje monastery** (*Samostan Olimje; www. olimje.net; tel. 03/582 91 61; open Mon-Sat 9am-12pm & 1pm-7pm, Sun 1pm-7pm; admission €1 adults, €0.50 children*) is the square Renaissance fortress built by Count Tattenbach in 1550. A century later this was given to Pauline monks who in 1663-75 erected the adjoining **Church of Assumption**. The gray and white decoration of the church was extended to the whole complex giving it its memorable appearance. Inside of the church one can admire Illusionist paintings on the ceiling, several golden altars and the highly ornate chapel of St Francis, all from the mid 18th

Bistrica ob Sotli

The Doctor's House in Bistrica ob Sotli

emptied of its Slovenian population and resettled with Germans from Kočevlje. The place is also linked with the childhood of Josip Broz Tito, the lifelong communist ruler of Yugoslavia: born in Kumrovec just across the border with Croatia, he spent his summer holidays in Bistrica visiting his maternal grandparents, times he remembered as "the nicest moments of my youth". His cult of personality was such that the local primary school was named after Tito's Slovene mother, Marija. The fact that Kozjansko could boost a rebellious anti-feudal past, strong anti-Nazi sentiments and that it was the native place of Tito were all crucial factors in its nomination as the second Regional Park in socialist Slovenia.

▶ At the top of the hill is the parish **church of St Peter**, a gothic edifice remodelled in Baroque fashion. Next to it is the yellow **Doctor's House**, with naïvely charming façades.

▶ The road towards **Podsreda** follows the Bistrica river where it enters a 3km

The church of St John the Baptist in Podsreda

long **ravine** (*Soteska Bistrice*), a corner of untouched nature. To approach it take the road branching left just after Zagaj, the first village next to Bistrica ob Stoli; note that the road ends in the middle of the gorge which is impassable for all but the most experienced hikers.

▶ Just under 4km from here is **Podsreda**, a perfectly preserved medieval marketplace where, judging by its name, on Wednesdays (literally "Under Wednseday"), peasants from the local area would come to sell their produce and buy

Handmade pottery

locally made pottery. All of its houses are arranged in an elongated square ending with a parish church. Not much of their medieval appearance survived the 1798 fire but a well preserved **pillory** inscribed with date 1667 still stands in the middle of the square, a sign of the judicial rights of the local mayor whose house faces it. Wrongdoers would be chained to the column while the metal tablet above it was used to inscribe their name and crime.

▶ The marketplace developed beneath **Podsreda Castle** (*tel. 03/58 06 118; open 1 Apr - 31 Oct 10am-6pm except Mon; admission €4 adults, €2.50 children*) which still stands high above it. If taking the road to the castle, look out for a poorly marked left turn that leads between the farmhouses. The castle, originally known as Hörberg, was established in the 12th century by the Bishop of Krško. Luckily for today's tourists, it played no role in the tumultuous historic events of the region and is today almost unchanged from medieval times. Like all Slovenian castles it was neglected after becoming state property in 1945 but its reconstruction over the last three decades has made it into one of the best places for a genuine Slovenian castle experience. In the

Podsreda Castle, unchanged since medieval times

The inner courtyard of Podsreda Castle

narrow inner yard you will see Romanesque arches, half timbered floors and the newest addition - the Renaissance arcades. Most of the castle's maze-like interior is used an as exhibition space with permanent collections of glasswork and local history.

2 Rogaška Slatina

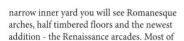

👥 4,800

ℹ️ Zdravliški trg 1, 03/581 44 14, open Mon-Fri 8-16h, Sat & holidays 8-12, Sun closed

🚆 Kidričeva 29, tel. 03/581 48 99

🚌 Kidričeva 1, tel. 03/81 92 510

👫 Rogaška Musical Summer, late June

The hotels of Rogaška Slatina

Due to its curative mineral waters Rogaška Slatina has been on the tourist map for centuries. It has long been the most fashionable resort in a region where well-being and relaxation have been as important as healing. Though not as exclusive as it once was, this old spa town tries hard to maintain this prestigious image, capitalising on the beautiful scenery surrounding it on all sides and offering active holidays that attract guests from around the world.

The first person known to have benefited from Rogaška's three mineral springs, rich in magnesium and sodium, was a Styrian count who visited it in 1574. The news spread and soon the first inn for the sick, also selling bottled water, was opened. It was around then that a legend emerged of Apollo ordering Pegasus to break open a spring in the rock with his hoof and drink to recover his health and strength. Today Apollo embellishes the bottled water "Donat Mg" and Pegasus the town Coat-of-arms. The early 19th century was a golden epoch for Rogaška Slatina, when it was frequented by the likes of Napoleon's brother Louis, Archduke Johann Habsburg, the King of

The Grand Hotel Rogaška

The music pavilion on Zdravilíski Trg

Netherlands and the Parisian Rothschilds, some entertained by Franz Liszt who held concerts here. In 1927 local craftsmen opened a glassworks and soon the glass and crystal from Rogaška became its second trademark.

▶ The heart of the spa is the airy **Zdravilíski Trg** with its neatly landscaped classicist park surrounded by the spa's grandest buildings. Among them "**Grand Hotel Rogaška**" with its long yellow façade and the impressive classicist portico with Styrian arms stands out. Built in 1912 for the Spa Centre, its sumptuous **Crystal Hall** (*Kristalna dvorana*), named after the chandeliers from the Rogaška Glassworks, contains four 1912 paintings showing milestones in the spa's development.

▶ At the upper part of the square you will find another building that draws its inspiration from antiquity, the "**Temple**" (*Tempelj*), a pavilion from 1819, which

stood above the spa's central "Styria" spring before it was capped deep underground in 1952 and redirected to the Pivnica (*see below*). Today it serves as a music pavilion and is the focal point of Rogaška Musical Summer festival.

▶ The 12-storey tall glass tower closing the square is the "**Therapy**" (*Terapija*) where most of the curative programs are concentrated. To the left of it is the **Pivnica**, a round glass hall where you can drink mineral waters directly from the Styria and Donat springs from numerous fountains (*open every day 7am-1pm & 3pm-7pm; free entry, get a glass from Terapija's reception*).

Rogaška Slatina is famous for its glassworks

The "Donat Mg" water here differs from the bottled water you may have seen in cafés and restaurants in its very high concentration of magnesium that might not quite suite everyone's taste. Nevertheless, it might be worth trying considering the lengthy list of its curative properties.

▶ Walk behind the Therapy building to find the **Chapel of St Anne**, the protector saint of the spa. There was a chapel here since the spa's founding but don't be mislead by its rustic appearance: this is its fourth incarnation, designed in 1926 by Jože Plečnik. Next to it is the Baroque statue of St John of Nepomuk, erected in 1732 by Viennese apothecaries to commemorate the finding of another mineral spring.

▶ At the other end of the square from Terapija is a low secessionist building from 1904 which houses the **Glass Showroom** (*open Mon-Fri 8-16h*); here you can buy or just admire various pieces of cut crystal and glass from stemware to vases produced in Rogaška's famed glassworks. An even a wider choice of products can be seen in the outlet by the factory, south of spa center (*Ulica Talcev 1*). You can also arrange a group visit to the glassworks where you will see the skilled workers moulding and cutting the melting glass.

The Therapy building on Zdravilíski Trg

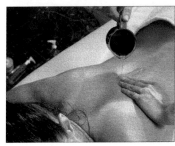

Enjoying a relaxing massage at Lotus Terme

▶ Zdraviliški Trg is also where most of the activities connected with **taking in the waters** take place. The "Therapy" is

Strmol Castle in Rogatec

where people visiting the spa with health problems come but it also offers various baths for casual visitors. To the left of the Therapy and Pivnica is the top-notch **Lotus Terme** (*www.rogaska.si*) where you can indulge in thermal baths, massages and saunas. There is a similar offer (including thermal waters pool, health bar and gym) at the **Vis Vita Wellness Centre** between the Styria and Strossmayer hotels (*www. terme-rogaska.si; open Sun-Thu 8am-8pm, Fri & Sat 8am-11pm*).

▶ Just 6km to the east of Rogaška Slatina is the townlet of **Rogatec** from which the spa got its name. It lies

One of the halls of Strmol Castle

next to the Sotla River, which today forms a border with Croatia while in previous centuries it was a border between the Holy Roman Empire (of which Slovenia was part) and the Hungarian state.

▶ Rogatec's focal point is a sizable square, simply called **Trg**, surrounded by two-storied houses and adorned by a late 17th century Marian column. On the hill above it stand two 18th century churches; the lower one is the parish **church of St Hieronymus** with fine frescoes from 1743 while the upper one, **St Hyacinth**, hosts the town cemetery. The benefit of climbing up to them is predominantly in the view over the town centre.

▶ The main attraction of the town is the picturesque **Strmol Castle** on its northern edge. In the 19th century it housed the local court with the town jail conveniently located in the cellars while after WWII it was turned into flats. Inside you can find a wine cellar, restaurant or take a look at one of temporary exhibitions (*open 1 Apr– 31 Oct Tue-Sun 10am-6pm*). Guided tours are available, covering its two classicist halls and the Baroque chapel (*€3 per person, contact 03/81 072 86*).

The Church of St Hieronymus looks down on Strmol Castle

▶ Most people come to Rogatec to see the **Open-air Museum** (*03/81 86 200; open 1 Apr – 31 Oct Tue-Sun 10am-6pm; admission adults €3, students €2.60, families €6*) located a few minutes walk up the road from Strmol Castle. Though rather small, the museum offers an insight into peasant life, with lot of details that you will learn about such as why the girls' sleeping room had barred windows and a squeaky door.

▶ Heading westwards from Rogaška Slatina for 12km you can reach **Šmarje pri Jelšah,** a small town in a pleasant hilly setting that

The church of St. Roch in Šmarje pri Jelšah

▶ The **Church of St Roch** on the hill above the town is its most important sight. Dedicated to the saint protector against the plague it was erected after Šmarje got rid of the deadly disease in 1645. The nicest way to reach the church is to follow the winding path up the steep hill starting with the St Roch's Chapel. The church is an austere edifice done in a (very) late Gothic style, its **interior**, however, is a different story. Decorated in 1738 it is a real explosion of playful rococo forms and sparkling details. Note the excellent stucco work as well as the paintings depicting the life of St Roch but also Šmarje during the time of plague.

developed in the shades of Jelšingrad, a 15th century fortification remodelled in a curious mix of neo-Gothic and oriental styles in 1860. The castle, in dire need for repairs, is sadly not open to public.

3 Ptuj

👥 23,250

ℹ️ Slovenski trg 5,
www.ptuj.info
02 77 960 11; open Mon-Fri 8-16h,
Sat & holidays 8-12, Sun closed

🚆 Osojnikova cesta 2,
tel. 02 292 47 34

🚌 Osojnikova cesta 11,
tel. 02 77 11 491

👫 Kurentovanje Carnival, February

A view of Ptuj across the Drava

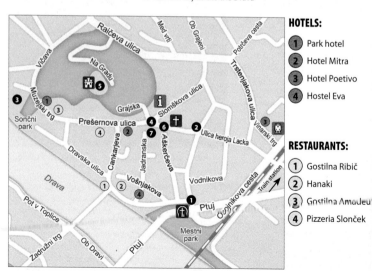

HOTELS:

① Park hotel

② Hotel Mitra

③ Hotel Poetivo

④ Hostel Eva

RESTAURANTS:

① Gostilna Ribič

② Hanaki

③ Gostilna Amadeu

④ Pizzeria Slonček

① Minorite Monastery
② Mestni Trg
③ Dominican Monastery
④ Slovenski Trg
⑤ Ptuj Castle
⑥ Church of St. George
⑦ City Tower

The resplendent lights of Ptuj at dusk

Ptuj ranks as one of the most beautiful towns in Slovenia and is arguably its most historic, with a plethora of Roman, medieval and Baroque monuments packed along its charming streets, in its fine churches and excellent museums. If you are not a museum hound, you will find the surrounding countryside, especially the Haloze hills and vineyards, reason enough to visit Ptuj and enjoy the tranquil pace of life here. The city also hosts Slovenia's most famous carnival, the Kurentovanje (see box on p. 229).

Ptuj is one of the oldest inhabited places in Slovenia, continually settled since Neolithic period, thanks to its position where the Drava River is slow, wide and is easy to cross. The **Romans** conquered the local Celts around 15 BC and established a military camp on the right bank of the river. It was here that in AD 69 the Pannonian Legions declared their support to Vespasian and helped him to become the Emperor of Rome. This momentous event described by Roman historian Tacitus put **Poetovio** (Roman Ptuj) on the historical map. During the 3rd and 4th centuries, with more than 10,000 inhabitants and a stone bridge, Poetovio was the most important

A view across Ptuj

Roman city in present day Slovenia. These prosperous times came to an end in 452 when Poetovio was sacked by the Huns on their way to Rome.

Though the city now lay in ruins the crossing was still there and it attracted the new Slavic settlers. In the 9th century the small town was one of the most valued possessions of the **Archbishops of Salzburg**, protected by their local vassals, the Lords of Petau, as it was called in German. By the mid 13th century Petau would have looked fairly familiar to us: two monasteries, a parish church and numerous burghers' houses surrounded by town walls. In **1376** it was declared a city in a long statute, the oldest surviving legal document of this kind in Slovenia.

The golden age of Ptuj came to an end during the 1500s as the Turks cut the old trade routes and threatened the city. Great fires in 1684 and 1705 sealed its fate though the burned down houses were rebuilt in an opulent Baroque style. When the railroad connection passed through Maribor, Ptuj's greatest trade rival, in the mid-19th century it was clear that the city's future lay in its glorious past: a Society for Care of Town

An illustration of medieval Ptuj

and Tourism was established as early as 1886.

Prior to WWI ethnic Germans were a majority in the town and they were not the least bit happy when their city became part of a South Slav state in 1918. As the tables turned in 1941 the Nazi occupiers were willingly embraced here and, to make place for ethnic Germans resettled here from elsewhere in Slovenia, the Nazis forced more than 1,200 Slovenes out of their homes. In 1945 it was the local Germans' turn to run and German Petau became Slovene Ptuj.

Ptuj Town Hall

The interior of the church of St Paul in the Minorite Monastery

Considering its rich history you might be quite surprised how small the old town is. It is still much the same as it was during the town's golden age in the Middle Ages, squeezed between the Drava and the crest of Castle Hill.

▶ The best place to embark on a tour of the old town is from Minoritski Trg, close to the river. The square takes its name from the **Minorite Monastery**, *Minorite* being another name for Franciscans. The monastery was established in 1239 and its Gothic church was the first edifice of that style in Slovene lands. It survived all of the town's perils, not least the reforms of Joseph II, only to be abolished in 1941 by the Nazis who sent the friars off to Croatia. As if tied to its friars' fate, the monastery was almost destroyed by Allied bombing raids in 1944. What remained served as a post office and a

library in communist times. The renovation that took the best part of the last two decades gave it back its church including the late 17th century frontage, the earliest example of Baroque on such a scale in Slovenia. Inside the monastery (*open by prior appointment, tel. 059/073 000*) the most precious sight is the first-floor summer **refectory** with a rich stuccowork and paintings

▶ A short walk along Krempljeva Ulica will bring you to **Mestni Trg** (Town Square) whose most prominent feature is the new City Hall. Built in 1907 it features all the obligatory elements (such as a clock tower) and its style reflects the German fashion of the period. Rising from the centre of the square is he **Column of St Florian**, the saint protector against the fires that ravaged the city before and after it was built in 1745. Note his little helpers spilling water onto the burning castle at his feet.

▶ The short Murkova Ulica leads to **Slovenski Trg**, the historic core of the

Ptuj City Tower and the small theatre at it's base

old town. Here you'll find one of the best known sights in town, the tall white marble block called the **Orpheus Monument**, named after the central relief depicting the hero grieving for his beloved Eurydice with laments so beautiful they charm even wild beasts. This was a funerary stone of Marcus Valerius Flerus, the 2nd century major of Poetovio. Shortly after it was discovered in the 16th century, the monument was put to use as a pillory with holes for the chains seriously damaging the inscription.

▶ Behind the monument are the tiny **Theatre** from 1892 on the right and the **City Tower**, a notable part of the cityscape, on the left. Initially a church belfry, it was heightened to serve as a watchtower at the pinnacle of the Turkish scare in the 16th century. Roman tombstones found around the city built into its base in the 1830s now serve as a sort of primitive open-air museum.

The Church of St George

▶ The parish **Church of St George** is the city's most cherished architectural monument. It is probably as old as the Christian faith in Ptuj: this was the site of a basilica in Roman times and of a church built below the castle in the 9th century. The present day church dates back to the early 12th century with a superimposed Gothic guise and Baroque details such as the side chapel. Note the Renaissance tombstones built into the church walls.

▶ At the end of **Prešernova Ulica** is the former **Dominican Monastery**, clearly discernable by the playful Baroque stuccowork of its façade, which makes it resemble a huge cake. The well established monastery was dissolved by Joseph II and turned into a hospital, later becoming a barracks until it was bought by the city authorities in 1926 and turned into a **regional museum**.
   Scattered throughout the monastery you will find the Museum's rich **archeological**

The Orpheus Monument on Slovenski Trg

collection (*open April 15th – Dec 1st 10-17h; combined ticket with the castle collection child/adult €3/5*). Look out for the fine **Gothic cloister** with modest remains of 15th century frescoes and the exhibition of Celtic and Roman coins including the two clay piggy banks in the **old refectory**. The highlight of the collection is in the former church, now turned into a **lapidarium**: sarcophagi, mosaic floors, altars to various deities, sculptures from the famous shrines of Poetovio dedicated to sun god Mithra, as well as busts of emperors Tiberius and Hadrian, regarded as the finest in the whole of Slovenia.

▶ The steep climb up to the **Ptuj Castle**, the historical treasure chest of the city, starts from the Monastery. Construction of the castle started around 1140 and in the 16th century it was additionally fortified against the prospect of a Turkish attack, most of what we see today dates from this and the next centuries. The castle changed hands between a number of noble families, notably Leslies (Scotts in Habsburg service) and Herbersteins, until it was taken over by the state in 1945. Today it houses most

Detailed carvings at Ptuj Castle

The inner cloister of Ptuj Castle

of the exquisite **Regional Museum of Ptuj**, one of the best loved museums in the country (*open May 1ˢᵗ - Oct 15ᵗʰ daily 9-18, otherwise 9-17, except on weekends in July and August 9-20h; admission as above, guided tours €10*). On the ground floor of the castle is the **Armory**, filled with weapons from Medieval times to WWII and the **Music Collection** (across the courtyard), the largest in Slovenia with over 300 different musical instruments, including a Roman flute from the 2ⁿᵈ century AD. Rooms on the first floor have been fitted with stylish furniture from the mansions around Ptuj displaying different fashions (such as a Chinese salon) and several highly valuable works of art. The second floor is home to the **ethnographic collection**, showing rural way of life from the 19ᵗʰ and early 20ᵗʰ centuries. You can also see the **Sluga Collection** presenting life from the early 19ᵗʰ century, and the **France Mihelič Collection** of graphics and drawings.

▶ The Church of **Ptujska Gora**, crowns a hill in the village of the same name 13km south from Ptuj on the road to Rogatec.

Ptujska Gora church is an important destination for pilgrims

This is one of Slovenia's most important destinations both for pilgrims and for art lovers who flock here to see this gracious Gothic church and the relief of the Virgin of Mercy. Founded around the year 1400 where there was no church before and named Neustift in German ("New Foundation"), Nova Štifta in Slovenian. Its Latin name Mons Gratiarum ("The Hill of Mercy") denotes its importance as a pilgrimage site that a also became a place for weekly markets and annual fairs. Another name for the area is Črna Gora ("Black Hill"), from the legend that, in order to protect it from a Turkish attack, the Virgin Mary covered the hill in a black cloud. The church interior is

A view of the rooftops of Ptuj from the Castle

simple and unruffled but is overflowing with precious artwork. The **high altar** is an exquisite Baroque work as is the relief of the Virgin Mary with her cloak held up by angels to shelter the faithful. Also note the Gothich **altar of Fridrich II of Celje** and the detailed **Gothic frescoes** including an unusual scene of St Dorothy helping a young Jesus pick flowers.

▶ For those arriving by public transport, Ptujska Gora is accessible by a number of buses heading daily from Ptuj to Majšperk. Alight at the station of the same name from where it is a ten minute walk uphill to the church.

The exquisite high altar in Ptujska Gora church

Chasing out the Winter

Every February or early March, ten days before the start of Lent, a carnival called Kurentovanje takes place in Ptuj. This is the largest carnival in Slovenia, with crowds of up to 100,000 taking part in processions. The event's origins come from the ancient South Slavic traditions of chasing away the winter and welcoming the spring. This custom was adapted by the Church which allowed it as a period of merry making, eating and reckless fun culminating on Shrove Tuesday. The Shrovetide processions in villages around Ptuj were slowly dying out when they were revived by ethnographers and enthusiasts in 1960 as a carnival of village masks. The carnival was named Kurentovanje ("kurenting") after its most impressive and most popular figure – the Kurent, a spirit of unrestrained partying and merry making. The mask, previously worn only by young unmarried men, is made out of sheep skin, with cow bells, a long tongue and topped with horns or feathers. Kurents go about in groups, dancing and whirling their clubs with hedgehog spikes to scare off evil spirits and are led by deamons with nets to catch wayward souls. Local masks were soon joined by similar carnival characters from the region and today Kurentovanje has carnival guests from around the world. Nowadays, the main event – the procession of masks through Ptuj – takes place on Shrove Sunday while on other days there are numerous performances in the Town Hall or in a large carnival tent.

4 Maribor

	120,000
ℹ	Partizanska 6a, www.maribor-pohorje.si 02/234 66 11, open Mon–Fri 9am–7pm, weekends and holidays 9am–6pm
🚆	Partizanska Cesta 50, 02/29 22 164
🚌	Mlinska 1, 02/23 50 212
🎉	Lent Festival, late June–early July

Fine architecture in Maribor's old town

Slovenia's second city in size and in overall importance, Maribor is the economic and cultural centre of the

A statue of Bacchus on Slovenska Ulica

Štajerska region and indeed of the whole east of the country. However, do not call it a *provincial* centre - Mariborčani see their city as equal, if not superior, to the capital. This is mostly thanks to the town's industrial might, largest theatre festival, first Slovene daily and Slovenia's most successful football club since the country's independence. Its attractive pedestrianised town centre, river walkways, museums, festivals and a nightlife fuelled by a large student population make it a worthwhile stop.

The seed from which Maribor grew emerged in the 12th century when Marchburch (later Marburg), the "March Castle", was built north of today's city centre. Merchants, including Jewish traders, engaged in wine and timber trade by the Drava river, however, the city's heyday ended with the arrival of an economic crisis and the Turkish threat in the 15th century.

HOTELS:

1. Hostel Uni
2. Hotel Piramida
3. Hotel Bellevue
4. Hotel Lent
5. City hotel Maribor

RESTAURANTS:

1. Pizza Verdi
2. Art restaurant Andre Petan
3. Kitaski Žad restaura
4. Restaurant Gala Žar
5. Takos
6. Baščaršija

1. Water Tower
2. Synagogue
3. Oldest Vine
4. Main Square
5. Plague Column
6. Town Hall
7. Slomškov Trg
8. Cathedral
9. Slovene National theatre
10. Grajski Trg
11. The column of St. Florian
12. The Castle
13. National Liberation monument
14. Trg Svobode
15. Franciscan church
16. Titov most
17. Mestni park

The prosperous Jewish community was forced out and a century later the same fate befell those who opted for Protestantism. Already shaken, it was crippled during the 1600s as three plague epidemics eradicated a third of the population. In 1846 Maribor was one of the first cities of the Habsburg Empire to get a rail connection with the imperial capital, triggering rapid growth.

The old coat-of-arms of Maribor

At the beginning of the last century Maribor was an overwhelmingly German town, with Slovene spoken only by one fifth of its inhabitants (in fact, its present-day name was coined only in the mid-19th century by poet Stanko Vraz). It was, however, the centre of the Slovenian nationalist movement in the province of Styria. In the turmoil at the end of the First World War it only narrowly escaped becoming a part of Austria. Between the two World Wars Slovenes were favoured in public service so that when the German army marched into the town in 1941 the local Germans greeted it with open arms. The task set by Hitler during his visit to the town was to turn it back into Marburg by resettling thousands of Slovenes, inflicting grave terror against all who resisted the Nazi regime. The last of the Germans left in 1945, their place taken by Slovene workers as the Yugoslav communists turned the town into an industrial centre. The loss of the Yugoslav market and the privatisation of state-owned industrial giants in the early 1990s shook Maribor's economy so seriously that the population shrank by 10,000, but in recent years the city has recovered.

Maribor is very much a student town thanks to Maribor University

▶ **Lent**, Maribor's old harbour on the northern bank of the Drava was the commercial heart of the city for many centuries as rafts and ships transporting wood downriver docked here every day. Since river trade has declined Lent has become a place of leisure with several cafés and restaurants that fill up fast on sunny days.

A view of Titov Most

▶ Starting from Titova Cesta and Titov Most the first sight is the **Water Tower**, a hefty piece of defensive architecture built in 1555 by Italian masters to protect the wharf from Ottoman invaders.

▶ Across the road is the **Synagogue and the Jewish Tower**, the only remains of a once thriving community that had commercial connections across Central Europe. The 14th century synagogue, a square edifice with long Gothic windows, is one of the oldest in Europe. After the expulsion of the Jewish community in 1497 it was turned into a church, then a warehouse and in the end into flats, but today it houses a **collection** on the life and

culture of Jews in Maribor (*02/252 78 36; www.pmuzej-mb.si; open Mon-Fri 8am-4pm, Sun 9am-2pm; free entry*). The monument in front is dedicated to the Jewish victims of WWII.

▶ A few steps further along the embankment will bring you to the Old Vine House. It's not the house, but the vine that stretches out along the front that is of interest here: tests and research of old documents show it to be more than 400 years old and it is certified by the Guinness Book of Records as **the oldest vine in the world**. In recent years it has become the centrepiece of a wine festival, when wine made from its grapes is bottled and sold dearly or presented to important visitors to the city. There is also a **museum** dedicated to this extraordinary vine (*02/251 51 00; open every day 1 May[i] – 31 Oct 10am-8pm, 1 Nov – 30 Apr 10am-6pm; free entry*).

▶ Despite still being an important traffic artery, the handsome **Main Square** (*Glavni Trg*) has an air of antiquity. Its focal point is the glorious **Plague Column**, erected by the town council to plead for mercy with the saints after an especially ghastly epidemic of 1680/81.

The oldest vine in the world!

The Plague Memorial on the Main Square

▶ Among the Square's ensemble of old houses the **Town Hall** with its clock tower stands out. Built in 1515 it was remodelled half a century later in true Renaissance spirit by artists of the Dell'Allio family. The nice balcony with the town coat of arms was used for public proclamations, of which the most infamous was Hitler's "make this land German again" during his visit to the freshly occupied town in April 1941.

▶ Praised as the most harmonious square in the city, the leafy **Slomškov Trg** was, until 1797, used as a graveyard spreading around the **Cathedral**. Built in the late 12th century, it was overhauled in the Gothic and Baroque eras, while the newest addition is the classicist top of its tall belfry. By its main entrance stands a **monument to Anton Slomšek** (1991), a bishop and Slovene patriot, hailed for his 1859 transfer of the seat of the bishopric from Sankt

The Main Square and Town Hall

Andrä in the German part of Styria to Maribor. During his visit to the town, Pope John Paul II beatified Slomšek, the first Slovene to reach that level of canonisation. The cathedral's interior is surprisingly sober; of interest are the rib vaulted Gothic presbytery and its Baroque choir stalls with scenes from the life of St John the Baptist, the protector of the church, as well as the **chapel of the Holy Cross** (from 1775) where bishop Slomšek is buried.

▶ Back in the open air on the north side of the square is the **Slovene National Theatre**. The older section was built in a neo-Classicist style back in 1852 to suit the needs of a German language troupe and the German club. After WWI the building was taken over by the professional Slovene theatre.

Maribor Cathedral

▶ The triangular Grajski Trg lies in what was once a corner of the enwalled town but today it enjoys a very central position. It is a popular meeting spot and several summer cafés spill out onto it. In the middle of the square is the **column of St Florian**, whose protection was very much needed for a

The Slovene National Theatre

The unusual "baldhead" monument on Freedom Square

town that used to burst into flames every few decades.

▶ The square gets its name from the **"Castle"** (*Grad*), a curious multifaceted building started in 1487 to enforce a weak point in the town's defences. For many centuries the castle was for the most lavish residence in town and as such has seen its share of famous guests – Liszt, who held a concert here in 1846, Pope Pius VI and, yes, Hitler.

In winter Freedom Square hosts a popular ice rink

▶ The *Grad* is home to the **Regional Museum** (*02/228 3551; www.pmuzej-mb. si; open Tue-Sat 9am-4pm, Sun 9am-2pm;*

entrance adults €3, children 2) whose rich collections have long ago ceased to be of regional interest. Don't miss the *kurent* costumes (see p. 229) and the painted beehives as well as models of boats and rafts that once navigated the Drava. There is also a fine collection of costumes and uniforms from the 19th and 20th centuries and a collection of arms in the cellar of the bastion. Be sure to visit the grand **Knights' Hall** with its incredible stucco work and a huge 1763 ceiling painting of a clash of Christian and Ottoman forces.

Cafés spill out onto Maribor's Grajski Trg

▶ Connected with Grajski Trg is the broad **Freedom Square** (*Trg Svobode*), the best part of which is a small market. Also note the **National Liberation Monument** (from, 1975), the round metal structure called "baldhead" (*kojak*) by locals. On this unconventional communist monument you will find scenes from the town's resistance to the Nazis, portrayals of fallen citizens and, of course, Tito.

▶ More interesting than the square itself are the extensive **"Vinag" wine cellars** dug underneath the square in the 19th century (*entrance from the northeast corner of the square; open Mon-Fri 9am-7pm, Sat 8am-1pm*). Part of the 20,000m² of wine cellars, is open to the public in a guided tour. Also

The Baroque staircase in the Regional Museum

The Knights' Hall of the Regional Museum

The Franciscan church, atonement for the sins of Maribor ladies?

guided group tours around the city. The length and cost of the tours depends on the size of the group (*1h tour for up to 5 persons at €50, up to 10 persons €60; 2h tour up to 25 persons €80, up to 50 persons €90*). Alternatively, hire a bike and ramble around on your own (*€2 for 2hrs, €5 for the whole day*).

▶ After a few villas the northern side of Maribor's city centre gives way to the green vastness of the **City Park** (*Mestni Park*). Landscaped in 1872 it was a perfect playground for the bourgeoisie, dotted with fountains, flowerbeds and remarkable tree species crowded with friendly squirrels.

▶ Among the most astonishing sights in Maribor are the vineyard covered hills **Piramida** and **Kalvarija**. The south face of the Piramida hill (384m) provided good conditions for wine growing but the centuries old vineyards have disappeared with the rapid growth of the city. The long rows of Rhine Riesling we see today were planted in 1986 by the town's wine company

worth inspecting is Vinag's shop that sells regional whites as well as plonk from the barrel at bargain prices.

▶ South of the square stands the large **Franciscan Church**, one of the town's best known buildings. Constructed at the turn of the 20th century its neo-Romanesque forms in red brick aimed at bringing northern German architectural traditions to Maribor. A local legend tells that the Franciscans called for each woman in Maribor who has sinned to bring two bricks in order to receive atonement and that the quantity of bricks was enough for a church of this size!

A genteel cruise along the Drava

▶ Directly in front of the church is the **Tourist Office kiosk**, the starting point of the tourist train (*€7.20 per person*) and

Vinag and have since yielded excellent award winning wines. The top of the hill is the birthplace of Maribor, as it was here that Marchburch castle stood until it was raised so thoroughly in 1784 that even its foundations are barely visible. A pyramid of its stones was built as a reminder and gave the hill its name but was replaced in 1824 by a small chapel.

▶ For a genuine trip back in time head to the **Maranovo Estate** (*Posest Meranovo*). A group of small houses enjoying views over the vineyards and south to the city that are hard to match. The estate was founded in 1822 by Archduke Johann, brother of Habsburg

The vineyards on Piramida Hill

The wine cellar of the Vinag wine producer

The Meranovo Estate founded by the brother of a Hapsburg Emperor

Emperor Franz I. The Archduke married the daughter of a post office superintendent and denounced the life of the court to pursue happiness by helping Styrian culture, industry and agriculture. In front of the estate his wooden statue overlooks the vineyards. Today the estate is managed by the Faculty of Agriculture that continues to make its own wine, which you can try in the house's historic cellar (*02/613 22 11; open noon-8pm, except Tue*).

▶ The mountain massif of **Pohorje**, the easternmost tip of the Alps, is Maribor's most incredible feature, a genuine heaven for lovers of active holidays. It is hard to decide whether it is more interesting in summer when you can hike or bike along its many marked trails, or in winter when you can glide down 33km of ski slopes. It is best known for its "Golden Fox" world cup competition for women, held in mid-January, and Europe's longest night run (10km long!). Most importantly, it is all within easy reach: a few minutes

drive or a short ride on the No.6 bus from the city centre and you will be in the suburb of Zgornje Radvanje in front of the cable car ready to transport you to a totally different setting. All of this is even more fun if you

Hiking trails abound in Pohorje

look at it from the reverse angle: how about spending a holiday in Pohorje and then in the evenings descending to unwind in Maribor's restaurants and clubs.

▶ From mid-December to early April the cable car (*Vzpenjača*) runs every half hour

The so-called Black Lake, one of the attractions of Pohorje

Skiing at the Pohorje Ski Centre

The small museum at Areh

between 8am and 8pm (*one way/return ticket adults €8/10, children €7/8*).

A smaller ski-lift which starts by the "Habakuk" hotel and the Snow Stadium (*Snežni Stadion*) takes you to the **Adrenaline Park** half way up the mountain and the beginning of the **"PohorJET" track** and its "MiniJET" kids version, where you descend on a one track sledge.

Biking in Pohorje

▶ At **Bolfenk**, the upper terminus of the *Vzpenjača*, you will find yourself in the centre of a veritable mountain resort, with hotels, a ski school where you can hire skiing or snow-boarding equipment and even a horse-riding centre "Hlev" offering carriage or horseback rides. Look for a disused church, now used by a small **museum** presenting Pohorje's natural and geological past. Another skiers' hub, **Areh**, is located to the west and best reached by the free ski-bus. Between the two you will find cross-country tracks as well as several "hidden" slopes.

▶ In summer, the best way to explore Pohorje is along its 75km long biking transversal but there are tens of kilometres of other biking roads to be explored (get a free copy of the *Pohorje Cycling Map*). Those who are in for a heart pounding experience will visit the **Bike Park**, where the world cup races take place every June.

5 Celje

50,100

Krekov Trg 3,
www.celeia.info
03/42 87 936, open Mon-Fri 9am-5pm, Sat 9am-1pm, closed Sun

Krekov trg 1,
03/29 333 156

Aškerčeva 20,
03/4 25 3400

Medieval days, last Fri & Sat in August

Celje old town

For anyone arriving in Celje for the first time it might come as a surprise that it is Slovenia's third largest town and one of the strongest industrial centres in the country. Lying half way between Ljubljana and Maribor and with no university of its own, Celje is slower paced than these two and has a quiet, almost provincial feel about it. Yet its rich history has left it with an admirable heritage that can be observed in its historic town centre and its rich museums.

Celje lies where the Savinja River suddenly changes its lowland flow turning into the mountains to the south, a region that has been settled since prehistoric times. The Celts developed a trading settlement here with an active silver mint, called Kelea, the town's first name, recorded by Greek historians. The Romans came in 15 BC and promoted it to the rank of *municipium* under the new name Claudia Celeia. These were the glory days of the prospering town as can be judged from Roman ruins found during any construction works in the old town or in the fact that the adapted Roman sewage system is still used today! This all came to an end in 452 when rampaging Huns pillaged the town so thoroughly that it disappeared from historic records for the next 700 years. It appears again in the 12th century as a market for the nearby castle.

Celje Castle sits on a hill above a bent in the Savinja River

It grew in importance in the 14th century together with the rise of the castle's owners, the Counts of Cilli.

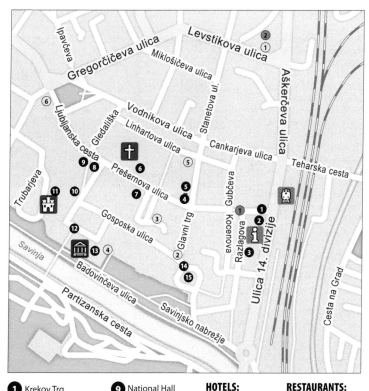

1 Krekov Trg
2 Celjski dom
3 Pelikan photo atelier
4 People's loans society
5 Metropol cinema
6 St. Mary's assumption church
7 Former Town Hall
8 Trg Celjskih Knezov
9 National Hall
10 Wall of Scorn
11 Lower Castle
12 Muzejski trg
13 Regional Museum
14 Slomšek Square
15 Cathedral of St. Daniel

HOTELS:
1 Hotel Evropa
2 MCC Hostel

RESTAURANTS:
1 MCC Kavarna
2 Kavarna Oaza
3 Kavarna "Scotch"
4 Kavarna Miško Knjižko
5 Kavarna Žan Težak
6 Gostilna Asado

The Counts of Celje permanent exhibition at the Regional Museum

After the Counts died out, the town became the domain of Habsburgs who built the strong town walls just in time to prevented Turks and rebellious peasants from taking it. Population growth spurred by the arrival of the railway in 1846 led to clashes between the German majority and the Slovene minority. The Germans held the upper hand until 1918 when the new state of Yugoslavia helped the Slovenes take over. During WWII the situation was reversed once again and the town became one of the centres of the Nazi terror in the country as well as a centre of Slovene resistance. This all ended in 1945 with the expulsion of almost all of the town's Germans. In the socialist era Celje continued to develop and had at one time 17 large factories that employed almost all of its inhabitants and produced brands known throughout Yugoslavia, a prosperity that is still sometimes remembered with a longing sigh.

▶ The **Old Town** is compact and easy to navigate and is where almost all of the sights are. Most of the commercial activities have, however, moved away to shopping malls and the nightlife seems to be moving out too, leaving the centre alarmingly calm some nights.

▶ The most notable building on **Krekov Trg**, which opens in front of the train station, is **Celjski Dom**. Built in 1907 in a mixture of historic styles, "The German House" (as it was originally called) was the response by local Germans to the Slovene National Hall at the other end of town. Today it is the home of Celje's **tourist board** and several other cultural institutions.

Krekov Trg at the heart of the old town

▶ Also nearby is the **Pelikan Photo Atelier** (*Razlagova 5; tel. 03/548 58 91; open Tue-Fri 10am-2pm, Sat 9am-12pm, Sun 2pm-6pm; admission: adults €3, schoolchildren €1.50, families €6*), a glass structure from 1899 complete with cameras, various photo developing devices and photos by the town's most distinguished photographer, Josip Pelikan. Visitors are even invited to pose on the original set for an old-fashioned black and white photo.

▶ Prešernova Ulica continues straight ahead from Krekov Trg. At the next intersection a **stone star** in the pavement marks the symbolic centre of the town, a favourite meeting spot. One corner to the right on Stanetova Ulica is the memorable building of the **People's Loans Society**, designed by Plečnik but built by one of his pupils in 1929. Its wing along Stanetova Ulica houses the **"Metropol"**, an art cinema that also hosts exhibitions and alternative music concerts in its foyer, while on quieter days you can enjoy a drink in its café, which attracts an arty crowd.

Celjski Dom on Krekov Trg

The Metropol arthouse cinema

The former Town Hall, now the Museum of Recent History

▶ Back on Prešernova Ulica, which widens out into an elongated square, opposite the **Church of St Mary's Assumption** we find the **former Town Hall**. Originally this was an aristocratic manor that hosted Pope Pius VI on his way to Vienna in 1782 in his unsuccessful attempt to bring to a halt reforms by Emperor Joseph II. Bought by the town in 1830, the manor was used as the seat of the municipal authorities until 1953. Today it houses the **Museum of Recent History** (*Prešernova 17; tel. 03/428 6410; www.muzej-nz-ce.si; open Tue-Fri 10am-6pm, Sat 9am-1pm, Sun 2pm-6pm; admission €3 adults, €6 families*) with exhibits presenting different aspects of life in the town.

▶ Prešernova Ulica ends in **Trg Celjskih Knezov** (Dukes of Cilli Square). The yellow corner edifice is the **National Hall** built in 1897 in a neo-Renaissance style. The Hall was a hub for the local Slovene community and its activities against "Germanisation" in Habsburg times, while today it is the seat of the regional and city authorities. Just next door is the **"Wall of Scorn"** where in 1942 captured Partisans were tortured and humiliated by the Nazis. The square ends with the back view of the **Lower Castle**, the seat of the Counts of Cilli from the start of the 15th century, later turned

into a barracks, and used as such until 1981. Nowadays it serves as the **Gallery of Contemporary Art** (*Trg Celjskih Knezov 8; tel. 03/42 65 160; open Tue-Fri 11am-6pm, Sat 10am-12pm, Sun 2pm-6pm; free entry*).

The "Celeia, the Town Underneath the Town" exhibition in the Gallery of Contemporary Art

In its cellar and courtyard is a permanent **exhibition "Celeia, the Town Underneath the Town"** which presents archaeological layers of Celje from Roman times to World War II (*tel. 03/4280 960; www.pokmuz-ce. si; open Tue-Fri 10am-12pm & 4pm-6pm, Sat 10am-12pm; admission: €2 adults, €1 schoolchildren*).

▶ Further south is **Muzejski Trg** that takes its name from the **Regional Museum** (*Pokrajinski muzej; tel. 03/4280 962; www. pokmuz-ce.si; open March 1st to Oct 31st Tue-Sun 10am-6pm, closed Mon and holidays; admission: €3.50 adults, schoolchildren €2*) housed in the **Old County Hall**, an attractive building, with arcades stretching the full length of its two storeys, built at the turn of the 17th century. The museum is a rich depository of archaeological

The Counts of Cilli Square

Museum Square and the Regional Museum

findings, art and everyday items, arranged in rooms with period furnishing. Special attention is paid to the Counts of Cilli whose skulls brought from Mary's Church are also on display. Since its completion in 1670s, however, the highlight has been the **Celje Ceiling** in the main hall. Painted by an unknown Italian artist, its central section is a typical *trompe l'oeil* painting creating the illusion of a courtyard with people looking downwards from balconies with the heavens in the form of a cross opening above it. Around it are the four seasons, two battle scenes of Greeks and Trojans and four characters from ancient mythology.

▶ The focal point of the Old Town the is cobbled **Glavni Trg** (Main Sq.), surrounded by old burgher houses and, in the summer months, several open air cafés. In the middle of the square, where a pillory once stood, is the **Plague Column** from 1776, topped by the gilded statue of the Virgin Mary. The south side of Glavni Trg is adjoined by **Slomšek Square**, once the yard

of the **Cathedral Church of St Daniel**, built in the 13th century but thoroughly reconstructed in a Gothic style in the 14th and 15th centuries. Along its outer walls you can see a number of tombstones from various epochs. Inside, the highlight is the **Chapel of the Sorrowful Mother of God** (to the right of the entrance), a Gothic addition financed by the Counts of Celje around 1400, distinguished by rich stone masonry, especially the stone seats with baldachins, the famous pieta (1415) and frescoes from the same period.

▶ The most famous sight in Celje is the **Old Castle** (*Stari Grad, 03/544 3690; open Sun-Thu 9am-8pm, Fri-Sat 9am-9pm in summer, 9am-4pm in winter, admission €2 of*

The Cathedral, built in the 13th century but later reconstructed in a Gothic style

which €1 can be used in the castle café), the ruins of a grandiose fortress perched on a tall hill to the southeast of the town centre. The Romanesque castle was acquired by

The Celje Ceiling in the Old County Hall

The Plague Column dedicated to the Virgin Mary

The Old Castle dominates a rise above the town

the future Counts of Cilli in 1333 (see p. 16) and soon became their seat of power. Over the next hundred years they built and rebuilt extensively turning it into one of the largest castles in the region. Later it was sold to a local farmer as a stone quarry. Its devastation was halted in 1846 when the ruins were bought by the local governor who began its reconstruction, which continues to this day.

▶ In the middle of the Castle's courtyard is the massive **Frederick's Tower**, now an interesting gallery space – head to the top to enjoy sweeping views over Celje.

▶ The small town of **Šempeter**, 14km west of Celje, is known for rich archaeological findings from Roman times when it was positioned on a prominent road between Emona (present day Ljubljana) and Petovio

Frederick's Tower rises above the ramparts of the Old Castle

The Roman Necropolis in Šempeter

(Ptuj). The road to Šempeter leads through the broad and fertile valley of the Savinja river, once compared by an Italian traveller to the Promised Land. The vicinity of the Šempeter is especially known for hop growing. The most important site is the **Necropolis**, just south of the town centre (*open 16 Apr – 30 Sep every day 10am-6pm; admission adults €4, children €3*), displaying over a hundred tombstones, including some of the most impressive and best preserved in Central Europe. During the 1st and 2nd centuries AD rich patricians of Celea/Celje were buried here along the road as was Roman custom.

6 Laško

👥 3,800

ℹ️ Trg Svobode 8 (next to the bus station), *www.stik-Lasko.si* 03/733 8950, open Mon-Fri 9am-5pm, Sat 9am-1pm, closed Sun

👥 Beer & Blossoms, second weekend in July; *www.pivocvetje.com*

A view over Laško

The name of this small town has been made famous throughout the world by "Laško Pivo", the beer made in the country's largest brewery. This is the reason many come here today, but there is more to this place than a sip of good beer at the source.

Laško developed on the Savinja river, sheltered by sparsely populated mountains, like Mount Hum (583m), rising above the town. It lived off petty trade and mining, passing from the hands of one feudal lord to another and trying to survive Ottoman raids. Then in 1816 a road from Celje to Zidani Most was built and everything changed. Taking advantage of the abundance of clear water a brewery was opened in 1825. The healing potential of the thermal springs, known since time immemorial but not properly utilised because of flooding, were noticed immediately. In 1858 the first spa facilities and covered pools began to welcome guests. Today it might seem that everything of any importance in this clean and pretty town is owned or sponsored by the brewery but, after all, you won't hear anyone complaining about it.

▶ The focal point of Laško's miniature old town of just a few snaky streets is the spacious **Aškerčev Trg** with its **Virgin Mary Column** from 1735. The town's main sight, the **Church of St Martin**, also lies on the square. Inside one can see several Renaissance tombstones and several lushly gilded Baroque altars.

Laško Museum

▶ **Laško Museum** stands on the same square (*Aškerčev Trg 5; 03/734 0 236; open Tue-Sat 9am-5pm; admission €3 adults, €2 students, €6 families*), presenting the town's past from fossils and prehistory to brewing and spa tourism. To climb to **Tabor Castle** take the street leading uphill from the square, then the first (unmarked!) left turn and then the dirt path indicated by a green arrow. The fort, laid out in 1328, was burnt down by the Turks, in 1487. With the danger of Ottoman invasion gone, the castle

The church of St Martin on Aškerčev Trg

fell into disuse, from which it was revived in the mid-1980s by the Laško Brewery which turned it into a luxurious restaurant with a winery and a popular wedding hall. The castle's position offers great views of the town, however, for truly unmatched vistas reaching all the way to Pohorje in the north, take the walking **trail to the top of Mount Hum**, starting just behind the castle.

▶ Head north past the Town Park to the **Laško Spa** complex. With two recently renovated hotels, outdoor and indoor pools, thermal waters from 32 to 35˚C, different saunas (Roman, Turkish, Finnish…) as well as all the different kinds of massage, health and fitness programs you can imagine.

▶ **Laško Brewery** was founded by local gingerbread and mead producer Franz Geyer. Its rise to a beer industry major was not swift or without pitfalls: in 1889 it went bankrupt, in 1924 it was bought by the rival Union Brewery from Ljubljana

The point of Mount Hum rises above Laško

The famous Laško brewery

The church of the Holy Mother of God in Marija Gradec

and, to top it all off, in 1945 it was bombed by the Allies, but it survived. To hear more about these and other stories and to see its brewing premises take the guided tour, arranged through the tourist office. For the price of €6.50 per person you will be taken to see the Laško Museum, its modern brewing facilities and, of course, to sample its produce along with a small snack.

▶ Just a few minutes walk to the south of the brewery you reach the village of **Marija Gradec**. At the entrance of the village is the **church of the Holy Mother of God**. The church is famous for its frescoes from 1526 influenced by the Italian Renaissance, note God the Father with St Anne surrounded by angels in the vault. If you haven't had enough of grand views of the town head to the **Church of St Michael** in **Šmihel**, its twin towers rise above the town at a height of 442m.

7 Žiče Monastery

The ruins of the **Carthusian monastery of Žiče** as well as the church in the hamlet of Špitalič are among the most important (and most impressive!) medieval monuments in Slovenia. While the church serves the needs of Špitalič the ruins of the monastery have been conserved and are run as a museum. After purchasing a ticket every visitor receives an audio guide, while groups get a guided tour, both of these will provide you with detailed information that

The Carthusian monastery of Žiče

goes beyond what we could fit into this guide.

One of the towers of the rather well fortified Charterhouse

▶ The **Žiče Charterhouse** lies at the bottom of a peaceful and secluded valley, sheltered on all sides by dense woods and quite far from any larger settlement, perfect for the Carthusians who try to keep away from worldly matters. The monastery was founded in 1160 as the first monastery of the order outside of Romance language speaking countries. According to the rules of the order the monastery was built following the layout of the monastery at Chartreuse in Burgundy (hence the name "charterhouse"). The so called Upper Monastery (now in ruins) was reserved for monks who spent their days in solitude, working and praying, while the Lower Monastery (today the Špitalič church) was built for lay brothers who took care of the fraternity's everyday needs. The well respected monastery attracted learned monks whose main activity was copying (or even writing) books and with

Hymns recorded by Žiče monks

time Žiče boosted a library with over 2000 manuscripts, the largest in the region. The Charterhouse survived the Turkish incursions and the peasant uprisings of the 16th century but was finally dissolved in 1782 by order of Emperor Joseph II.

To reach the monastery by car or bicycle head for the village of Žiče and continue through the valley. You will first arrive at Špitalič, the Upper Monastery follows 2.5km later. There is a large car park to the right of the road but if there are not too many people around you can also drive up a bit closer. Local buses run from Konjice to Spitalič, though you will have to cover the rest of the road on foot.

The ruins are open from 1 April to 30 November, 9am-6pm in spring and autumn and 9am-8pm in summer. Tickets are purchased in the bulky medieval building by the road that houses the tourist office. A restaurant called **Gastuž** (from the German *Gasthaus*; tel. *03/752 3700; open Tue-Thurs 10am-6pm, Fri-Sun 10am-8pm*) has been reinstated here and serves specialties prepared in the monastic kitchens. Dating from 1467, the inn claims to be the oldest in Slovenia and even Central Europe.

The Gastuž inn from 1467, certainly one of the oldest in Central Europe

8 Upper Savinja Valley

> **Mozirje**, Smihelska Cesta 2 (on the roundabout), 03/8 39 33 34, open Mon-Fri 9am-5pm, Sat 9am-1pm, closed Sun
>
> **Gornji Grad**, Attemsov trg 3; 03/839 18 50
>
> **Ljubno o/S**, Plac 3; 03/838 14 92; open 9-12h & 13-16
>
> **Luče**, Luče 106; 03/839 35 55; open Mon-Wed 7.30-10.30 & 11-15, Thu 12-15, Fri 7.30-10.30 & 11-13, closed on weekends
>
> **Solčava**, Solčava 30 (across the post office); www.solcavsko.info; 03/83 90 710
>
> **Lôgarska Dolina**, Plesnik Hotel; www.logarska-dolina.si, 03/838 9004

The upper reaches of the Savinja river, from its source in Logarska Dolina to the flatlands around the townlet of Šempeter (see p. 241) are regions whose natural beauty is beyond doubt. With its green meadows, prosperous villages set against a backdrop of deep forests

The Savinja River

and towering Alps it is an idyllic landscape often found on the front-pages of tourist brochures. From the deep glacier valleys to gentle hills crowned with white churches, the mantle of its beauty keeps changing with every bend of the Savinja.

A rural corner of Slovenia without major settlements, Upper Savinja remains difficult to reach by public transport, even in high season. There are regular buses from Ljubljana and Kamnik for Gornji Grad wherefrom you can continue to Radmirje or Mozirje. From Celje there is only one daily bus in this direction but it's still your best bet since it runs the whole length of the valley to Solčava.

Astounding mountain views in the Upper Savinja Valley

too much even for garden-loving Slovenes, the park also features a small open air ethnographical museum.

The breathtaking landscape of the Upper Savinja Valley

▶ If coming by car along the Ljubljana-Maribor highway you will reach an exit for **Mozirje,** the largest settlement in the valley. Mozirje's main sight is **Mozirski Gaj** ("Mozirje Grove"; *03/583 27 19; open early Apr – mid Oct 8am-7pm; admission €5 adults, €2.50 children*). Apart from a multitude of flowerbeds so orderly that at moments they seem

▶ The second exit on Mozirje's roundabout sets you on the road towards the **Golte Ski Centre** (*www.golte. si*). The winding road climbing upwards to some 1,070m offers excellent views to the south but can't equal those from the cable car starting from the village of Radegunda (*same road, first left*) and departing on the hour, every hour between 8am and 6pm. Though Golte is primarily a ski centre it makes sense to visit in summer for mountain biking, a trip into the icy Ledenica Cave or paragliding across the valley.

▶ Take time out to visit the **Museum of Forestry and Logging** in **Nazarje** (*03/839 16 13; open Apr-Nov Tue-Sun 9am-5pm, Dec-Mar Tue-Fri 8am-2pm; admission €3 adults, €2 schoolchildren & students, kids free*). The museum, where you will learn just about everything on the industry that kept the Upper Savinja region going for

The quaint little village of Mozirje

The Golte Ski Centre is equally charming without the snow

One of the sawmills along the Savinja

centuries, is housed in the greatly restored Vrbovec Castle, of whose nine-century history sadly very little remains. The Savinja, a fast and unpredictable Alpine river, used to power hundreds of sawmills, an activity that ended with the advent of better roads and trucks.

The wondrous Snežna Jama

who built their summer residence here and were soon spending more time here than in the capital of Carniola. The grand new Baroque **Church of Ss. Hermagoras & Fortunatus**, the largest church in Slovenia, was built in the mid-18th century modelled on the Ljubljana cathedral. To the right of the entrance is a remaining part of the St Andreas altar, a 1527 masterpiece showing influences of late Gothic and early Renaissance styles.

▶ Beyond **Ljubno**, with its pretty white houses and **collection on Savinja log-rafting** (*open Mon-Fri, 9am-noon & 1pm-4pm; admission €1.50 adults, €1 children*), the scenery changes as the mountains draw closer in to the road. Before entering the village of Struga (3km from Ljubno), note the car park opposite the restaurant; this is where a small road branches off towards the **Snežna Jama** ("Snow Cave"), 17km up the mighty Raduha mountain (*03/572 48 66; open 1 June-30 Sept on weekends, 15 July-31 Aug every day 9am-5pm; admission €7 adults, €5 children & students*). At 1500m Snežna Jama is the highest cave in the country and its interior is a combination of rock and ice formations.

▶ Back on the main road leading to Logarska dolina, after some 10km take a left turn for Radmirje, climbing up through rustic scenery of great beauty leading to **Gornji Grad**. This townlet consists of a few streets clustered in the shadow of a large church. Originally the location was occupied by the only Benedictine monastery on the territory of present-day Slovenia. After its dissolution in the 15th century the location was taken over by the bishops of Ljubljana

Luče in winter

▶ Back down by the Savinja, the road suddenly narrows as you enter **Luče** and continues as the main street of this Alpine village. Luče is the starting place of many rafting tours, site of the only camp in the area ("Smiča", 1km along the road) and the best place to stock up on supplies, get some more money from the bank or have a drink in one of its village bars.

The magnificent landscape of Logarska Dolina

▶ If short on time, head directly to the breathtaking **Logarska Dolina** (Logger Valley) a few kilometres down the road. With its floor

Rinka Waterfall is Slovenia's tallest

covered in green meadows contrasted against the craggy sides this glacially shaped valley seems to have popped out straight of a geography textbook. Its fairytale beauty draws tourists from far and wide, not least Slovenes paying homage to one of the iconic sights of their homeland.

At the entrance to the valley is the small info point where you will have to pay €4 if you would like to continue on in your car (note that this is valid for one entry only). Not only do cyclists and pedestrians enter for free but they are further rewarded since every few meters there is another stunning view to behold. Along the 7km of the valley's length lie long-established farms, the predominant form of accommodation in the area.

▶ At the valley's head look out for signs directing you on a 15min walk up to the **Rinka Waterfall** (Slap Rinka), just

beneath the source of the Savinja. At an impressive 90m it is the country's tallest, however, its gushing springtime vigour dies down to a thin drip down the rocks in summer. From here experienced climbers can proceed to a number of peaks, the most attractive walks being past the source of the Savinja to Frischaufov Dom cabin at 1,392m, on to Kamniško Sedlo pass (1,884m) with great views over Logarska valley and Mrzla Gora (2,203m) on the border with Austria.

▶ If you get tired of fellow tourists, the two refuges near at hand are the two valleys running almost parallel with Logarska Dolina and of comparable beauty. To the west is the deep **Matkov Kot** ("Matk's Corner") where you can walk to the 50m deep ice abyss of **Matkov Škaf** (1,500m), shaped by falling water . On the other side is **Robanov Kot** ending with several sharp peaks such as Ojstrica (2,350m).

Logarska and Solčavsko are not just for hikers and cyclists: inquire at the tourist office for horse riding and carriage rides, paragliding, rock climbing, archery or kayaking. In winter, there are only two small ski-lifts (keep in mind that this is a protected natural area) but there are around 15km of cross-country tracks.

Matkov Kot runs parallel to Logarska Dolina

9 Brežice

6,600

Cesta prvih borcev 18,
07/49 66 995, open Mon-Fri 10am-
5pm, Sat 10am-2pm

Trg vstaje 3; 07/49 61 293

Cesta svobode 11; 07/499 42 80

Brežice Castle and the town's jolly red rooftops

The southernmost town of Styria, Brežice is in the centre of the lower Sava valley, right next to the famous Čatež spa, and a great place from which to explore the Bizeljsko region, known for its excellent wines and welcoming farmsteads.

Exhibits in the Posavski Museum

▶ **Brežice Castle** (*Brežiški Grad*), the focal point of the town's historic centre, closes the long main street, Cesta Prvih Borcev, on the south side. During the great peasants' revolt of 1515 the castle was burned to the ground not to be rebuilt until 1529 when Emperor Ferdinand Habsburg wanted to strengthen his defences against Turkish raids. In the next 20 years Italian masters built what we see today – a quadrangular renaissance

A view of Brežice with the water tower in the foreground

fort, a combination of practicality and geometrical harmony. The new fortification served its purpose well and Brežice was the only castle for miles around that survived the peasant rebellion of 1579. The counts of Attems, who owned the castle in the 18th century, are to be thanked for the **grand staircase** decorated with trompe ľoeil paintings, just a warm up for the magnificent **Knights Hall**, completely covered in Baroque frescoes depicting themes from classical mythology.

▶ The castle houses the **Posavski Museum** (*www.posavski-muzej.si; tel. 07/46 60 517; open Mon-Fri 8-14.30h, weekends and holidays 10-14; admission €2.50, children €1*) with exhibits on the peasant uprisings, World War II and archaeological and ethnographical collections.

The Bizeljsko region is famous for its wines

▶ The region to the north of Brežice, the **Bizeljsko** region is well known for its wine production. You can obtain a brochure from the Brežice tourist information on the local wine road but, on the other hand, that is not essential since heading for any of the villages in this hilly but tame region you will find at least one or two wine cellars. Heading straight north will lead you past the scenic village of Bizeljsko to Orašje (to the right of the main road), above which looms the 16th century **Bizeljsko Castle**. Head for the castle's cellar, where you can taste and buy local wines.

🔟 Koroška

👪 74,000

ℹ️ **Slovenj Gradec**, Glavni Trg 24, 02/88 12 116; open Mon-Fri 8am-4pm, weekends 9am-12pm

Dravograd, Trg 4. Julija 7, 041/318 973

Ravne n/K, Trg Svobode 21, 02/82 21 219; open Mon-Fri 8am-4pm, Sat 8am-12pm

Črna n/K, Spodnje Javorje 8, 02/870 48 10

The valley of the Drava river in Koroška

Koroška is the smallest Slovenian province, consisting of three river valleys surrounded on all sides by mountains. This backwater region is all that Slovenia got of the Dutchy of Carinthia, nine tenths of which ended up as Austria's Kärnten. Small and isolated, with its unintelligible dialect and rough men, Koroška seems distant and different even to other Slovenes.

What it lacks in size, Koroška makes up for with unexplored beauty. Long known as a mining region, in recent decades transformed it into a heaven for outdoor activities lovers, known for its extensive biking routes, scenic hiking paths, alpine and free climbing, a ski centre, even two small sport air fields.

▶ Though historically not part of Koroška, **Slovenj Gradec** is today included in the statistical region with the rest of the province. In the late 15th century it was unfortunate enough to be plundered first by the Turks and then by the Hungarians but

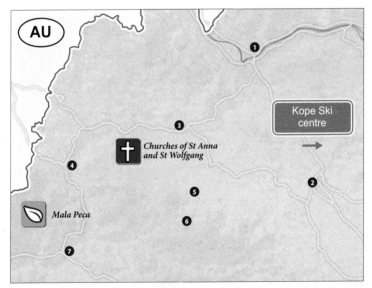

Churches of St Anna and St Wolfgang

Kope Ski centre

Mala Peca

1 Dravograd

2 Slovenj Gradec

3 Ravne na Koroškem

4 Mežica

5 Ivaračko jezero

6 Uršlja gora

7 Črna na Koroškem

Koroška

continued to thrive mainly due to its many skilled craftsmen and artists, for which it was famous throughout the region. After the First World War many ethnic Germans, previously a majority in the town, left for Austria, while the reminder fled before Slovene Partisans in 1945. Today Slovenj Gradec is still known for a relatively large number of painters and sculptors, who safeguard its title as the culture capital of Koroška.

▶ Still, do not expect to find yourself in an art Mecca – Slovenj Gradec hides its talents well, behind its mask as a run-down small town. Its core is the pedestrianised **Glavni Trg** lined with old two-storied burgher houses. The house at No. 24 is the former Town Hall, now the local tourist office and the **Koroška Regional Museum** (*www. kpm.si; tel. 02/884 20 55; open Tue & Thu*

The winter sun catches the top of Mount Peca

A display at the Koroška Regional Museum

10am-1pm; admission €2, children €1.50). Its archaeological collection displays finds from the Roman settlement of Colatio, an ancient necropolis and a Slavic burial ground while the second floor presents local and regional history. The first floor is home to the **Fine Arts Gallery** (*02/88 22 131; open Tue-Fri 9am-6pm, weekends 9am-12pm & 3pm-6pm; admission: €2.50, concessions €1.7*) whose exciting collection of modern art could be the envy of much larger town. Its main hall has rotating exhibitions, focusing on interesting local talent, such as Karel Pečko and the cheerless Jože Tisnikar.

▶ Facing the Museum and Gallery are two old churches. The larger one is the parish **church of St Elisabeth of Hungary**, built in 1251 and later remodelled in a Gothic style, while its interior is almost fully Baroque. Of more interest is the smaller church, **Holy Spirit**, built in the 15th century as a part of a hospital complex. In the rectory facing the main entrance you will find the **Soklič Museum** (*Trg Svobode 5; open by prior arrangement at the Regional Museum; donation*) a collection of artefacts and local art amassed by the local

priest, more interesting for the ambiance they create than their artistic value.

▶ The nicest day trip from Slovenj Gradec is westwards to the peak of **Uršlja Gora** (1,699m). You can walk any section of it on the Slovene Alpine Path (4½h) or reach it by car via the village of Kotlje, with the last 45min covered on foot. Just beneath the highest peak lies a mountain cabin and the grand **church of St Ursula**, started by the parishioners of a now deserted mountain village in 1570. The secret of the building's survival on top of a mountain for four

The church at Uršlja Gora

centuries lies in its construction, akin to a local house with steep roof as well as in its bulky walls. On your way down, don't miss the small but scenic lake, **Ivaračko Jezero**, just a few minutes drive from the main road.

▶ Slovenj Gradec is situated conveniently close (15km) to the **Kope Ski-centre** high up in the Pohorje massif to the east. Here snow comes early and does not melt until late spring, making almost six months of skiing possible on its 8km of slopes or twice as long cross-country trails. During the ski season there are regular buses from the town to Kupe.

Regular buses operate from Slovenj Gradec to the Kope Ski resort

Dravograd hugs the banks of the Drava riverrresort

▶ North of Slovenj Gradec is **Dravograd**, Koroška's communication hub. Set in attractive natural surroundings where the Meza and Mislinja rivers join just before spilling into the Drava. Established as a market beneath a 12th century castle, it lived quietly from levies, rafting timer down the river and later as a railway junction. Then in 1918 it was the prize in a long struggle between the new Yugoslavia and Austria that ended in 1921. The history of these times can be seen in the small **exhibition** housed in the parish of **Libeliče** (*open by prior arrangement via the Museum in Slovenj Gradec, see above; admission €4, children €2*). In the same place you will see reconstructions of daily peasant life in

Libeliče as well as a section on local cuisine. Dravograd's defiance was punished when it was occupied by the Nazis in 1941. Memory of these gruesome days is preserved in the **Gestapo Prison** in the cellar of the town hall, now a museum (*Trg 4. julija 7; open by prior appointment with the Regional Museum in Slovenj Gradec; admission €1, children €0.50*).

▶ The town's main sight is the **Church of St Vitus** at the end of the main street. This stone pre-Romanesque edifice from the 12th century

The Church of St Vitus in Dravograd dates back to the 12th century

has a robust belfry with choirloft, a local particularity of Koroška (*ask for the key at the tourist office next door*).

▶ At Dravograd's tourist office you can arrange for three-hour **rafting trips** down the Drava (*€20 including food and drinks*) The downside is that with all the hydroelectric plants on the Drava the trips are pretty slow and adrenaline-free.

▶ Head westwards from **Ravne na Koroškem**, a small mining town and the capital of the region for the village of **Leše**. Follow signs leading up to the **churches of**

Rafting on the Drava river

The churches of St Anna and St Wolfgang

St Anna and St Wolfgang, a picturesque whole found in all the brochures on Koroška. Their isolated position with nice views of vicinity adds to the rustic beauty of their 15th century mature Gothic style. In the white-painted St Anna there is a splendidly painted ceiling (1689) and a gilded high altar (1644).

▶ Beyond Prevalje in a few minutes ride you reach **Mežica**, where the woody hills and snow covered peaks of Mt Peca make one easily forget that this is a town making its living from mining. Today, the mine on the south side of the town has been turned into a unique museum of mining named **"Peca Underground"** (*Podzemlje Pece; Glančnik 8; www.podzemljepece.com; 02/87 00 180; see the website for opening times and admission prices*). There are three different options here; the first one is a visit to the museum where you will see reconstructions of the day-to-day life of miners 80 years ago as well as many colourful crystals and minerals. The other option is to visit to the mine for a tour by miners' train deep into the mountain and then a walking tour to see how this painstaking work was done. The last and the most attractive option is to embark on a guided bicycle

tour through the mine, starting from near Črna (*see below*) and ending by the Mining Museum, where you will be riding on a bumpy, narrow road in darkness lit only by your headlamps. The only downside to this adventure is that the track is only 5km long, ending just as you start to love it.

▶ A few miles behind Mežica lies **Črna na Koroškem**, a picturesque townlet that rewards bountifully all who come here. In the last half a century Črna, previously a mining town, has been developing as a centre for outdoor sports and is home to several of Slovenia's top skiers, the most recent and most successful being Tina Maze, nine times gold medallist in alpine ski racing.

A view of meadows and foothills leading to Mt Peca

▶ Črna is most famous for its numerous opportunities for **hiking and cycling**. With almost 1,000km of marked paths, this is a real heaven for those who are into mountain-biking. There are plenty of hiking tours to choose from as well but one that all nature lovers should take is to Mala Peca (1713m, 3hrs) with magnificent views of the rugged south side of Kordeževa Glava (2129m, 1hr more), the highest peak around, marking the border with Austria.

Cycling opportunities abound in the countryside around Črna

11 Murska Sobota

👥 12,500

ℹ️ Zvezna 19; tel. 02/534 11 30; open Mon-Fri 10-16h, Sat 9-12

🚂 Ulica arhitekta Novaka 23; 02/29 25 802

🚌 Slomškova 40; 02/530 1661

👪 Days of Sobota (*Soboški dnevi*), last weekend of June

Murska Sobota is Prekmurje's main town

Murska Sobota (*Sobota* or *Subota*, in the local dialect, for short) is the administrative centre of Prekmurje as well as its economic and geographic centre. Although you wouldn't be able to tell from its climate, it is also Slovenia's northernmost town. It is by no means a remarkable place (most of it doesn't look too different to a large Prekmurian village), but due to its location it is the best spot from which to explore Prekmurje.

The name Sobota ("Saturday") suggests that weekly markets were held here once upon a time. It was only at the end of the 19th century that the town started to change and stand out from the surrounding

The Victory Monument, commemorating the Red Army's victory over Fascism

villages. In WWII Sobota was occupied by the Hungarians who in 1944 together with Nazi troops cleared the town of its Jewish community, which made up a good deal of the local bourgeoisie.

▶ The town's focal point is **Trg Zmage** (Victory Square), honouring the Red Army's victory over fascism in WWII. In the middle of the square is the white **Victory Monument**, designed by Russian architect Arončik with sculptures by brothers Boris and Zdenko

Kalin and unveiled just two months after liberation. With real guns on the sides, sculptures of a Slovene Partisan and a soldier of the Red Army, this is the prime example of Socialist Realism in the country.

Sobota Castle

▶ Behind the Victory Monument is the English-style **Town Park**, with a number of impressive 200 year-old oaks and the rectangular **Sobota Castle**. A tower on each of its sides is a reminder of its defensive role when it was built in the 16th century but it now houses the **Regional Museum** (*tel. 02/52 717 06; www.pok-muzej-ms.si; open Tue-Fri 9am-pm, weekends 9am-1pm,; admission adults €3, children & students €2*) presenting the history of the town and the surrounding region.

▶ From Slovenska Street continue left into Slomškova for the Catholic **Church of St Nicholas**. This is the oldest church in town dating back to the 14th century and standing

The Church of St Nicholas is the oldest in town

The 14th century parish church in Martjanci

where an older church built on the site of pagan temple once stood. However, the church was rebuilt on several occasions and what you see is all from 1910-12 in a distinctively Hungarian Art Noveau. The interior of the church was not drastically changed during renovation so that it still treasures valuable **Gothic paintings** (including the Holy Trinity represented as a person with three heads!) and a late 18th century altar.

▶ Just to the north of Murska Sobota is the village of **Martjanci**, famous for the **church of St Martin**. It was built in 1392 with frescos painted by Johannes Aquila, a local artist of considerable importance. Aquila is mostly famous as the first painter from Slovene lands whose name is still known today but he was also much sought after in his own time. A good deal of the interior of the church is still covered in **paintings**, including Aquilla's self-portrait as a middle aged bearded man in prayer.

▶ **Moravske Toplice** complements neighbouring Murska Sobota almost

perfectly – while the latter has history, Moravske Toplice has good hotels, hot waters and fun. And that is about all there is to it. Moravci was an ordinary Prekmurian village until the state oil company by pure chance found a source of sizzling sulphuric water in the early 1960s, transforming it into the biggest tourist magnet in Prekmurje. Now known by the flashy name **"Terme 3000"**, the spa has Slovenia's hottest thermal water, 72˚C, that has to be cooled to body temperature for use in one of the 18 outdoor and indoor pools, in which you will never be cold (*open 8am-9pm 1 May – 1 Oct, otherwise 9am-9pm; day ticket adults/ children €12.90/ €8.90*). Here you can enjoy all kinds of water slides and flumes (watch out for the near vertical *Kamikaze* and the breathtaking 360° loop!) as well as jacuzzis and sun-beds (*€5.90 per hour*) and two health centres. Don't miss a dip in a pool filled with thermal water as it comes from the ground – black and smelly!

There are no real attractions in Moravske Toplice itself but its position at the foot of the rolling Goričko hills offers

The black sulphuric water – valued for its health benefits

great opportunities, especially for cyclists. There are 10 cycling tours that start and end in Moravske Toplice, ranging from 5 to 50km in length.

▶ It is an easy 5.5km ride over flat terrain to one of the biggest attractions of the region, the **Church of the Ascension**, easily spotted in its snow-white guise at the edge

The Terme 3000 aqua park

The Church of the Ascension in Bogojna

The interior of the church

of the village of **Bogojna**. Nicknamed the "White Dove", this is yet another brilliant work from the ever-surprising Jože Plečnik who was asked in 1924 by a local priest to extend his small parish church. Entry is through the old church, which Plečnik used as a vestibule, after which comes a nave with a number of bare arches supported by a single plump column forming a three-dimensional cross. The high altar is a wonder in its own right, resembling a Greek temple and adorned with jugs made by local potters whose plates of diverse designs also adore the wooden ceiling.

12 Prlekija

12,500

Ljutomer, Jureša Cirila 4;
www.jeruzalem.si;
02/58 111 05; open Mon-Fri 8am-
4pm, Sat 8am-noon

Jeruzalem, Jeruzalem 8
(in "Dvorac Jeruzalem");
02/729 45 45; open every day
9am-6pm

Ormož, Kolodvorska 9 (Ormož
Manor); 02/741 53 56;
www.slovenia.info/ormoz; open
Tue-Sat 8am-4pm

Trgatev ("Grape picking"), late Sep
- early Oct

The winding vineyards of Prlekija

You will search for Prlekija on maps in vain: this region is defined more by a set of social characteristics and dialect than by provincial borders and geography. Bordered by the Mura, Drava and Pesnica Rivers, it is a region of rolling hills covered with vast vineyards known jointly as Slovenske Gorice (literally "Slovene Hills") giving way to wheat covered plains. The region takes its name from its inhabitants, *Prleki* known for their specific dialect that is closer to that of Prekmurje than official Slovene, as well as for their joviality, humour, songs and even noisiness. This is undoubtedly connected to the region's bountiful fertility which feeds their love of eating and drinking, their good nature and warm hospitality.

▶ The capital of Prlekija and its largest town is **Ljutomer** (called *Lotmerk* by locals). Its development as a town was initially hampered by frequent Turkish raids, looting by Hungarian anti-Habsburg insurrectionists in 1708, and several great fires, the last big one in 1828. In the mid 19th century its fifty-fifty divide between ethnic Germans and Slovenes made it fertile ground for the growth of nationalism and it was here in 1868 that the first mass gathering (*tabor*) of Slovene nationalists took place demanding the unification of Slovene lands. On a lighter

A view over Ljutomer

Detail of the Column of the Virgin Mary in Ljutomer

with wonderful views. The place takes its name from an icon supposedly brought here during the Crusades. On the other hand, local legend claims that passing Crusaders liked the area so much that they declared to have reached the Promised Land and decided to stay. Jeruzalem is what most tourists come to see, but with around 50 inns and farmsteads involved in wine making and twice as many good vistas scattered around

note, in the same period the region's horse breeding traditions were institutionalised with the founding of the first racing society in Slovene lands. The Ljutomer trotters became the best known Slovene racehorses, a tradition that you can still witness four times a year at town's race grounds.

▶ The centre of the town is the recently revamped **Glavni Trg** surrounded by two storied burghers' houses and with the **Virgin Mary Column** from 1729 at its centre. On the square are also the **Town Hall**, built in 1833 after the last great fire, and the large **Church of St John the Baptist**. In front of the richly decorated Baroque entrances of the church is a bust of Franc Miklošič (1813-1891), a famous local Slavist and philologist.

The church of St John the Baptist

The rolling hills and vineyards of Jeruzalem

the area there is also much to explore. There are two marked wine routes for walkers and one for cyclists and several maps that you can get in local tourist offices. Don't miss a chance to try the local wine variety, Šipon, including famous blends such as Ljutomerčan and Jeruzalemčan or to sample hearty Prlekian cuisine.

The best time to visit is of course during picking time, generally in early October. If

▶ The most beautiful part of Prlekija are the hills between Ljutomer and Ormož. Due to its favourable location with an abundance of sunshine, good soil and ample humidity this is one of the best known vine growing areas in the country, producing an array of fine white wines. With its long rows of vineyards on curvy terrace hills, scattered farms and patches of woodland it is arguably also the most picturesque. The centre of the region is **JERUZALEM**, a group of houses around a church (note the fine Baroque interior) and a small hostel

The vineyards of Jeruzalem are reminiscent of Provence or Tuscany

Winding rows of vines near Jeruzalem

A *klopetec* wind powered rattle

you arrive between August and October, amidst the endless sea of golden vines you will notice tall wooden rattles called *klopotec*, whose sound, announcing the arrival of new wine, frightens away birds and delights the soul of men. Your second best bet is 11 November, the famed Martinovanje festival, when young wine is first tasted.

▶ To the south of the vine-covered hills the Drava plain opens out. On a terrace above the river stands the town of **Ormož**, on the other side of the river is Croatia.

The courtyard of Ormož Manor

The town's most memorable building is **Ormož Manor**, standing on the eastern edge of the old town. The stately quadrangle building was begun in 1278 by Frederic of Ptuj; its oldest part, dating from this period, is the tower. The entry gate, decorated with the arms of the Wurmbrand family, the manor's later owners, leads to a pretty arcaded courtyard with an old well. Today it houses the **Regional Museum** (*tel. 02/741 72 90; www.pok-muzej-ptuj. si; open Mon-Fri 8am-3pm, Sat 9am-2pm, closed on Sun and holidays; admission €1.50 adults, €1 children*) whose collections include the archeological legacy of Prlekija, art collections and

a small exhibition on the history of the Slovenian War of Independence in 1991 in which Ormož, played a noteworthy role. Be sure to see the wall paintings by Alois Gleichenperge on the first floor of the west wing; they are amongst the best classicist works in Slovenia.

▶ On the main road to Ptuj, some 4km from Ormož is the village of **Velika Nedelja**. From the main road take the turning heading north to the church and castle, both visible from afar. Local legend tells that the unusual name of the village, meaning Great Sunday, comes from a victory won here by Frederic II of Ptuj against the Hungarians on Easter Sunday 1199 with the help of the Knights of the Teutonic Order. Due to this the Order was bestowed with vast estates in the area.

▶ The **Church of Holy Trinity** in Velika Nedelja was built shortly after 1200 in a Romanesque style but was later expanded. The **castle** dates from the same period as the church. The western part is Medieval while the eastern wing was added in 1612-19 yet both parts form a harmonious whole. Today the castle is home to an **ethnological collection and a historical exhibition** on Velika Nedelja's past but, more surprisingly, also to several families!

The church of the Holy Trinity in Velika Nedelja

Due to the abundance and diversity of accommodation available in Northeast Slovenia – not to mention the difficulty of keeping printed listings current – we chose to provide just a quick overview. For full up-to-date listings of hotels, hostels and other accommodation we recommend you go online. You also can get accommodation advice and bookings from **Slotrips.si**.

Maribor

	Name	Website	Address	Tel.
★★★★	Hotel Bellevue	www.termemb.si	Ulica heroja Šlandra 10	+386 2 234 43 01
★★★★	Hotel Piramida	N/A	Gregorciceva 38a	+386 5 673 25 55
Hostel	Hostel UNI	www.termemb.si	Volkmerjev prehod 7	+386 2 250 67 00
★★★★	City Hotel Maribor	www.cityhotel-mb.si	Ulica kneza Koclja 22	+386 2 621 25 00
★★★	Hotel Lent	www.hotel-lent.si	Dravska ulica 9	+386 2 250 67 69
Hostel	Vila Mira	www.vilamira.com	Lešnikova ulica 6	+386 2 250 14 53
★★★	Hotel Bau	www.hotel-bau.net	Limbuška cesta 85	+386 2 421 63 10
★★★	Hotel Tabor	www.hoteltabor-maribor.si	Ulica heroja Zidanška 18	+386 2 42 16 410
Hostel	Hostel Pekarna	www.youth-hostel.si	Ob železnici 16	+386 591 80880
★★★	Hotel Bajt Garni	www.hotel-bajt.com	Radvanjska cesta 106	+386 2 332 76 50

Ptuj

	Name	Website	Address	Tel.
★★★	Park Hotel	N/A	Prešernova ulica 38	+386 2 749 33 00
★★★★	Hotel Mitra	www.hotel-mitra.si	Prešernova ulica 6	+386 2 78 77 455
★★★	Hotel Poetivo	www.hotel-poetovio.si	Vinarski trg 5	+386 2779 82 11
Hostel	Hostel Eva	hostel-ptuj.si	Jadranska ulica 22	+386 31 667 606
Hostel	Hostel Sonce	N/A	Zagrebška cesta 10	+386 31 361 982

Celje

	Name	Website	Address	Tel.
★★★★	Hotel Evropa	www.hotel-evropa.si	Krekov trg 4	+386 3 426 90 00
Hostel	MCC Hostel	www.mc-celje.si	Mariborska 2	+386 3 490 87 42
★★★	Hotel Štorman	www.storman.si	Mariborska cesta 3	+386 3 426 04 26
★★★	Celjska Koča	www.celjska-koca.si	Pecovnik 31	+ 386 590 70 400

Murska Sobota

	Name	Website	Address	Tel.
★★★★★	Hotel Livada Prestige	www.slovenia.info	Kranjčeva ulica 12	+386 2 512 50 55
★★★	Hotel Diana	www.hotel-diana.si/	Zvezna ulica 1	+386 2 514 12 00
Hostel	Hostel Murska Soboto	www.youth-hostel.si	Tomšičeva ulica 15	+386 2 530 03 10

Other

	Name	Website	Address	Tel.
★★★★	Hotel Breza	www.terme-olimia.com	Zdraviliška cesta 24, **Podčetrtek**	+386 3 829 78 36
★★★	Hotel Zeleni Gaj	www.sava-hotels-resorts.com/	Banovci 1A, **Veržej**	+386 4 206 60 47
★★★★	Sun House	soncna-hisa.si	Banovci 3c, **Veržej**	+386 2 588 82 38
★★★	Hotel Ormož	N/A	Vrazova ulica 5, **Ormož**	+386 2 741 08 30
★★★★	Hotel Korosica	www.korosica.si	Otiški Vrh 25d, **Dravograd**	+386 2 878 69 12
★★★★	Laško Health Spa	www.thermana.si	Zdraviliška cesta 4, **Laško**	+386 3 734 51 11
Hostel	Hostel Brežice	www.youth-hostel.si	Gubčeva ulica 10a, **Brežice**	+386 590 83790
★★★★	Hotel Cateski Dvorec	www.cateski-dvorec.com	Dvorce 3, **Brežice**	+386 7 499 48 70

MARIBOR

Kavarna Q   Gorkega ulica 45, Maribor ☎ 02/805 13 90

Delicious, healthy 'fast food' - perfect for a quick lunch.

Restavracija Mak   Osojnikova 20, Maribor

It may be a little pricier but this is a wonderful place to really wind down and enjoy amazing 'slow food'.

Gostilna Pec   Spodnja Selnica 1 | Selnica ob Dravi, Maribor ☎ 02/674 03 56

Great place to enjoy innovatively modernised Slovenian cuisine. A little pricier but great for a special occasion.

Restavracija/kavarna/vinoteka Rozmarin   Gosposka ulica 8, Maribor, ☎ 02/234 31 80

Good food and great wine in a modern but friendly atmosphere ensure that Rozmarin is very popular with locals and travellers alike.

Pizzeria and Spaghetteria La Cantina   Pohorska ulica 60, Maribor ☎ 02/417 88 36

A nice little rustic Italian restaurant with a warm feel.

Baščaršija   Postna ulica 8, Maribor,

Excellent Bosnian cuisine, but beware – the portions are enormous. Reasonable prices.

Pizzeria Verdi   Dravska 8, Maribor

Good pizza, good service and reasonable prices.

Gala Žar   Loška Ulica, Maribor

The best Serbian food in Maribor with a great choice of Balkan drinks accompanied by merry Balkan music.

Cantante Café   Vetrinjska 5, Maribor ☎ 02/252 53 12

Great food, nice and cheap, plenty of veggie options and pleasant service. Wonderful cosy atmosphere and very reasonable prices.

Picerija/pub/restavracija Ancora   Jurciceva ulica 7, Maribor 02/250 20 33

Kick back and enjoy a local beer or a choice of different dishes or pizzas.

Novi Svet Pri Stolnici   5 Slomskov Trg, Maribor ☎ 02/250 04 86

Excellent, authentic local fish restaurant just next to the Franciscan Church.

Čajnica Čajek   Slovenska ulica, Maribor,

A great range of teas and other drinks too in a homey, old fashioned atmosphere.

Štajerc   Vetrinjska ulica, 30, Maribor,

Ever tried green beer? If not Štajerc is a must. In the summer there is live music in the garden.

Tako's   Mesarski prehod 3, Maribor ☎ 02/252 71 50

Maribor's best Mexican restaurant, good food and good Mexican beer.

Fuego - latino club   Mesarski prehod 3, Maribor

Latin American food but also cocktails, shooters and fantastic Latin beats to dance the night away.

PRACTICAL HELP

Getting Around
Communications
Money & Banking
Health & Security

Getting Around

ARRIVING BY AIR

Slovenia has no fewer than three international airports - Ljubljana, Maribor and Portorož - however, unless you're on a charter flight or have your own private jet you will be landing at Brnik, some 19km north of **Ljubljana** (and only 11km from Kranj). There are shuttle buses connecting the airport to Ljubljana, Kranj, Kamnik, Bled and Bohinj. See also p. 70

Ljubljana airport

If you flew to **Trieste airport** get a 14.30 bus to Portorož or take no. 51 bus to Trieste bus station where there are plenty of departures for Slovene towns, especially Koper.

The Piran-Trieste Ferry

ARRIVING BY SEA

Arriving on **your own boat** you will have to head for the ports of Koper or Piran (also Izola from May through to October). Upon mooring, find the border authorities to declare the vessel and its passengers. For this you will need a document of ownership, a skipper's license and IDs of all the people on board. You can moor your boat in the **marinas** of Koper, Izola or Portorož, all are well equipped. The one in Izola also features a repairs centre.

High-speed **hydrofoils** operated by *Trieste Lines* connect Piran with Trieste in Italy and Rovinj and Pula in Croatia from late April to late September.

TRAVELLING BY TRAIN

Slovenian trains, all run by the state owned *Slovenske železnice*, are a highly reliable means of transport. The railway network links almost all of the major towns and is centred on Ljubljana. Ljubljana is well connected with major cities in Austria and Croatia as well as with Munich, Zurich, Prague and Belgrade but there are no direct trains to Italy or to Budapest in Hungary.

International lines as well as one from Ljubljana to Maribor are served by fast IC, EC trains as well as their local variants - ICS and MV. Slovene towns are linked by LP trains that stop only in larger towns as well as by regional RG trains, the latter being of a considerably lower standard. Note that there are no domestic night trains.

Trains are more affordable than busses and cheaper than their western European counterparts. Tickets purchased onboard cost €2.50 more than those bought before boarding. This fee will not be charged if a station is so small that it does not have a ticket office. At such a station you might find yourself in front of a timetable only in Slovene. Here *odhod* means departures and *prihod* arrivals.

Slovenian Railways, *Slovenske železnice*, are reliable and comfortable

Ljubljana coach station (*Avtobusna Postaja*)

Bicycles are allowed on trains marked with a matching icon, one needs only to buy a separate ticket for them (*kolesarska vozovnica*) that costs €3.20 no matter how far you go.

Small **dogs** that can sit in a passenger's lap travel at no cost and so do all other animals carried in their boxes; larger dogs travel at half a 2nd class fare.

TRAVELLING BY BUS

No matter how comprehensive the train network is, you will need buses to reach many of the smaller places of interest. Bus services are provided by a number of private companies resulting in a number of combined timetables at stations.

TRAVELLING BY CAR

Driving around Slovenia is a pleasure since almost all roads, including minor rural ones, are in excellent condition. They are appropriately signposted so that you will easily find your way without Sat Nav. Furthermore, since Slovene towns are mostly very small, parking places are not hard to find.

To enter the country by car you will need a valid registration card and drivers license (with a photo!) – a national one for drivers coming from EU member states and international driving permits for others. Green Card motor insurance is obligatory for drivers coming from outside the EU. Don't forget a national sticker for the back of your car.

Many of the major routes are toll roads and you will need to obtain a **vignette** sticker (*vinjeta*) as soon as you enter the

A vignette (*vinjeta*) sticker is necessary on the motorways

Slovenian roads, even in remote areas, are of good quality

Timetable Decoder

D — Mon-Fri
D+ — Mon-Sat
N — Sundays
NP — Sundays and holidays
PP — Mon-Fri
SN — Sat-Sun
Šr — School days
V — Daily

country. These are sold at the border crossings or in kiosks immediately beyond the border as well as at most petrol stations. At the time of writing a weekly vignette costs €15 and a monthly one €30. There are no toll gates but you need to keep the sticker displayed on your windshield.

The AMZS is the main roadside assistance organization

Speed limits are 130km/h on motorways, 90 on non-urban roads and 50 in built-up areas. Police can impose a fine on the spot. If you pay the fine within eight days it will be reduced by half. You will also need to keep a reflective jacket, first aid kit and a warning triangle in the car. Dipped headlights are compulsory even during daytime and seat belt use for both front and rear seat occupants is required by law. From November 15 to March 15 all vehicles must have either winter tires or summer ones with tread depth of at least 3mm plus snow chains. The permitted blood-alcohol limit is 0.05% - roughly equivalent to two small drinks for an average male - but please avoid drinking and driving all together!

Unleaded petrol, diesel and LPG are readily available. Petrol prices are similar to the EU average, considerably lower than in Italy and somewhat higher than in Hungary, Austria and especially Croatia.

Auto Moto Zveza Slovenije (AMZS) is your best resource for **help on the road**. Dial 1987 for a 24-hour roadside emergency service.

There are plenty of **car rentals** in major towns, including all the big international brands. If on a tighter budget consider renting from a local company which offer slightly older vehicles at more than competitive prices. To rent a car you will need an ID with a photo, valid national or international drivers' license and a credit card to pay with. You will also have to be above 21. Some companies charge an additional fee for "young drivers", namely those between the age of 21 and 25.

TRAVELLING BY BICYCLE

With its bike-friendly destinations, lots of designated bike paths, accommodation and campsites, Slovenia is a genuine heaven for cyclists. There are a lot of good roads with light to moderate traffic connecting almost all destinations so that there is no problem traversing the country on a bike. Biking is very popular here and most people have bikes and ride them frequently, even if only for recreation. Having this in mind it comes as no surprise that Slovene drivers are by and large very considerate. Tourist offices provide details on trails and guided rides.

Helmets are obligatory only for kids under 14 years of age.

Slovenia is uber-bike-friendly and cycling is very popular

Communications

Making a **local call** in Slovenia is easy, you only have to dial the subscriber's number with no area code. When calling long-distance within Slovenia, you need to add the area code at the beginning (for instance Ljubljana 01, Maribor 02, Koper 06). For **international calls**, first dial 00, followed by the country code and the area code thereafter (for example 00-49-30-xxxxxxxx, 49 for Germany, 30 for Berlin). Slovenia's country code is **386**.

Due to the rapid proliferation of mobile telephones, making cheap domestic calls without your own phone has become substantially more difficult in recent times; **public payphones**, once fairly common, have largely disappeared over the last ten years. Nevertheless, there are some still around, at least in the more prominent parts of major towns. They do not, however, accept coins and can be used only with pre-paid **telephone cards**, which are sold in four different versions (25 units, called impulses, for €2.92, 50 impulses for €4.18,

Due to the popularity of mobile phones, phone boxes are increasingly rare

A Slovenian post office

100 for €7.09 and 300 for €14.60). One impulse here corresponds to approximately one minute for local landline calls but only to 10 seconds when calling a mobile. The phone cards are also needed to make calls from the phone booths found in post offices. **Post offices** are open 8am to 7pm on workdays and from 8am to 1pm on Saturdays.

When calling from your hotel or guesthouse make sure you check the charge before making the call as these can vary substantially. Most hotels also provide fax and internet services, the better or larger ones usually have free Wi-Fi.

Postage stamps can be bought at the post offices and cost €0.40 for a postcard or small letter inside the EU. Letters can be posted either at the post office or in post boxes, usually found just outside the post office or near many supermarkets. The usual mail delivery time to EU countries is 3 to 5 days but sending letters to other countries will take longer, depending on the country. To ensure safe arrival of a letter or shipment, it is advisable to send it by registered post (*priporočeno*).

Foreign newspapers, except for some Croatian, Serbian and German ones, can be bought only in the larger hotels and a few of the better stocked newsstands and bookshops in the centres of major towns and resorts. It is worth noting that most newsstands close very early – around 7pm in city centres and even earlier elsewhere.

TV channels in English, German, Italian, French and Serbo-Croatian are just about everywhere as cable television is very common.

Mobitel is the largest mobile phone operator

Use of the **internet** is widespread and above the European average with most users having home connections. As a consequence, **internet cafés** are almost non-existent and quite costly (in Ljubljana one hour of internet usage can cost up to €3). For that reason the best option might be to go to a public library, where one can present some ID and ask for a guest password to access the internet for free but with a time limit (30-60 minutes). Furthermore, a growing number of cafes and bars in urban centres have recently also begun to provide free Wi-Fi. The exact location of **Wi-Fi points** can be checked at *http://wifi-tocke.si*.

As already mentioned, **mobile phones** are widely used and have already surpassed landlines in terms of numbers. If staying for a longer period, it might therefore be more economical to obtain a SIM card with pre-paid credit (around €10) from one of the Slovenian service providers, rather than rely on public phones. Major mobile companies are Mobitel, Si.mobil Vodafone and Tuš mobil. In addition, Izimobil is a smaller company offering a range of cheap pre-paid packages which can be bought at newsstands, gas stations, post offices and in many supermarkets. GSM and EDGE signals cover most of the country, except for the remote mountain areas.

Money & Banking

In 2007 Slovenia adopted the **Euro** as its currency. The best place to change foreign cash into Euros is in a bank as they charge no commission. Commission at exchange offices (*menjalnica*), travel agencies and tourist offices varies, it's usually around 3%. You will be worst off if you change money in a hotel. Banks are also the best places to cash in the travellers' cheques, they take a commission of 1%.

Banks are open 9am-noon and 2pm-5pm on workdays and some also open on Saturdays, from 9am to noon.

Visa, Master/EuroCard and American Express **credit cards** are widely accepted, Dinners Club cards somewhat less frequently. ATMs (*bančni avtomat*) are to be found all around the country, even in the smallest of towns. Visa holders can get cash advances from any branch of Abanka, Master/EuroCard holders from NLB or SKB banks.

If you come from outside the EU you are eligible for a **refund of VAT** (known as *DDV* in Slovene) of 20%. This applies to any shopping above €50. Your best options are the affiliated shops displaying the "Tax Free" logo that will issue refund cheques with your bill. At shops outside of this system you will need to ask for a special

A Slovenian €2 coin commemorating France Prešeren

invoice for foreigners which should be made out to you personally. This invoice must be stamped by customs officials as you leave the country and can be reclaimed at any Global Refund Office around the world.

Tipping is not customary in Slovenia but rounding up the sum at a café or in a taxi as well as rewarding any extraordinary service will be appreciated.

Slovenia is more expensive than countries to its South and East but is considerably cheaper than neighbouring Italy or Austria.

Health & Security

Slovenia's health care system can be considered completely reliable. EU citizens are covered for most **medical care** by their health insurance card (EHIC). Other nationals are recommended to take out travel insurance that will cover some or all of the immediate payments expected in

hospitals. No vaccinations are necessary for travel to Slovenia.

Tap **water** is safe to drink throughout the country, though it may vary in quality and will often be "hard water".

Pharmacies (*lekarna*) working round the clock are to be found only in the larger towns.

In terms of crime, Slovenia is one of the safest countries in Europe. Violent crime is almost unheard of and the greatest danger facing visitors – except the usual petty crime like pick pocketing - is **vehicle break in** or **theft**. If travelling with an expensive car try leaving it in well lit areas or at guarded car parks. Try to keep any valuables out of sight while away from your vehicle.

Always carry your passport or at least a copy with you. If you are staying with a friend or self-catering note that the law requires your host to **register** you at the nearest police station within three days of your arrival.

At the time of writing Slovenia has been experiencing a wave of **demonstrations** against government austerity measures. Most of these are peaceful, though several have involved minor clashes with the police so be careful if joining a demonstration or just passing by.

Emergency tel. 112
Police tel. 113

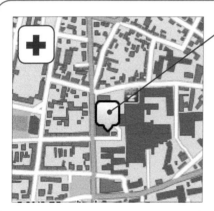

Ljubljana:
Lekarna pri Polikliniki,
Njegoševa cesta 6K,
tel. 01 230 61 00

Maribor:
Tabor, Ljubljanska 9,
tel. 02 320 79 10

Koper:
Lekarna Koper, Kidričeva 2,
tel. 05 611 0000

Ambulance in a hurry in Ljubljana

Female travellers are perfectly safe in Slovenia and are unlikely to get any more unwanted attention than male travellers. Despite a number of **gay and lesbian** friendly venues and the Ljubljana Pride Parade, public displays of affection by same sex couples are still regarded as awkward even in the larger towns.

Possession of any quantity or kind of **drugs** is illegal but in practice cannabis is widely enjoyed and its use is rarely penalised.

We wish you a pleasant journey!

Tours made by photographers for photographers

Planning to visit Slovenia? Join our photography tours and workshops,
improve your camera skills and bring back stunning photos!

More information on **adriatic2alps.com** and **facebook.com/adriatic2alps**

ΔDRIΔTIC2ΔLPS
PHOTOGRAPHY TOURS

CIP - Каталогизација у публикацији
Народна библиотека Србије, Београд

338.48(497.7)(036)

DULOVIĆ, Vladimir, 1978-
    Slovenia in Your hands : travel guide /
[Vladimir Dulović, Adele Gray ; photos Miha
Gantar ... [et al.]. - Beograd : Komshe, 2013
(Beograd : Publikum). - 269 str. : fotogr. ;
22 cm

Podatak o autorima preuzet iz kolofona. -
Tiraž 1.500.

ISBN 978-86-86245-16-8
1. Gray, Adele, 1978- [аутор]
а) Словенија - Водичи
COBISS.SR-ID 199453452